Key Terms
in
People Management

Steve Flinders

with Tom Gamble

YORK
ASSOCIATES

For Lorenza

Published by: York Associates International Ltd.
Cover design: Hutton Peach Design Consultants, York.
Typesetting: Celtic Publishing Services, Wrexham.
Printed in the UK by: The Russell Press Ltd, Russell House, Bulwell Lane, Basford, Nottingham.

ISBN 1 900 99 1 13 6

The authors

Steve Flinders is a director of York Associates and specialises in training European politicians, HR managers and trade unionists. He also acts as a consultant for building effectiveness in European works councils. He has special responsibility for the company's marketing in France and for its publications and teaching resources. His special professional interests include international human resources, trade union and political communication, and coaching. For training enquiries, contact: steve.flinders@york-associates.co.uk.

Tom Gamble, who has contributed the exercises, discussion questions and case studies to this edition, has an MA in industrial relations and human resource management, and has been living and working in France for fifteen years. He worked as an EFL trainer at primary, secondary and university levels and in business schools and as a freelance translator and copywriter for a variety of international companies before setting up his own professional development and communication business in 1998. He currently works as a management coach for the Thales Group and as a corporate trainer for the Anglo-French company, AMEC SPIE. He has also published a collection of poetry and regularly develops EFL and HR courseware. Contact: contact@tomgamble.net.

The publisher

The mission of York Associates is to help people develop internationally. In addition to its publishing activities, it offers a wide range of training in management, communication, intercultural and language skills to private and public sector clients worldwide. It is accredited to administer instruments which support international professional development: The International Profiler (TIP) – a psychometric support tool for the development of intercultural management competencies; and others provided by Team Management Systems Development International (TMS). It offers coaching and training to individuals and groups at its main training centre at Peasholme House, an eighteenth century town house close to the historic centre of York in the north of England, and in-house worldwide.

Contact:
York Associates International Ltd.
Peasholme House, St Saviours Place, York YO1 7PJ, England
Tel: 00 44 (0)1904 624246
Fax: 00 44 (0)1904 646971
E-mail: training@york-associates.co.uk
Website: www.york-associates.co.uk.

Contents

Introduction

People management today

Key Terms in People Management is not just for people in HR and for employee representatives but for anyone involved in people management who needs to communicate in English. It is the new edition of Key Terms in Human Resources and has been significantly expanded and reorganised to include two new chapters on employment law, and on culture and communication. Employment law has grown in importance for the HR function since the appearance of the earlier edition in 1999. The importance of both culture and communication for people working internationally is becoming increasingly acknowledged, although understanding of the processes involved in both culture and communication is developing more slowly. Perhaps these two themes symbolise one of the tensions at the heart of people management and HR practice. On the one hand, we need to communicate more effectively across national, corporate and occupational boundaries. On the other, there is at least a general feeling that people are increasingly resorting to litigation in order to resolve conflict. At the moment, HR people – at least in the UK – spend more time talking about the law than about culture and communication. My own hope is that the next five years will see a shift in favour of the theme of the other new chapter.

The book

This book is a glossary of people management terms designed to help anyone who works internationally – but particularly HR managers and employee representatives – to learn and use the words they need to communicate in English. It contains key terms together with definitions written in simple English, supported by examples of how the words are used and which other words they combine with. The book is for:

- anyone who is involved in the management or representation of people in the workplace internationally whose first language is not English
- business students, both native and non-native speakers
- business English trainers
- translator and interpreters.

The organising principles of the book are that:

1 people only need a limited number of key terms to communicate successfully on people management questions;
2 learning how to use these words means learning how they typically go together with certain other words, for example: a binding agreement, a fatal accident, take early retirement;
3 these word groups form the vital bridge between individual words and sentences.

The context of the book is:

- international, although the bias towards European practice has been unavoidable;
- generally neutral about HR, although the definitions and examples may support the belief that companies which invest in the skills and development of their employees will gain long term competitive advantage.

The language model is British English but most British terms without wider application have been excluded.

What is included

The terms are directly relevant to people whose work involves the management or administration or representation of other people in the workplace. Most general business terms and also very technical terms are excluded although the degree of generality or specificity varies from chapter to chapter:

- In chapter 4, I have added a number of terms relating to benefits – pensions, in particular – to reflect the growing importance of this area of HR;
- In chapter 8, I have included a number of general legal terms which are not specific to employment law but which are nevertheless necessary to know to be able to talk about employment law cases and procedures;
- In chapter 9, I have selected terms with which I think most people working internationally should be familiar. Specialists will be dissatisfied both with the limited number of terms and with the drastically over-simplified definitions I have provided for many of those which are

included. But the whole aim of the glossary is to keep things simple. Users who are encouraged to find out more will develop their own views about the terms as they learn to use them.

- Some of the terms – like milk round, leapfrog, Mcjob and golden handcuffs, have been included not just because they are useful but also because they are fun.

How to use it

The book is divided into nine chapters. Each chapter deals with a different area of people management. Dictionaries are not usually organised in chapters. This one encourages you to look around within each area and to see how terms group together. There is a full A-Z index at the end of the book. So you can either look up a particular term in the index and then turn to the right page, or you can work intensively in one particular area.

If you want to work on a certain theme, either on your own or with a group (with or without a trainer), you can work like this:

1   Choose the chapter you want to work on.
2   Look at the list of headwords on the first page. Tick the terms you know and can use, cross the words you do not know or cannot use, and put a question mark by the ones you are not sure about. If you working with other people, you can now help each other to understand unknown terms.
3   Work through the exercises at the end of the chapter a first time.
4   Look through the glossary in order to complete the exercises and then check your answers against the key at the back of the book.
5   Take more time to read through the glossary again.
6   Discussion topics: (on your own) make notes or (in a group) compare ideas and experiences with colleagues.
7   Case studies: the same.

Business English trainers of HR or trade union groups doing intensive courses can use this formula for a daily 60 – 90 minute specialist vocabulary and discussion session.

Collocation

Collocation (also referred to as word groups, word families or word associations) is the way words typically group together. It forms the bridge between the individual word and the formation of sentences and so is an essential key for successful communication. Much of this dictionary is given to showing which other words typically group with key terms in people management so that users can begin to recognise how the terms really work.

Appendix 6 is designed to help readers build these bridges between the language of people management and the language of general professional communication; and also between the specialist terms and complete sentences.

Entry key

Each entry consists of some or all of the following:
1   The headword + part of speech.
2   The phonetic transcription of the headword.
3   Useful derivations from the headword with parts of speech.
4   A definition of the headword written in simple English.
5   A cross-reference to other related terms.
6   Collocations which require their own definitions.
7   A list of typical collocations (word groups). Note: the verb comes at the start of the collocation if it is a very important part of the collocation (as in: invite the candidate to attend an interview) and at the end of the collocation if it is less important (as in: the final interview, reach ~ stage)
8   An example, in italics, of the headword in context to show meaning and use.

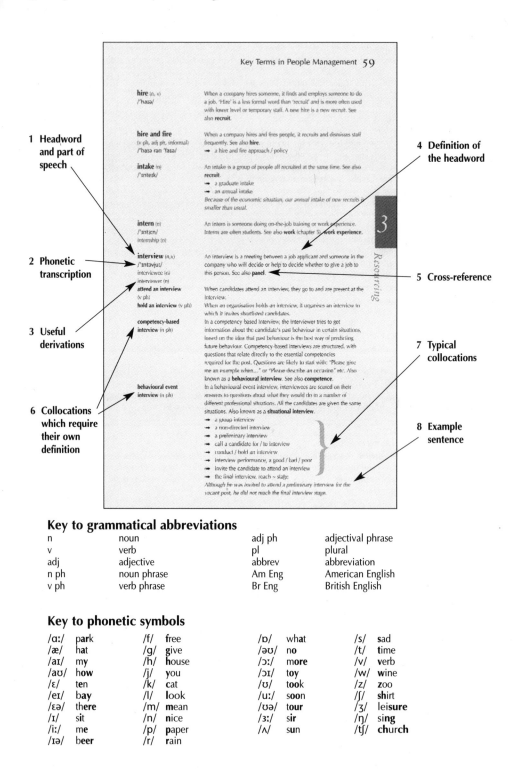

1 Headword and part of speech

2 Phonetic transcription

3 Useful derivations

6 Collocations which require their own definition

4 Definition of the headword

5 Cross-reference

7 Typical collocations

8 Example sentence

Within the image:

Key Terms in People Management 59

hire (n, v) /ˈhaɪə/
When a company hires someone, it finds and employs someone to do a job. 'Hire' is a less formal word than 'recruit' and is more often used with lower level or temporary staff. A new hire is a new recruit. See also **recruit**.

hire and fire (v ph, adj ph, informal) /ˈhaɪə rən ˈfaɪə/
When a company hires and fires people, it recruits and dismisses staff frequently. See also **hire**.
➡ a hire and fire approach / policy

intake (n) /ˈɪnteɪk/
An intake is a group of people all recruited at the same time. See also **recruit**.
➡ a graduate intake
➡ an annual intake
Because of the economic situation, our annual intake of new recruits is smaller than usual.

intern (n) /ˈɪntɜːn/ internship (n)
An intern is someone doing on-the-job training or work experience. Interns are often students. See also **work** (chapter 5), **work experience**.

interview (n,v) /ˈɪntəvjuː/ interviewee (n) interviewer (n)
An interview is a meeting between a job applicant and someone in the company who will decide or help to decide whether to give a job to this person. See also **panel**.

attend an interview (v ph)
When candidates attend an interview, they go to and are present at the interview.

hold an interview (v ph)
When an organisation holds an interview, it organises an interview to which it invites shortlisted candidates.

competency-based interview (n ph)
In a competency based interview, the interviewer tries to get information about the candidate's past behaviour in certain situations, based on the idea that past behaviour is the best way of predicting future behaviour. Competency-based interviews are structured, with questions that relate directly to the essential competencies required for the post. Questions are likely to start with: "Please give me an example when..." or "Please describe an occasion" etc. Also known as a **behavioural interview**. See also **competence**.

behavioural event interview (n ph)
In a behavioural event interview, interviewees are scored on their answers to questions about what they would do in a number of different professional situations. All the candidates are given the same situations. Also known as a **situational interview**.
➡ a group interview
➡ a non-directed interview
➡ a preliminary interview
➡ call a candidate for / to interview
➡ conduct / hold an interview
➡ interview performance, a good / bad / poor
➡ invite the candidate to attend an interview
➡ the final interview, reach ~ stage
Although he was invited to attend a preliminary interview for the vacant post, he did not reach the final interview stage.

Resourcing
3

Key to grammatical abbreviations

n	noun	adj ph	adjectival phrase
v	verb	pl	plural
adj	adjective	abbrev	abbreviation
n ph	noun phrase	Am Eng	American English
v ph	verb phrase	Br Eng	British English

Key to phonetic symbols

/ɑː/	park	/f/	free	/ɒ/	what	/s/	sad
/æ/	hat	/g/	give	/əʊ/	no	/t/	time
/aɪ/	my	/h/	house	/ɔː/	more	/v/	verb
/aʊ/	how	/j/	you	/ɔɪ/	toy	/w/	wine
/ɛ/	ten	/k/	cat	/ʊ/	took	/z/	zoo
/eɪ/	bay	/l/	look	/uː/	soon	/ʃ/	shirt
/ɛə/	there	/m/	mean	/ʊə/	tour	/ʒ/	leisure
/ɪ/	sit	/n/	nice	/ɜː/	sir	/ŋ/	sing
/iː/	me	/p/	paper	/ʌ/	sun	/tʃ/	church
/ɪə/	beer	/r/	rain				

References

Websites:
- www.cipd.co.uk
- www.peoplemanagement.co.uk
- www.humanresourcesmagazine.com
- www.personneltoday.com

The definition of Business Process Re-engineering is taken from Hammer M. and Champy J. 1993. *Re-engineering the Corporation.*

Transforming Learning, compiled by Susan Norman and published by Saffire Press (ISBN 1 901564 06 1) was helpful in identifying and defining new terms for chapter 5.

Intercultural Business Communication by Robert Gibson and published by Oxford University Press (ISBN 0 19 442180 5) was helpful in identifying and defining new terms for chapter 9. So also was *Business Across Cultures* by Jeremy Comfort in the *Down to Business Minimax* second series published by Falcon Press (ISBN 983 9672 66 5).

Acknowledgements

Thanks to friends, colleagues and family who have helped produce this book:

- Tom Gamble, who wrote a completely new set of exercises, discussion questions and case studies for this edition and tolerated the vagaries of his co-author without complaint;
- Tony Cornish of Celtic Publishing Services who not only wrote the phonetic transcriptions but who designed and page set the whole text with saint-like patience from start to finish;
- Nick Brieger of York Associates for his major contribution to the chapter on employment law;
- Peter Franklin of Konstanz University of Applied Sciences in Germany and the driving force behind www.dialogin.com, the Delta Intercultural Academy, a knowledge and learning community for all those interested in intercultural business and management communication, for generously allowing me to use his own glossary of terms in intercultural communication for chapter 9;
- Lesley Bers, HR consultant and Chair of the North Yorkshire branch of the Chartered Institute of Personnel and Development for her expert comments;
- John King, training consultant for York Associates and the University of York, for help with appendix 5;
- Jim Chamberlain of the Fachhochschule Bonn-Rhein-Sieg, Germany, for his suggestions for the chapter on culture and communication;
- David Knowles, Tutor in English as a Foreign Language at York College, for proof reading and help with phonetics;
- William Birdwell, of the Birdwell Institute, Lyon, France, for suggesting the inclusion of case studies;
- Martina Wehry of TFL Ledertechnik , Germany, for her suggestions on the organisation of this edition;
- Mike Seymour, of Corporate Language Training and Translation, Bonn, Germany, for his enthusiasm in identifying new HR terms;
- Mike Barker and Josephine Bakke of the Norwegian Workers' Educational Association, who have made possible so many of my exchanges on trade union issues and for their feedback on chapter 7;
- Michael Flinders, for his assiduity in reformatting all the entries for the new edition and for his attention to detail in helping to check the final text;
- other colleagues and staff of York Associates for their suggestions and, above all, for their patience during the long wait for this edition to appear;
- all those managers and employee representatives who have attended York Associates courses in York or elsewhere over the last twelve years and who have contributed terms, ideas and, above all beliefs about how people can work together to achieve extraordinary things.

Steve Flinders, York, England
January 2005

1

The individual at work

Key terms to talk about your job and other people's, the way work is organised, and basic conditions of employment.

The individual at work

1

These are the key terms in this chapter. Which of them do you understand? Which of them can you use?

Assignment
atypical
Blue-collar
Cadre
casual
clock in
conditions of employment
consultant
counterpart
co-worker
Day off
direct report
director
duties
duty
Employ
entitlement
expatriate
Flexible working
following partner
freelancer
full-time
function
Gangmaster
grade
Half-time
holiday
homeworking
hours
Incumbent
interim
Job
Labour
leave
line manager

Mcjob
manual
moonlighter
Occupation
operative
Part-time
peer
position
posting
predecessor
psychological contract
Quit
Resign
retire
returner
Seasonal
shift
shop floor
sideways move
skill
stand-by
subordinate
successor
superior
supervisor
Team
temporary
third country national
time off
Unemployed
Vacation
White-collar
work
work-life balance

assignment (n)
/ə'saɪnmənt/
assign (v)
assignee (n)

An assignment is a particular job that you are given to do. If your employer **reassigns** you, then you are given a different job to do.
➡ an international assignment
➡ an expatriate assignment
➡ a written assignment
➡ a special assignment

atypical (adj)
/eɪ'tɪpɪkəl/

If something, for example behaviour, is atypical, then it is not normal or standard.

atypical employment (n ph)

If you have an atypical employment contract, then you have a non-standard contract which can be, for example, for temporary and/or part-time work. Some employers prefer atypical employment contracts because they give them with flexibility.

atypical worker (n ph)

A typical worker is one with a normal contract of employment. As working practices change, new relationships develop for atypical workers. Workers in this category include the self-employed, temporary workers, freelancers, agency workers, homeworkers, subcontractors, part-timers and job sharers, casual and seasonal workers, fixed-term and contract workers. See also **casual**, **employ**, **freelancer**, **homeworking**, **job**, **part-time**, **seasonal**, **temporary**.
There are so many atypical workers in some job markets today that being atypical is almost typical.

blue-collar (adj ph)
/'blu: 'kɒlə/

A blue-collar worker is someone who works in a manual job or in a job on the factory floor. See also **manual**, **white-collar**, **single status agreement**.

cadre (n)
/'kɑːdə/

A cadre is, in France, a manager with special status relating to pension rights, etc. Other non-French European companies sometimes use this term to talk about executives above a certain level within the organisation.

casual (adj)
/'kæʒuəl/
casualisation (n)
casualised (adj)

Casual work is work done for a short period. A casual worker is someone who works for an employer on a less than full-time basis. We talk about the **casualisation** of the workforce when more and more of the employees of a company are part-time or temporary workers. Workers are **casualised** when they change from being permanent or full-time to temporary or part-time workers. See also **seasonal**, **temporary**.
➡ a supply of casual labour
➡ a casual job
Companies use casual labour to increase production when there is a sudden increase in demand.

clock in (v ph)
/'klɒk 'ɪn/

If your company wants to know the time when you arrive at work, you have to clock in, using a clock card or badge. When you leave work, you **clock out**. Also known as **clocking on** and **clocking off**.
Clocking-in machines used to stamp clock cards with the employee's arrival time mechanically, but it is now usually done electronically.

The individual at work

The individual at work

1

conditions of employment (n ph)
/kən'dɪʃənz əv ɪm'plɔɪmənt/

Your conditions of employment state what you have to do in your job and the rules that you and your employer must follow. These conditions are usually stated in a contract of employment. Also known as **conditions of service**. See also **contract**, **terms**, **work**.
➡ enjoy good conditions of employment
➡ have good / bad conditions of employment
Under the conditions of employment in this company, all staff have a 40 hour working week and 25 days' paid holiday per year.

consultant (n)
/kən'sʌltənt/
consult (v)
consultative (adj)
consultation (n)

A consultant is someone whom you pay to give you specialist or expert advice. See also **consultation**, **cowboy**.
➡ an internal consultant
➡ call in a consultant
➡ charge for a consultation
➡ internal consultancy
➡ use a consultant

counterpart (n)
/'kaʊntəpɑːt/

A counterpart is someone who does the same kind of job as you in another organisation or another part of the same organisation. Also known as an **opposite number**.
➡ a counterpart visit, make / go on

co-worker (n)
/'kəʊwɜːkə/

Some less hierarchical companies call their employees co-workers. Sometimes also known as an **associate**. Employees of The Walt Disney Company are called **cast members** like a group of actors in a film or a play. See also **employ**.
Companies which talk about their co-workers or associates are trying to create an image of greater equality, and also of greater commitment to and from the workforce.

day off (n ph)
/deɪ 'ɒf/

A day off is a day when you do not go to work.
➡ have / take a day off
Her employer lets her take a day off now and then because she does a lot of unpaid overtime.

direct report (n ph)
/dɪ'rɛkt rɪ'pɔːt/

A direct report is an employee who is one level under you in the organisation and so who reports directly to you. See also **subordinate**.

director (n)
/dɪ'rɛktə/
direct (v)

A director is:
➡ a senior manager who works for a company full-time, for example The managing director, the marketing director, the director of research and development; or
➡ a person who represents the shareholders of the company on its board of directors.

executive director (n ph)

An executive director is a member of the board of directors who is also a full-time manager in the company.

non-executive director (n ph)

A non-executive director is a member of the board of directors who comes from outside and who is not an employee of the company.

duties (n pl)
/'dju:ti:z/

Your duties are the different parts of the job that you have to do, especially for a lower grade job.
- ➡ allocate / assign duties
- ➡ carry out / perform duties
- ➡ essential / non-essential duties

duty (n)
/'dju:ti/

You are on duty when you are at work. You are off duty when you are not at work. In particular we talk about people in the public services – for example, soldiers, police, doctors and nurses – being on or off duty. See also relieve.

duty of care (n ph)

Employers' duty of care towards their employees gives them a general responsibility to make sure they do not come to harm while at work.

employ (v)
/ɪm'plɔɪ/
employee (n)
employer (n)
employment (n)
employable (adj)
employability (n)

When you **employ** people, you give them a job. An **employer** gives jobs to people. An **employee** is someone who works for an organisation. People who work for themselves are **self-employed**. If you are **employable**, you have skills which employers want. Your **employability** is the measure of how employable you are. See also **employee, employee assistance programme, employee value proposition, employee segmentation, employer branding, employers' association, employment agency, employment tribunal, industrial relations, unemployed.**

core employee (n ph)

A core employee works full-time for a company.

peripheral employee (n ph)

A peripheral employee works part-time for a company.

employee attitude survey (n ph)

An organisation can find out what its employees think about a range of issues by asking them to answer questions in an employee attitude survey. Some organisations administer these on an annual basis.

employment break (n ph)

If you agree to stop working for a period as an alternative to redundancy, you agree to take an employment break. See also **career, secondment.**

full employment (n)

There is full employment when everyone who wants a job has one.

lifetime employment (n ph)

A company offering lifetime employment guarantees jobs for its employees for the whole of their working lives.

suitable alternative employment (n ph)

When an employer offers suitable alternative employment to an employee, the employer offers the employee a different job as an alternative to redundancy.
- ➡ a salaried / non-salaried employee
- ➡ an employee attitude / opinion survey
- ➡ an employee handbook
- ➡ an employers' organisation
- ➡ an employment right
- ➡ employee recognition
- ➡ employment conditions
- ➡ employment contract
- ➡ employment legislation
- ➡ full employment, a period of
- ➡ good / bad employee representation, have

The individual at work

⇒ involve employees, employee involvement
⇒ monitor employees
⇒ seasonal employment
⇒ strong / weak employee representation
The level of participation in the annual Deutsche Telekom employee attitude survey rose to 76% in 2003 with a general level of employee satisfaction of 7 on a scale of 1 to 10.

entitlement (n)
/ɪn'taɪtəlmənt/
entitle (v)

An entitlement is something you have a right to at work. See also **conditions of employment, holiday.**

holiday entitlement (n ph)

Your holiday entitlement is the number of days' holiday which your contract of employment says you can take per year.
⇒ entitlement to rest periods and breaks
⇒ entitlement to paid annual leave
⇒ legal entitlement

expatriate (adj, n)
/ɛks'pætriət/
expatriation (n)
expat (n, Br Eng informal)

Expatriates work abroad for their companies. See also **posting, third country national.**
⇒ an expatriate assignment

flexible working (n ph)
/'flɛksɪbəl 'wɜːkɪŋ/

Flexible working is:
1 choice in the times when you start and finish work. Also known as **flexible hours, flexitime, flextime** (in US English) and (informally) **flex.** See also **benefits, family-friendly.**
2 a general approach to working hours which maximises productivity and reduces non-productive time to a minimum, through the agreement of employees to work when work needs doing.
⇒ a flexible working week / year
⇒ a flexitime scheme, operate
⇒ flexible work patterns, implement
⇒ flexible working hours

following partner (n ph)
/'fɒləʊɪŋ 'pɑːtnə/

Following partners are people who give up their own jobs to follow their husbands or wives when their partners relocate to a new job in another city or country. Also known as a **trailing partner.**

freelancer (n)
/'friːlɑːnsə/
freelance (adj, v)

Freelancers are self-employed, usually professional people, who may work for one company for a limited period, for example as a consultant, but who normally have a range of clients. See also **outsource.**
⇒ work freelance
⇒ go freelance, decide to

full-time (adj, adv)
/'fʊl 'taɪm/
full-timer (n)

When you work full-time, you work the standard working week, normally between thirty-five and forty hours a week in rich countries. A full-timer is someone who works full-time. See also **half-time, part-time.**

➡ full-time employment
➡ on a full-time basis
Although the total number of employees in this company is increasing, there are now fewer full-timers and more part-timers than in the past.

function (n)
/ˈfʌŋkʃən/

A function is a job, a position or an area of responsibility. See also **position**. See also **functional silo**, **position**.
➡ the human resources function
➡ carry out / exercise / fulfil / perform a function

gangmaster (n)
/ˈgæŋmɑːstə/

A gangmaster organizes groups of low-paid workers – who may be illegal immigrants or working illegally – to do unskilled jobs.

grade (n)
/ˈgreɪd/

A grade is a class or level of a job within the structure of a company's workforce. See also **downgrade**, **regrade**.
➡ a grading scheme / system
➡ a low grade, a low-grade worker
➡ a pay grade
➡ a skilled / semi-skilled / unskilled grade
➡ move to a higher grade
➡ the bottom / top grade
A London hospital reduced staff turnover and absence with a grading scheme which linked pay and competencies to staff development.

half-time (adj, adv)
/ˈhɑːf ˈtaɪm/
half-timer (n)

When you work half-time, you work half the standard working week. Someone who works half-time is a half-timer. See also **full-time**, **part-time**.
➡ on a half-time basis
Some couples share the same job, with each partner working half-time, so that each can spend more time with their children.

holiday (n)
/ˈhɒlɪdɪ/
holidays (n pl)
holidaymaker (n)

A holiday is a period of time when you do not have to go to work. See also **leave**, **vacation**.

holiday carried over (n ph)

If you carry over some or all of your holiday, you do not take it in one time period but can take the unused holiday in the next.

working holidaymaker (n ph)

A working holidaymaker is someone who is allowed to work in a country while on a visit without having a work permit.
➡ a holiday replacement
➡ a national holiday
➡ a public holiday
➡ be owed holiday
➡ holiday money
➡ paid / unpaid holiday
➡ statutory public holiday
➡ use up one's holiday entitlement

The individual at work

1

homeworking (n)
/ˈhəʊmwɜːkɪŋ/
homeworker (n)

Homeworkers are people who work at home. They often have a connection to their employer's computer and use telephones, email and the organisation's intranet to work and to communicate with colleagues and clients; but homeworkers can also work in manufacturing jobs, for example employees on piecework in the clothing industry. Homeworking is also known as **remote working**, **telework** or **telecommuting**. See also **piecework**.
There are now more than two million remote workers in the UK – people working mainly at home. While this does not affect their employment status, it does raise issues relating to data security and risk assessment.

hours (n pl)
/ˈaʊəz/

Your hours are the length of time you spend at work per day, per week or for some other period.

annual hours (n ph)

If you work under a system of annual hours, your employer agrees to employ you for a certain number of hours in the year. Also known as **annualised hours**.

core hours (n ph)

If you work flexible hours, your core hours are the times in the day when you must be at work. See also **flexible working**.

unsocial hours (n ph)

Someone who works unsocial hours does not work at the same time as most other people. For example, if you work through the night, you work unsocial hours.

working hours (n ph)

Your working hours are the number of hours your contract says you should work per day, and the time when you should start and finish work each day.
⇒ a forty-hour week
⇒ a long hours culture
⇒ flexible hours
⇒ maximum working hours
⇒ normal hours
⇒ work long hours

incumbent (n)
/ɪŋˈkʌmbənt/

An incumbent is a person who holds a particular job.
We need to find a replacement for the marketing director since the present incumbent has told us he is planning to leave.
⇒ a job incumbent
⇒ the present / previous incumbent

interim (n, adj)
/ˈɪntərɪm/

An interim or interim manager is a temporary executive who works on a short-term basis for different companies. See also **temporary**.
⇒ an interim management agency
Interim managers can be taken on to manage projects, to manage change, to define strategy or because they are familiar with a particular culture. They must be able to adapt to new environments and new markets at short notice.

job (n)
/ˈdʒɒb/
jobless (adj, n)

A job is a position of regular paid work. Someone who does not have a job is **jobless**. See also **job** (chapters 3 and 5), **occupation**, **occupational**, **unemployed**.

Jobcentre (n ph, Br Eng)   A Jobcentre is a local office of the British government's employment
                                 service helping unemployed people to find work.
job hopping (n ph, informal) A job hopper is someone who often changes job.
job security (n ph)   If you have job security, you are sure that you will keep your job for a
                                 long time.
job insecurity (n ph)   If you have job insecurity, you think there is a good chance that you
                                 will lose your job.
job sharing scheme   A job sharing scheme is a plan which lets two or more people share
(n ph)   the same job between them. Job sharers may work split days, split
                                 weeks or work alternate weeks. See also **half-time**.
job tenure (n ph)   Your tenure of a job is the length of time you are in it.

- a badly-paid / well-paid job
- a demanding / undemanding job
- a flexible job market
- a job analysis
- a job code
- a job description
- a job family
- a job for life
- a job holder
- a job incumbent
- a job profile
- a job seeker
- a job summary
- cut a job, cut jobs, job cuts
- do a job
- find a job
- get a job
- hold down / hold onto a job
- job classification, a ~ scheme
- job conditions
- job content
- job creation, a government job creation programme
- job design
- job enrichment
- job evaluation, a job ~ scheme
- job grading
- job objectives
- job performance
- job prospects
- job protection
- job rating
- job reclassification
- job regulation
- job satisfaction
- job security
- job stress
- keep a job
- lose a job

The individual at work

1

The individual at work

→ take on a job
→ the job market
→ the jobless rate

labour (n, v)
/'leɪbə/
labourer (n)
sweated labour (n ph)

A company's labour is its people - the human resources of the organisation. A **labourer** is an unskilled general worker. See also **manpower**.

Sweated labour is hard, low-paid work. Clothes sold by retail chains in the rich world are often produced by sweated labour in LEDCs (less economically developed countries).

→ a flexible labour market
→ a rigid labour market
→ casual labour
→ child labour
→ high / low labour mobility
→ high / low labour turnover
→ labour law
→ labour standards
→ manual labour
→ organised labour
→ the labour market

leave (n)
/'liːv/
adoption leave (n ph)

Leave is holiday or permission to be away from work. This term is often used for expatriates. See also **holiday**, **vacation**.

When you adopt a child, you become the legal parent of someone else's child. Adoption leave is the time off work that you get when this happens.

ante-natal leave (n ph)

Ante-natal leave is time off for a parent before the birth of his or her own child.

compassionate leave (n ph)

If your employer grants you compassionate leave, you have permission to be absent from work for some strong personal reason, for example because a close relative is ill or has died.

discretionary leave (n ph)

Discretionary leave allows an employee to decide how much (unpaid) leave to take up to a specified limit.

garden leave (n ph)

Garden leave is an informal term for the period of notice of departing employees who are paid but who do not attend work so that they do not learn confidential information about the company.

maternity leave (n ph)
paternity leave (n ph)

Maternity leave is the time a woman can take off work to have a baby. Paternity leave is the time a man can take off work to look after a baby or small children.

→ a leave schedule
→ additional maternity leave
→ be on leave
→ domestic incident leave
→ emergency leave
→ exceptional leave
→ extended leave
→ flexible leave
→ go on leave

➠ grant leave (of absence)
➠ leave entitlement
➠ ordinary maternity leave
➠ paid leave
➠ parental leave
➠ post-natal leave
➠ relaxation leave
➠ sick leave
➠ unpaid leave

line manager (n ph)
/ˈlaɪn mænɪdʒə/

A line manager is directly involved in production or in providing a service, and is usually responsible for a department or a team.
Many jobs which used to be the responsibility of the human resources function in companies are now carried out by line managers.

Mcjob (n, informal)
/məkˈdʒɒb/

A Mcjob is a low-paid, unskilled, short-term job with poor security, reflecting a common view of the employment conditions offered by fast food chains like McDonald's.

manual (adj)
/ˈmænjʊəl/
manual record (n ph)

Manual workers work with their hands. See also **blue-collar, manual handling**.
A manual record is a paper file containing, for example, information about an employee.

➠ a skilled / an unskilled manual worker
➠ manual labour

moonlighter (n, informal)
/ˈmuːnlaɪtə/
moonlight (v)
moonlighting (n)

A moonlighter is someone with more than one job. Very often the main employer does not know about the other(s).

occupation (n)
/ɒkjəˈpeɪʃən/
occupational (adj)
occupational segregation (n ph)

An occupation is a job or a class or category of job.
See also **job, occupational**.

There is occupational segregation when there is a concentration of men and women in different jobs.

operative (n)
/ˈɒpərətɪv/

An operative is someone who works a machine, for example in a factory.

➠ a machine operative
➠ a plant operative

part-time (adj, adv)
/ˈpɑːt ˈtaɪm/
part-timer (n)

When you work part-time, you work only part of the standard working week. A part-timer is someone who works part-time. See also **full-time, half-time**.

➠ part-time employment
➠ part-time work
➠ work on a part-time basis

The individual at work

1

peer (n)
/'pɪə/

Your peers are the people at more or less the same level in the organisation as you.
➡ peer group
➡ peer group attitudes
➡ peer group pressure, to refuse to give way / give in to
➡ peer pressure, to give way / give in to
Business unit managers at BP developed "peer assist" and peer challenge processes whereby they could first challenge and then spend time helping colleagues in the running of their operations.

position (n)
/pə'zɪʃən/

A position is a job. Also known as a **post** (n). See also **function**.

reserved position (n ph)

A reserved position or post is one given to a special category of employee, for example to a disabled person. A **reserved post policy** can be used, for example, to increase the number of disabled people in the workforce. See also **affirmative action**.
➡ a key position
➡ a vacant position, fill
➡ apply for the position of
➡ appoint someone to the position of
➡ occupy the position of
➡ take over the post of
The HR department invites interested staff members to apply for the vacant position of assistant to the marketing director.

posting (n)
/'pəʊstɪŋ/
post (v)

A posting is a job in another location. When your company posts you somewhere, it sends you to work somewhere else, usually abroad. A posting can last from a few months to several years. See also **expatriate**, **position**, **third country national**.

hardship posting (n ph)

A hardship posting is a job location for an expatriate where life is significantly more difficult or dangerous than at home. People in hardship postings often get paid more.

single status posting (n ph)

A single status posting is one where employees must go without their families.
➡ a foreign posting
➡ a posting abroad, send someone on

predecessor (n)
/'priːdɪsɛsə/

Your predecessor is the person who did your job before you. See also **incumbent**, **successor**.

psychological contract (n ph)
/saɪkə'lɒdʒɪkəl 'kɒntrækt/

The psychological contract is the unwritten agreement between an organisation and an employee about the obligations of each to the other. See also **contract**.
The psychological contract used to be based on career and job security. Today it is based more and more on the employer's promise to – among other things – provide interesting work, pay related to performance, opportunities for training and development, respect, a safe working environment; and the employee's promise – among other things – to work hard, be flexible, uphold the organisation's reputation, and maintain high levels of punctuality and attendance.

quit (v, informal)
/'kwɪt/

When you quit your job, you leave it. See also **resign**.

resign (v)
/rɪ'zaɪn/
resignation (n)

When you resign, you tell your employer that you want to give up your current job and (usually) to leave the company. See also **notice**, **quit**, **termination**.
➡ accept someone's resignation
➡ hand in your resignation
➡ offer your resignation
➡ tender your resignation

retire (v)
/rɪ'taɪə/
retirement (n)

When you retire, you give up your job because you have reached the age – often 60 or 65 years old – when the government or the company says you must stop working. See also **termination**.
➡ a mandatory retirement age
➡ approach retirement
➡ early retirement, take
➡ retirement age, reach
➡ compulsory retirement
➡ phased retirement
➡ retirement plan

returner (n)
/rɪ't3:nə/
return (v)

A returner is a woman who rejoins a company after having spent some years away from work, raising a family. See also **engaged**.
Companies are now trying hard to recruit returners because of their maturity and experience.

seasonal (adj)
/'si:zənəl/
season (n)

Seasonal work is work that is available at some times of year but not at others. See also **casual**, **temporary**.
➡ a seasonal job
➡ seasonal employment / unemployment
➡ seasonal recruitment

shift (n)
/'ʃɪft/

A factory that runs a shift system has different groups of employees working at different times of the day, and possibly at night, so that one group starts when another group stops.

continental shifts
(n ph, Br Eng)

Someone on continental shifts changes regularly from one shift to another.

double-day shift (n ph)

The double-day shift is a two shift system, from, say, 06.00 to 14.00 and from 14.00 to 22.00.

permanent night shift (n ph)

A permanent night shift worker always works at night.

three-shift working (n ph)

Three-shift working is from, say, 06.00 to 14.00, from 14.00 to 22.00 and from 22.00 to 06.00.

continuous shiftwork (n ph)

A factory with a continuous shiftwork system operates 24 hours a day, seven days a week with two or three shifts per 24 hours.
➡ a shift worker
➡ a split shift
➡ an eight-hour shift
➡ do shift work / work shifts

The individual at work

1

⟹ shift working
⟹ the day / night shift, be on

shop floor (n ph)
/'ʃɒp 'flɔː/

The shop floor (or shopfloor) is the place in the factory where goods are produced.
⟹ a shop floor worker / a worker on the shop floor

sideways move (n ph)
/'saɪdweɪz 'muːv/

A sideways move is a job change which is neither a demotion nor a promotion. See also **career**.

skill (n)
/'skɪl/
skilled (adj)

A skill is a special ability or capacity. See also **multi-skilling**, **skills** (chapter 5).
⟹ a high level of skill
⟹ a (serious) skills shortage
⟹ a skilled / a semi-skilled worker / an unskilled worker
⟹ a highly skilled worker
⟹ acquire skills
Training and qualifications are very important because new industries often demand high levels of skill from their employees.

stand-by (adv ph)
/'stændbaɪ/

When you are on stand-by, you are not working but you are ready to work if asked. You can also say that you are **on call**. See also **contract**.
⟹ stand-by arrangements, make adequate
⟹ be on stand-by

subordinate (n)
/sə'bɔːdɪnət/

Someone below you in the organisation is your subordinate. Note: this term is less used in flatter, more democratic organisations. See also **co-worker**, **direct report**, **superior**.

successor (n)
/sək'sɛsə/
succeed (n)
succession (n)

When you leave a job, the person who takes over from you is your successor. You succeed someone when you take over a job from another person. See also **incumbent**, **predecessor**.

succession planning (n ph)

Succession planning is planning in advance who will take over a job and when.
⟹ draw up / formulate a succession plan

superior (n)
/suː'pɪərɪə/

Someone above you in the hierarchy of an organisation is your superior. Note: this term is less used in flatter, more democratic organisations. See also **co-worker**, **direct report**, **subordinate**.

immediate superior (n ph)

Your immediate superior is the person directly above you in an organisation.

supervisor (n)
/'suːpəvaɪzə/
supervise (v)
supervisory (adj)
supervision (n)

A supervisor is (usually but not always) someone in charge of a number of other, usually blue-collar workers. The supervisor was also traditionally known as the **foreman**.
⟹ supervisory staff
⟹ a supervisory position, an employee in

1

team (n)
/'tiːm/

A team is a small group of people, usually between four and fifteen, which works together most of the time or on a special project to achieve a common goal. In many companies flexible teams have become the basic unit of organisation.

virtual team (n ph)

A virtual team is a group of people who work in different places and communicate with each other via e-mail, video conferencing, etc. In international organisations, virtual teams can function 24 hours per day. A member of a virtual team is a virtual worker. Also known as a **remote team**.

➡ a high performance team
➡ build / develop a team
➡ create a team
➡ team-based pay
➡ team building
➡ team working
➡ teamwork
➡ work in teams

temporary (adj)
/'tɛmpərəri/
temp (n, v, informal Br Eng)

A temporary employee is an employee who does not have a permanent contract and who will therefore work for a company for only a limited period. A **temp** is someone who does temporary work, often through a private employment agency, especially someone doing temporary secretarial work. See also **agency**, **casual**, **seasonal**.

➡ temporary staff
➡ a temporary contract
➡ temporary employment

A major British supermarket chain reduced the number of temporary staff from 10% to 3% of its workforce as a way of improving customer service.

third country national (n ph)
/'θɜːd 'kʌntri 'næʃənəl/

A third country national (TCN) is someone with a passport from one country who is employed in another country by a company from a third country. See also **expatriate**.

time off (n ph)
/taɪm 'ɒf/

If you take time off work, you do not do your usual work for a period which could vary from just a few minutes up to several months.

➡ paid / unpaid time off
➡ reasonable time off
➡ take time off work to
➡ time off during a redundancy notice period
➡ time off for ante-natal care
➡ time off for dependants
➡ time off for pension trustees
➡ time off for public / union / European works council duties
➡ time off for study or training

unemployed (adj)
/ʌnɪm'plɔɪd/
unemployable (adj)

People who do not have jobs are unemployed. If you are **unemployable**, you do not have the skills which employers want and so it is difficult for you to find employment. If a lot of people do not

1

The individual at work

unemployment (n)	have jobs, then the rate of **unemployment** is high. See also **employ**.
	⇒ high / low unemployment
	⇒ the unemployment rate / the rate of unemployment
vacation (n, v)	A vacation is a period of time when you do not have to go to work.
/vəˈkeɪʃən/	See also **holiday**, **leave**.
	⇒ a long / short vacation
	⇒ go on / take a vacation
white-collar (adj phr)	A white-collar worker works in an office. See also **blue-collar**, **single**
/ˈwaɪt ˈkɒlə/	**status agreement**.
work (n, v)	See also **employ**, **job**, **overwork**, **welfare to work**, **work** (chapter 5),
/ˈwɜːk/	**work-to-rule**, **works council**, **worker director**,
worker (n)	**workforce**, **working environment**, **workholder**, **working time**, **work-**
working (adj)	**life balance**, **workshadowing**, **workshop**.
boomerang worker	You boomerang when you return to a job you left before.
(n ph, informal)	
clerical worker (n ph)	A clerical worker is a lower grade office worker.
itinerant worker (n ph)	Itinerant workers go from place to place looking for work.
mobile worker (n ph)	Mobile workers travel a lot and spend a lot of time away from the company: they may spend more time with clients than in their own company.
nomadic worker (n ph)	Nomadic workers are, culturally and technologically, able and ready to work anywhere – at the company, at home or while travelling – and at any time.
off work (adv ph)	If you are off work, you are absent from work, for example because you are sick.
out of work (adv ph)	If you are out of work, you are unemployed.
work permit (n ph)	A work permit is an official paper which gives you permission to work in a foreign country.
working conditions (n ph)	When you talk about your working conditions, you may refer to your conditions of employment and, more generally, to the physical environment in which you work. See also **conditions of employment**.
working group (n ph)	A working group is a temporary committee created to discuss and recommend how to solve a particular problem.
autonomous working group (n ph)	An autonomous working group is a team of workers, usually working in factory production, which can make more decisions than usual about the best way to work without asking a superior.
short-time working (n ph)	Someone on short time working works less than the normal full-time number of hours per week because there is not enough work to do.
	⇒ (flexible) working arrangements
	⇒ a (good / bad) working practice
	⇒ a flexible working practice
	⇒ a migrant worker
	⇒ a night worker
	⇒ a work environment
	⇒ a workplace
	⇒ autonomous working group

- be at work
- flexible working
- night working
- of working age
- the working day
- work for
- work on a project
- work routine
- work schedule
- working conditions
- working hours
- working patterns
- working time regulations
- working time, the European working time directive
- workplace bullying
- workplace learning
- workplace violence

work-life balance (n ph) /'wɜːk 'laɪf 'bæləns/ People with a good work-life balance keep a good balance between the amount of time they spend working and the time they give to their private and family lives.

The individual at work

The individual at work

1

Exercises

Exercise 1

Choose the best word or phrase (A, B, C or D) to complete each sentence. There are two gaps to fill in sentence 2.

1   The company recruited twenty _____ staff to meet an especially big order.
    A full-time   B long-term   C temporary   D personnel

2   In many countries, employers have to provide employees with paid _____ and _____ for personal matters.
    A meals   B holidays   C bonuses   D time off

3   The department organises its personnel into project _____ .
    A terms   B shifts   C teams   D services

4   The recent introduction of _____ for certain job categories has helped to lower costs by reducing office space.
    A teams   B homeworking   C labour   D morale

5   All of their employees, including senior managers, have to _____ at the start of their working day.
    A clock out   B swipe   C stand by   D clock in

6   The production line is staffed by _____ .
    A hands   B manpower   C manual workers   D human resources

7   Their conditions of employment include _____ contracts for all employees.
    A paid   B full-time   C variable   D complete

8   When the head of department left suddenly, she was replaced by an _____ manager until the company could recruit a successor.
    A associate   B employee   C interim   D operative

Exercise 2

Choose the word from the box which corresponds to each of the definitions (1 – 10).

unemployed	counterpart	shop floor	successor
leave	shifts	white-collar	direct report
	expatriate	retire	

1   A manager or office worker
2   A person one level below you in the organisation who answers to you.
3   Someone from the organisation's home country who works abroad.
4   Groups of employees working at different times during the day or night
5   When employees leave an organisation at the end of their career
6   The person who takes over your job when you leave it
7   Someone in another department or organisation with a similar job to yours
8   Holiday or permission to be away from work
9   Someone without a job
10   The main part of a factory

Exercise 3

Match the first half of each sentence (1 – 8) with a second (a – h) to form correct statements.

1   Shop floor workers are often referred to as
2   When employees decide to leave their jobs,
3   The company is aiming for better performance
4   Consultants were brought in
5   30% of their workforce is composed of
6   Big departments or divisions are usually
7   Employees in production usually
8   In the USA, employees may take two weeks

a   they resign.
b   statutory paid vacation.
c   blue-collar workers.
d   run by directors.
e   part-time and seasonal staff.
f   work on the shop floor.
g   through flexible working.
h   to advise management on how to build high performance teams.

1

The individual at work

Exercise 4

Match the definitions on the left (1-10) with the right term on the right (a - j).

1	When an employee decides to leave his or her job voluntarily	a	on standby
2	Someone working for the company at a distance, usually by internet	b	freelancer
3	Terms and clauses included in the contract of work	c	predecessor
4	When an employee is not working, but is ready to if asked	d	remote worker
5	A manager involved in the operations function in a company	e	supervisor
6	A self-employed worker working for different organisations	f	quit
7	Employees are not at work when they take a ...	g	line manager
8	A colleague at work	h	day off
9	A blue-collar worker in charge of a team	i	co-worker
10	The person who did your job before you took it over	j	conditions of employment

Exercise 5

Link each word in the circle to one of the headers in the box.

People	Contracts	Types of work	Departure

For discussion

1   What are the terms and conditions of employment for people in your organisation? What would you like to change?

2   Human resources management is about generating added value. In what ways does HRM add financial and human value in your organisation?

3   What motivates your people?

4   Does homeworking work? How does it affect HR?

Case study

The challenge of flexibility

Faced with increasing competition from domestic and foreign competitors, as well as pressure from its customers, Henson, an OEM (original equipment manufacturer) for several major car manufacturers, has to review its organisation. The company has been producing a full range of interior / exterior plastic moulded car parts for over thirty years and is a respected family firm.

Henson employs 650 people in three plants in Germany, France and the UK. French and German labour costs are high and hiring and firing is more complex than in the UK because of labour laws, and pressure from local government and employee representatives. However, these sites are the most productive and located in your most profitable markets. In addition, the company employs a large number of design and production engineers – approximately 35% of the workforce. Manual workers account for another 40%. The company currently works on a "proximity" basis, with sites supplying the local markets and car manufacturers. The organisation is strictly pyramidal, with each site possessing its own HR, sales, marketing and quality departments. The management at each site has great autonomy in applying its own, local strategy.

How can Henson adapt its organisation to the demands of its customers and market without damaging its reputation? How can it cut costs, while ensuring that quality is maintained? Consider:

*   the workforce
*   company structure and organisation
*   labour costs
*   locations.

2

Human resources policy and planning

Key terms to talk about the
management of an organisation's
human resources, including policies
on equality and expatriation and
against discrimination.

2

Human resources policy and planning

**These are the key terms in this chapter.
Which of them do you understand?
Which of them can you use?**

Absent
affirmative action
ageism
align
ancillary
attendance
Balanced scorecard
benchmark
business partner
business process re-engineering
Code
cover
cowboy
Delayer
demanning
demographic profile
demote
deploy
disability
discharge
discriminate
diversity
downgrade
downsize
Employee segmentation
empower
engaged
equal opportunities
equality management
exit
Family-friendly
free movement of labour
Glass ceiling
Headcount
human capital
human resources
Insource
Kiosk
Mainstreaming
man

manpower
market testing
motivate
Natural wastage
notice
Offshore
outplacement
outsource
overstaff
Performance
personnel
position analysis questionnaire
positive action
pre-retirement
promote
Quota strategy
Re-entry
regrade
relieve
relocate
removal
resettle
retain
roster
Seniority
service
sexual orientation
shared services
sheltered
short-time working
social dumping
staff
stagger
stakeholder
Termination
time and motion study
turnover
Welfare to work
workforce

absent (adj)
/'æbsənt/
absence (n)
absentee (n)
absenteeism (n)

When you are absent from work, you stay away from work because, for example, you are ill. An **absentee** is someone who is away from work. **Absenteeism** is the problem of frequent absence from work, often without a good reason.

absence without leave (n ph)

Absence without leave is being away from work without permission.

investigate absence (v ph)

When management investigates absence, it tries to find the reasons for the level of absence in the organisation, usually in order then to reduce it.

maternity absence (n ph)

If a woman has the right to maternity absence, then she can stay away from work for a longer period of time after the end of her maternity leave and then return to her job. Extended maternity absence is a period of absence which is even longer than the normal period of maternity absence. See also **leave**.

➡ a low / high rate / level of absenteeism, experience
➡ absence analysis
➡ absence control
➡ absent due to / owing to / through illness
➡ absent from work
➡ long-term absence
➡ monitor absence, absence monitoring
➡ repeated absence from work
➡ sickness absence
➡ sickness absenteeism
➡ unauthorised absence

Sickness absenteeism caused by personal or childcare problems, boredom and low morale costs the British economy £13 billion per year.

affirmative action (n ph)
/ə'fɜːmətɪv 'ækʃən/

A company which takes affirmative action makes extra efforts to recruit women and members of ethnic minorities as a way of reducing discrimination against these groups. See also **positive action**, **quota strategy**.

➡ an affirmative action programme
➡ take affirmative action

Some companies introduce affirmative action programmes as a way of improving the position of women and of ethnic minorities. Others believe that such groups do not need or should not receive this kind of support.

ageism (n)
/'eɪdʒɪzm/
age (n, v)
ageist (adj)

Ageism is unfair discrimination against older people.
As the values of pensions go down and working lives get longer, so ageism becomes an increasingly important issue for the HR function.

➡ age legislation
➡ an age-neutral policy
➡ an age-neutral workplace

2

Human resources policy and planning

Human resources policy and planning

2

align (v)
/ə'laɪn/
alignment (n)

When you align something, you put it in line with or make sure that it fits with something else. It is the job of human resources managers to ensure that HR policies are aligned with the objectives of the organisation as a whole. See also **business partner**.

ancillary (adj, n)
/æn'sɪləri/

Ancillary staff are usually support staff at lower levels in the organisation – for example cleaners, porters and canteen workers – who are not directly involved in the main activity of the organisation. See also **staff**.
➡ an ancillary worker
➡ ancillary staff

attendance (n)
/ə'tɛndəns/
attend (v)

If you have a good attendance record, it means that you are rarely absent from work.
➡ a good / poor attendance record

balanced scorecard
(n ph)
/'bælənst 'skɔːkɑːd/

With a balanced scorecard approach to measuring organisational performance and achieving its strategic goals, an organisation takes into account not just financial measures but also customer service, internal processes, and innovation and learning. The idea of the balanced scorecard comes from management writers Robert Kaplan and David Norton. See also **benchmark**.
➡ adopt a balanced scorecard approach
HR can use the balanced scorecard approach to align HR with organisational strategy and also to be proactive rather than reactive in moving the organisation towards its goals.

benchmark (n, v)
/'bɛntʃmɑːk/
benchmarking (n)

When a company benchmarks some part of its operation, it looks in detail at what other successful organisations do, defines a best practice, and then uses the information to improve its own performance in this area. You can benchmark against competitors, other organisations with similar functions, 'best in class' companies, or internally. See also **balanced scorecard**.
➡ benchmark against
Examples of HR benchmarks are training expenditure per employee, absence per employee, the ratio of permanent to temporary employees, and recruitment costs per employee.

business partner (n ph)
/'bɪznɪs 'pɑːtnə/
business partnering (n ph)

HR managers who are successful business partners add value to the organisation by making a genuine contribution to its strategy, at lower cost. See also **align**.
To be successful, HR business partners must understand the business and its strategy inside out and must also be able to communicate in terms that a company's board will understand. In particular, they must be able to show the financial gains to be made from HR policies and proposals.

business process re-engineering (n)
/'bɪznɪs 'prəʊsɛs riːɛndʒɪn'ɪərɪŋ/

Business process re-engineering involves analysing all the systems in an organisation in order to cut any system or process which does not add value. According to two of the management consultants mainly responsible for supporting this approach, Michael Hammer and James Champy, business process re-engineering is the "radical redesign of business processes to achieve dramatic improvements in critical measures such as cost, quality, service and speed."
At the time when BPR was most fashionable, some companies went so far as to dismiss all their employees, redraw the organisation chart, and invite old employees to apply for the new jobs.

code (n)
/'kəʊd/

A code is a list of rules about how to do things.

code of conduct (n h)

A code of conduct is a list of rules about how a group of working people – for example, employees or professionals – agree to behave, or about how an organisation wants its employees to behave.

code of practice (n ph)

A code of practice – for example, a code of practice for disabled people, ageism or health and safety – is a written set of rules for a certain area of work. Codes of practice propose models of good behaviour: they are not legally binding.
➡ comply with a code of practice
➡ implement a code of practice
We think the government's new code of practice on health and safety administration is good but we are worried about how much it will cost us to implement.

cover (n, v)
/'kʌvə/

When you cover for someone, you work in place of someone who is sick or on holiday. See also **cover** (chapter 4), **relieve**.
➡ provide cover for

cowboy (n informal)
/'kaʊbɔɪ/

A cowboy is a consultant (often unqualified or unaccredited), agency or company which provides bad service.
➡ a cowboy operator

delayer (v)
/di'leɪə/
delayering (n)

When a company delayers, it flattens the structure of the organisation by reducing the number of levels, and often by cutting jobs.
Delayering can lead to more job insecurity and fewer promotion opportunities.

demanning (n)
/di'mænɪŋ/

When there is demanning in a company, people lose their jobs. Note: using this term about women is sexist. See also **man**, **overman**, **redundant**.

demographic profile (n ph)
/dɛmə'græfɪk 'prəʊfaɪl/

The demographic profile of a workforce or of a population can give you information about the gender, age, educational background, ethnic origins, etc. of the group and is therefore useful for HR planning, development, equal opportunities, etc.

2

Human resources policy and planning

2

Human resources policy and planning

demote (v)
/dɪ'məʊt/
demotion (n)

When you demote someone, you give them a lower grade job.
See also **promote**.
➡ suffer a demotion

deploy (v)
/dɪ'plɔɪ/
deployment (n)
redeploy (v)
redeployment (n)

When an organisation deploys its staff, it sends them to the place
where it wants them to work. When an organisation **redeploys** its staff,
it sends them to another place to work.
*After the merger of Lloyds and TSB, the new bank said it would invest
in retraining and redeployment of staff as a way of trying to reduce the
number of redundancies.*

disability (n)
/dɪsə'bɪlɪti/
disable (v)
disabled (adj)
**accommodate a
disability** (v ph)

Someone with a disability has some kind of physical or mental injury,
handicap or illness. If you do not have a disability, you are **able-
bodied**. It is uncommon today to talk about disabled people as
handicapped. See also **sheltered**.
An organisation accommodates an employee's disability when it
adapts the working environment to fit the disabled employee's special
needs.
➡ a disability pension
➡ a disability plan / scheme
➡ a disabled person
➡ a partial disability, partially disabled
➡ disability benefit
➡ disability discrimination
➡ disabled employment
➡ physical disability
➡ provide adequate facilities for disabled people
➡ severely disabled
➡ suffer from a disability

discharge (n, v)
/'dɪstʃɑːdʒ/

1 To discharge a duty or a responsibility is simply to do that duty or
carry out that responsibility.
➡ discharge a duty / a responsibility / a function
2 If an employer discharges you, you lose your job. See also **discharge**
(chapter 6), **dismiss, fire, sack**.
➡ discharge a poor performer

discriminate (v)
/dɪs'krɪmɪneɪt/
discrimination (n)
discriminatory (adj)
indirect discrimination
(n ph)

If you discriminate against a person, you treat that person unfairly. See
also **disability, sexual orientation**.

Indirect discrimination happens when a group of people of the same
gender or an ethnic group is treated unfairly in the workplace or
because of a condition of employment which the employer cannot
justify.
➡ a discriminatory practice
➡ age discrimination
➡ an act of discrimination
➡ anti-discrimination law

⟹ discriminate against
⟹ discrimination on the grounds of race, creed or colour
⟹ race / racial discrimination
⟹ sex discrimination / sexual discrimination
⟹ unlawful discrimination
The aim of the British Sex Discrimination Act of 1975 is to encourage the equal treatment of men and women in employment and in other areas.

diversity (n)
/daɪˈvɜːsəti/
diverse (adj)

Diversity management not only aims at age, sex, disability, race and gender equality in the workplace but also encourages the employment of different kinds of people because it is good for business performance. See also **affirmative action**, **equal opportunities**, **positive action**, **sexual orientation**.
⟹ age diversity
⟹ encourage diversity
Diversity should be less about helping other employees cope in a white, male-dominated culture, more about valuing the differences which people have.

downgrade (n, v)
/ˈdaʊngreɪd/

If you are downgraded, you are given a lower grade job. Both jobs and people can be downgraded. The opposite of **downgrade** is **upgrade**. See also **grade**, **regrade**.
Are organisations using technology to improve, or to replace and downgrade the contribution made by people?

downsize (v)
/ˈdaʊnsaɪz/
downsizing (n)

When a company downsizes, it makes itself smaller by cutting staff. Also sometimes known as **rightsizing**.
⟹ initiate / undertake a (major) downsizing operation

employee segmentation (n ph)
/ɪmplɔɪˈiː sɛgmənˈteɪʃən/

Employee segmentation is a way of recruiting and organising groups of employees according to their profiles and the profiles of their jobs, especially in relation to customer service, so that employees who are good with customers go into the jobs which require more customer contact.
Many companies now use employee segmentation to divide the workforce into job families depending on their customer profile.

empower (v)
/ɪmˈpaʊə/
empowerment (n)

Empowered employees can make important decisions about how they do their work without having to ask a superior: they take more decisions, and have more control and responsibility for the work they do than unempowered employees. See also **engaged**.
⟹ an empowered organisation
Empowered employees believe that they share responsibility for the success of their company.

engaged (adj)
/ɪnˈgeɪdʒd/
engagement (n)

Engaged employees are committed to their jobs and to the organisations they work for. Engaged employees are more motivated, more productive and stay longer in their jobs than **disengaged**

Human resources policy and planning

2

engage (v)

employees. See also **engage** (chapter 3), **motivate**.
➟ highly engaged

equal opportunities (n ph)
/'iːkwəl ɒpə'tjuːnɪtiːz/

The objective of an equal opportunities policy is equal treatment for all of a company's employees.

equal opportunities employer (n ph)

Equal opportunities employers aim to remove discrimination on the grounds of sex, race, religion, marital status, disability and age.
➟ an equal opportunities statement
➟ an equal opportunities policy, be committed to
➟ equal opportunity monitoring
➟ equal opportunity targets
Equal opportunities policies should pay special attention, among other things, to selection and training procedures, promotion, pay and hours.

equality management (n ph)
/i'kwɒlɪti 'mænɪdʒmənt/

The objective of equality management is to achieve equal opportunities and diversity in the workplace. See also **diversity**, **equal opportunities**.

exit (n, v)
/'ɛgzɪt/

There is an exit from an organisation when someone leaves. Many organisations have exit procedures or processes in place to find out why people leave. See also **interview**, **retain**, **termination**.

exit data (n ph)

Exit data is information on the reasons why people leave a company. It can be obtained, for example, from exit interviews and leaver surveys. See also **data**.

exit interview (n ph)

You may have an exit interview with a manager before you leave a company.
➟ offer an employee an exit package

family-friendly (adj ph)
/'fæmɪli 'frɛndli/

A family-friendly policy is one that makes it easier for people with children or ageing relations to work. Flexible working, homeworking and additional maternity leave are examples of policies which can help such people. See **flexible working**, **homeworking**, **leave**.
Of the 40% of British women who do not work, most do not do so because of the high cost of child care so they need more family friendly policies from government and employers to help them into employment.

free movement of labour (n ph)
/'friː 'muːvmənt əv 'leɪbə/

When there is free movement of labour between two or more countries, workers of one nationality can get work in another country in the same way as in their own country.

glass ceiling (n ph)
/'glɑːs siːlɪŋ/

The glass ceiling is the invisible barrier which stops more women from getting promotion to top positions in organisations.
➟ break through the glass ceiling
The glass ceiling in industry is still strong since so few women are in senior management positions in major companies.

headcount (n)
/'hɛdkaʊnt/

An organisation's headcount is the number of people who work for it. *We have had an excellent six months and are planning to double headcount in sales by year end.*

human capital (n ph)
/'hjuːmən 'kæpɪtəl/

Human capital describes the contribution made by human skills and knowledge to the success of an organisation. Human capital management measures the value that people add to organisations.
- human capital management
- human capital measurement
- human capital reporting

Human capital management is not just about measuring added business value but also about understanding that employees who invest their own human capital in organisations expect a return, and about creating organisations which add value to the people who work for them. HCM should be about improving returns both for the business and for its people.

human resources (n ph)
/'hjuːmən rɪ'zɔːsɪz/

human resources practitioner (n ph)

The management of the human resources of a company is the management of all the people used by the company – from inside and outside – to achieve its objectives. See also **personnel**, **resource**. Anyone who works in HR is a human resources practitioner.
- a human resources audit
- a human resources information system
- allocate human resources
- deploy a company's human resources
- human resources cost management
- human resources development
- human resources management
- human resources planning
- human resources strategy
- manage a company's human resources
- the human resources contribution
- the human resources function

Personnel management is the day-to-day management of people; human resources management is the strategic management of people.

insource (v)
/'ɪnsɔːs/
insourcing (n)

Insourcing is when an organisation uses its own employees to provide a service, especially when the service had previously been outsourced. See also **market testing**, **outsource**.

kiosk (n)
/'kiːɒsk/
kiosking (n)

A kiosk, also called a **booth**, is a place with a computer terminal which employees can use to get information about flexible benefits, internal recruitment opportunities, etc. Kiosks are designed to give the user privacy. Employees can make calculations about benefits, get printouts, and, for example, tell the system to make changes to their own remuneration packages.
Employees of Alcatel Telecom UK, who have responsibility for their own flexible benefits packages, can check and change them at electronic kiosks in the workplace.

2

Human resources policy and planning

mainstreaming (n)
/'meɪnstriːmɪŋ/
mainstream (v)
gender mainstreaming
(n ph)

A company mainstreams an issue – usually to do with gender and equality – when it makes it a central part of all company policy and practice.
When a company makes gender mainstreaming an issue, it decides to give priority to ensuring equality of treatment for men and women.

man (v)
/'mæn/
manning (n)

When you man a task, you provide the men for the job to be completed. Note: using this term about women is sexist. See also **demanning, overstaff**.
➡ a manning agreement
➡ a manning level, a high / low

manpower (n)
/'mænpaʊə/

The manpower of a company is the total of all the people who work in it. Note: this term may be regarded as sexist. See also **personnel, staff, workforce**.
➡ a manpower shortage
➡ a manpower survey
➡ manpower demand
➡ manpower forecasting, ~ methods
➡ manpower needs / requirements
➡ manpower planning, carry out
➡ manpower provision
➡ manpower reductions

market testing (n ph)
/'mɑːkɪt 'tɛstɪŋ/

Market testing happens when a company compares the cost of a non-core function with the cost of having the function provided by an outsider. See also **insource, outsource**.

motivate (v)
/'məʊtɪveɪt/
motivation (n)
motive (n)
motivator (n)
extrinsic motivation
(n ph)
intrinsic motivation
(n ph)

When you motivate someone, you make them want to work hard and to succeed. See also **engaged**.

When you are extrinsically motivated, something outside yourself makes you want to work. Money is an extrinsic motivator.
When you are intrinsically motivated, something inside yourself makes you want to work. Interest in the content of your work is an intrinsic motivator.
One of the most important qualities in managers is the ability to motivate staff.

natural wastage (n ph)
/'nætʃərəl 'weɪstɪdʒ/

When a company's workforce gets smaller through natural wastage, it is because employees retire, die or leave the company and are not replaced.
We do not want to make anyone redundant so we hope we can reduce the size of the workforce by 20% over the next five years through natural wastage alone.

notice (n)
/'nəʊtɪs/

A period of notice is the length of time that you have to work between the date when you resign from or are dismissed from your job and the date when you actually leave the company. See also **notice** (chapter 6).

➡ a notice period
➡ a statutory period of notice
➡ give notice to quit
➡ hand in one's notice
➡ notice of dismissal
➡ receive notice
➡ serve notice
➡ serve out a period of notice
➡ three months' notice
➡ written notice

All our employees must give a minimum of one month's notice of their intention to leave the company.

offshore (adj, adv, v)
/'ɒfʃɔː/
offshoring (n)
**human resources
offshoring** (n ph)

Offshoring happens when a company reduces its workforce in its home country and employs workers in anther country where labour costs are lower. See also **outsource**, **social dumping**.
Human resources offshoring happens when HR functions are moved to a country with lower labour costs.

➡ an offshoring operation
➡ offshore a call centre

To deliver a successful offshoring programme, companies need – among other things – to think long term, consult closely with employee representatives, keep staff informed of what is happening, and not lose sight of the broader objectives of the organisation.

outplacement (n)
/aʊt'pleɪsmənt/

Outplacement is a support service for staff who are made redundant. During outplacement, the employer usually gives employees help in preparing themselves to find another job. See also **termination**.

➡ outplacement counselling

We provide outplacement support in the form of counselling, advice about how to write a CV, and retraining programmes for all staff made redundant.

outsource (v)
/'aʊtsɔːs/
outsourcing (n)

When a company outsources a service, it decides to stop employing people directly to provide the service and asks an outside agency to provide it instead. Also known as **outservicing**. See also **insource**, **offshore**, **transfer of undertakings**.

We decided to outsource our cleaning and canteen facilities to outside suppliers in order to cut costs.

overstaff (v)
/əʊvə'stɑːf/
overstaffing (n)

When a company is overstaffed, it has too many people working for it. Overstaffing is also known as **overmanning** but using this term about women can be considered sexist. See also **demanning**, **man**.

Human resources policy and planning

performance (n)
/pəˈfɔːməns/
perform (v)

When you talk about job performance, you talk about how well people do their jobs. When people **underperform**, they do not do their jobs as well as they could or should. See also **capability**, **performance-related pay**, **SMART objectives**.

performance attribute (n ph)

Performance attributes are qualities or skills that you can have, for example numeracy, a sense of responsibility, and stability. See also **competency**, **skill**.

performance consultant (n ph)

Performance consultants are trainers who work closely with line managers to understand their departments' needs and how they relate to the needs of the business, so that they can relate their training to these needs. See also **train**.

performance review (n ph)

Performance reviews are spoken or written summaries of how well people do their jobs. See also **appraise**, **assess**.

➡ a high / low level of performance
➡ a performance indicator
➡ a poor performer
➡ measure performance, performance measurement
➡ monitor performance
➡ perform a duty, perform duties
➡ performance appraisal
➡ performance improvement, achieve
➡ performance management
➡ raise / improve performance
➡ the performance review cycle

Raising people's performance is the single most important challenge facing HR and people managers.

personnel (n)
/pɜːsəˈnɛl/

The personnel of the company is the total of all the people who work for it. See also **human resources**, **manpower**, **staff**, **workforce**.

personnel management (n ph)

Personnel management is concerned with the administration of staffing, recruitment, training and development and other functions relating to the management of a company's workforce.

personnel practitioner (n ph)

Anyone who works in personnel is a personnel practitioner. See also **human resources**.

➡ keep / maintain personnel records

position analysis questionnaire (n ph)
/pəˈzɪʃən əˈnælɪsɪs ˈkwɛstʃənɛə/

A position analysis questionnaire (PAQ) is a detailed questionnaire used by a job analyst to describe a job. Also known as a **job analysis questionnaire**. See also **job**, **position**.

➡ fill in / complete a position analysis questionnaire

Some HR managers find the quantitative approach of the PAQ very useful in deciding on the pay for a particular job.

positive action (n ph)
/ˈpɒzɪtɪv ˈækʃən/

Employers take positive action to increase the diversity of their workforce or the balance among applicants for jobs with the organisation, not because they have to but because they want to. See also **affirmative action**, **diversity**.

Examples of positive action are comparing the profile of the workforce with the local population, encouraging job applications from members of under-represented groups, making company buildings accessible to the disabled, and helping staff with childcare arrangements.

pre-retirement (n)
/'pri: rɪ'taɪəmənt/

Pre-retirement is the period in your working life before you retire when you begin to prepare for retirement. See also **retire**.
Companies can offer pre-retirement counselling not only to employees retiring soon but also to their spouses.

promote (v)
/prə'məʊt/
promotion (n)
pass over for promotion (v ph)

When you promote someone, you give them a higher grade job. See also **demote**.

If you are passed over for promotion, someone else gets the higher level job that you had hoped or expected to get.
➡ automatic promotion
➡ good / poor promotion prospects
➡ miss (out on) promotion
➡ obtain promotion
➡ promote over someone's head
➡ promotion opportunities

quota strategy (n ph)
/'kwəʊtə strætədʒi/

A company with a quota strategy has a rule that some vacancies can only be filled, for example, by women or disabled or black people. See **affirmative action**, **diversity**, **positive action**.
Some people think that a quota strategy is a good way to help members of minorities to advance but others think that it can create a situation where vacancies do not always go to the best applicants.

re-entry (n)
/ri'ɛntri/

The re-entry of an expatriate manager is the manager's return to his or her home country and to a home workplace.

regrade (v)
/ri'greɪd/

When an organisation regrades a job, it changes its grade. See also **grade**, **downgrade**.

relieve (v)
/rɪ'li:v/
relief (adj, n)

1 You relieve someone on duty or at the end of a shift when you take over the work from them. A relief can also do the work of someone who is sick or on holiday. See also **cover**, **duty**, **shift**.
➡ a relief manager
➡ provide relief to
➡ relieve someone on duty
2 You relieve someone of their duties when you dismiss or suspend them. See also **dismiss**, **suspend**.
➡ relieve someone of his / her duties

relocate (v)
/rɪ:ləʊ'keɪt/
relocation (n)

When companies or people relocate, they move their place of work from one place to another. See also **assisted passage**, **removal**.
➡ a relocation allowance
➡ relocation expenses

2

Human resources policy and planning

Human resources policy and planning

2

Employees are often against relocation when they are first told that their company wants them to move from a city to a smaller town, but many of them are eventually very happy about the change.

removal (n)
/rɪˈmuːvəl/
remove (v)

1 A removals service is one which moves your furniture and other belongings from your old home to your new one. See **relocate**.
2 If you are removed from your post, you are either moved to another one or dismissed.
When a company relocates from the capital to the provinces, it usually pays the removal expenses of all its personnel.

resettle (v)
/riːˈsɛtəl/
resettlement (n)

When a company resettles you, it helps you to move back to the place where you used to live and work before you moved to live and work in another place.
➡ a resettlement allowance

retain (v)
/riˈteɪn/
retention (n)

A company which tries to retain staff makes efforts to keep its employees and to encourage them not to leave. See also **exit**.
➡ a retention strategy
Important features of a retention strategy are training, analysis of exit data, and recruitment of people with realistic expectations.

roster (n, v)
/ˈrɒstə/

A roster or **rosta** or **rota** is a list of employees and their duties or the times when they are on duty. When employees **self-roster**, they decide themselves who should work when.
➡ a duty roster
An IKEA store in Germany introduced self-rostering to help employees manage a better work-life balance for themselves.

seniority (n)
/siːniˈɒrɪti/

A company which operates a seniority rule promotes people according to how long they have worked for the company rather than according to merit. See also **ascription**, **service**.
➡ operate a seniority rule
➡ get promotion through seniority
Many European companies used to appoint managers to top posts by seniority but now it is done much more according to merit and ability.

service (n)
/ˈsɜːvɪs/
service award (n ph)

Your service is the length of time you have worked for an organisation. See also **seniority**.
A service award is a payment to an employee for having worked for the company for a certain period of time. See also **increment**, **seniority**.
➡ a lifetime's service
➡ a long service award
➡ length of service
We make a special service award to all employees who reach thirty years' service with the company.

sexual orientation (n ph)
/'sɛksjʊəl ɔːrɪɛnteɪʃən/

Your sexual orientation or **sexuality** or **sexual preference** refers to the gender of person you prefer to have sex with, and to your sexual identity – heterosexual, homosexual, bisexual, transsexual, etc. See also **discriminate**, **diversity**.
Under European law, employers may not discriminate against employees because of their sexual orientation.

shared services (n ph)
/'ʃɛəd 'sɜːvɪsɪz/

An organisation with HR shared services has a centralised system for providing information to its employees about different aspects of their working conditions, for example, information about payroll and pension administration, recruitment, career development, etc. Shared services can be provided internally or by an outsourced supplier and via call centres and the intranet.
➡ a shared service centre
➡ adopt a shared services approach
On the one hand, shared services can help cut the costs of HR support and make it more efficient. On the other, they can also be expensive to introduce and can move HR too far away from its internal customers.

sheltered (adj)
/'ʃɛltəd/

A sheltered situation is one specially designed for a disabled person. For example, a sheltered factory is one where a majority of the employees are disabled. See also **disability**.
➡ a sheltered job
➡ a sheltered placement scheme
Research in Britain shows that many disabled people prefer to work in sheltered jobs in sheltered factories rather than in "open" employment.

short-time working (n ph)
/ʃɔːt taɪm 'wɜːkɪŋ/

When a company puts some of its employees on short-time working, it employs them for fewer hours than usual each week because it does not have enough work for them to do.
➡ put someone on short-time working (and then: restore someone to full-time working)

social dumping (n ph)
/'səʊʃəl 'dʌmpɪŋ/

Social dumping is a critical way to describe offshoring – moving jobs to lower labour cost areas or countries; or employing low cost, non-unionised or illegal labour in a rich country. See **offshore**.

staff (n, v)
/'stɑːf/

The staff of the company is the total of all the people who work for it. See also **manpower**, **personnel**, **workforce**, **staff association**. When you staff a company, you provide it with the work people it needs.
➡ a (junior / senior) staff member / member of staff
➡ a (serious / severe) shortage of staff / staff shortage
➡ a skeleton staff
➡ a staff handbook
➡ contract staff
➡ core staff, non-core staff
➡ managerial staff

2

Human resources policy and planning

Human resources policy and planning

⇒ peripheral staff
⇒ secretarial staff
⇒ staff development / training
⇒ staff reduction
⇒ staff retention
⇒ staff turnover, reduce
⇒ supervisory staff
⇒ support staff
⇒ technical staff

stagger (v)
/'stægə/

When a company staggers the holidays of its employees, it organises them so that not everyone goes on holiday at the same time, in order to be sure that the work of the company goes on smoothly. See also **holiday, roster**.
⇒ staggered holidays
⇒ staggered hours
The summer holidays of our workforce are staggered from June to September so that not too many people are away at any one time.

stakeholder (n)
/'steɪkhəʊldə/

A stakeholder is anyone who has some interest in encouraging the success of a company. Stakeholders can include the shareholders of the company, its employees and their families, and its customers. See also **corporate social responsibility, workholder**.

termination (n)
/tɜːmɪn'eɪʃən/
terminate (v)

Termination is a general word for the different ways of ending a job, through retirement, resignation, redundancy, and so on. See also **dismiss, exit, fire, notice, outplacement, quit, redundant, release, resign, retire, sack**.
⇒ a termination interview
⇒ a termination payment
⇒ a termination report
⇒ notification of termination
⇒ settlement on termination of employment
⇒ terminate employment
⇒ terminate the employment relationship

**time and motion
study** (n ph)
/taɪm ən 'məʊʃən stʌdi/

Time and motion is a technique for studying how to increase the output from a job by measuring and analysing in detail how the job is done and how long each part of the job takes to do.
⇒ carry out / perform a time and motion study
Time and motion studies carried out by consultants have been very unpopular with workers in the past. More recent experiments with workers doing the measuring themselves have been more successful.

turnover (n)
/'tɜːnəʊvə/

The turnover of a company's workforce is the number of people being replaced each year expressed as a percentage of the whole workforce:

if a company has 100 employees and turnover is 10% for the year, it means that ten of the staff have left and have been replaced by new employees. Another word for turnover is **churn**.

➡ labour turnover

➡ high / low staff turnover

welfare to work (n ph)
/wɛlfɛə tə 'wɜːk/

Welfare-to-work programmes are run by government in Britain and the US to help unemployed people claiming state benefit to get training and find jobs. See also **welfare**.

workforce (n)
/'wɜːkfɔːs/
single status workforce
(n ph)

The workforce of a company is the total of all the people who work for it. See also **manpower**, **personnel**, **staff**.
A single status workforce is one which treats white-collar and blue-collar workers in the same way.

➡ a flexible workforce

Human resources policy and planning

2

Exercises

Exercise1

Read the corporate HR policy statement and fill the gaps with terms from the box.

diversity	equal opportunities	human resources	promotion
benchmark	absence	empowerment	
disabilities	attendance	family-friendly	

Our management of our (1) .... is based on three principles. The first is (2) .... : we aim to move decision-making to the people who have most opportunity to provide customer satisfaction. The next is (3) ....: women receive the same pay as men for the same work throughout the organisation and have the same chances of (4) .... The third is (5) .... : we believe that organisational strength comes from different views and ideas uniting in a common purpose and we are always trying to increase the number of people we recruit from ethnic minorities. Our policy of employing a certain percentage of people with (6) .... has helped to improve the status of handicapped people within our local community. Our (7) .... policies allow parents to spend more time with their children at times of the day when it is most important to them. And it works. (8) .... is high. (9) .... is low. Our aim is to be a (10) .... for the whole industry, viewed by our competitors as a reference for best practice as an employer.

Exercise 2

Match the HR terms (1 - 10) with their definitions (a - j).

1	Headcount	a	The period of time that you work between saying you are going to leave your job and leaving it
2	Absent	b	When a company reduces the size of the workforce without making anyone redundant
3	Turnover	c	The period near the end of your working life
4	Glass ceiling	d	Make people enthusiastic about their work
5	Natural wastage	e	The number of employees
6	Notice	f	Treat someone unfairly because of their sex, race or religion
7	Pre-retirement	g	Someone who has an interest in the success of a company
8	Stakeholder	h	The percentage of the workforce which needs to be replaced every year
9	Motivate	i	Off work
10	Discriminate	j	A barrier stopping people from certain groups (e.g. women) from getting promotion to the top jobs

Exercise 3

Choose the best term (A, B, C or D) to complete each sentence.

1 Many non-essential services such as maintenance, security and the company canteen have been contracted out as part of our _____ policy.
   A external   B part-time   C temporary   D outsourcing

2 Following a report on the company's structure, we decided to _____ , which involved removing several junior and middle management grades.
   A decrease   B delayer   C demote   D deploy

3 After five years in the centre of Paris, our organisation _____ to a greenfield site near Grenoble.
   A remained   B re-established   C returned   D relocated

4 Due to government pressure, many French firms offer _____ services when laying off employees.
   A firing   B rehabilitating   C outplacement   D relocation

5 We are not paying enough attention to the changing _____ profile of our workforce. We're getting old! We need to recruit some younger blood, and soon!
   A demographic   B democratic   C demagogic   D demotic

6 If the company continues to engage in a policy of social _____ and moves even more jobs to cheap labour locations abroad, we're all going to lose our jobs eventually.
   A security   B partnering   C dumping   D welfare

7 When companies run into financial difficulties, one solution is to _____ in order to cut the workforce and subsequent labour costs.
   A decrease   B reduce   C downsize   D miniaturise

8 Due to its customer commitment policy, management decided to _____ time off, holidays and working hours.
   A relocate   B introduce   C stagger   D shift

9 Companies in my country are required by law to have a minimum, fixed percentage of _____ jobs for disabled persons.
   A sheltered   B hidden   C protected   D opportunity

10 Negotiations ended when management and the unions agreed to _____ workers to the York site, in order to avoid redundancies.
   A regenerate   B redeploy   C return   D repatriate

Exercise 4

Which HR policy statement (1-10) does each of the words or phrases in the box refer to?

business partnering	retention	overstaffing	termination
sexual orientation		ageism	alignment
outsourcing	human capital	business process re-engineering	

1. We can expect the number of employees leaving the company to increase due to a rise in the number of people retiring or resigning: _____

2. Consultants came to the conclusion that there were too many people doing too little work in our department: _____

3. Dramatic improvements in quality, productivity, service and cost were made by completely redesigning the team mix: _____

4. Our new HR director has established a new credibility for us at board level by using stronger financial arguments for our policies: _____

5. Our HR policies are now much more in line with the overall strategic objectives of the company: _____

6. We decided to compare the cost of keeping our maintenance staff in the company with the cost of giving the function to an external provider:

    _____

7. We do not tolerate discrimination against homosexuals:

    _____

8. Too many people are leaving. We need to find out why and then we need to bring this figure down: _____

9. We need better measures of the value that our people add to the organisation:

    _____

10. Before the introduction of our equality management policy, the company treated many of our older people quite badly and certainly recruited very few people over the age of 50: _____

Human resources policy and planning

2

Exercise 5

Create word clusters (groups of words in the same family) from memory or by looking at the list of key terms at the start of this chapter.

1   Move someone within the organisation:

2   Change the structure of the organisation:

3   Improve equality in the workplace:

4   Develop HR and business strategy:

For discussion

1   Does HR have a future?
2   How strategic is your organisation's HR function? Should it be more strategic than it currently is? How can it become so?
3   Should a company totally outsource its HR requirements?
4   What is the ratio of male to female employees in your organisation? How far does this vary according to job type, department and level? Does the number of senior women managers reflect the gender balance as a whole? Should it?
5   What is your organisation's policy on diversity? Would you like to change it in any way?
6   Do you work for a family-friendly organisation? What makes it so?

2

Human resources policy and planning

Human resources policy and planning

2

Case study

Human resources management versus personnel management

Congratulations. You have just been appointed to the post of HR director of Jenson FaS. Jenson Facilities and Solutions was created seven years ago and has since grown rapidly, acquiring several well-established SMEs (small or medium-sized enterprises) around the country working in five sectors: air conditioning, electricity and cabling, safety and security services, IT networks, and sustainability services. You have been told that Jenson also has plans to make its first foreign acquisition soon.

Until now, Jenson operated a personnel department consisting of ten people, mainly dealing with the administration of pay, holidays and welfare-related subjects. Recruitment and career development was the direct responsibility of the founding directors. Appraisal was verbal and informal, relying on interpersonal skills and networking. All employees had direct access to top management.

Given the rapid growth of the company from a core of 150 people to 1,200 at present, you have been recruited to establish a human resources department. Top management wishes to see HR quickly become a strategic function within the company, covering not just areas such as motivation, mobility, training, recruitment and employee relations, but also closely linked to the business development of the organisation, especially in relation to profitability and the optimisation of resources. Your task is a challenging one: to build from zero a policy that puts the HR function at the heart of the company's strategy and which makes a clear contribution to profits.

Consider these questions:
* How will you organise your head office department?
* How will you organise HR in the five sectors?
* What systems and processes will you set up?
* How will you 'sell' HR to both employees and senior management?
* How will you ensure that HR adds value?

3

Resourcing

Key terms to talk about
recruiting, selecting and
retaining people for the
organisation and for managing
the overall size of the
workforce.

**These are the key terms in this chapter.
Which of them do you understand?
Which of them can you use?**

Advertise

apply

appoint

attract

Biodata

Candidate

CV

Degree

diploma

Employee value proposition

employer branding

employment agency

engage

executive search

experience

Fire

Gatekeeping

graduate

grande école

graphology

Halo effect

headhunter

high potential

hire

hire and fire

Intake

intern

interview

Job

Last in, first out

lay off

leapfrog

let go

Medical examination

milk round

Offer

old boy network

Panel

pick

pre-select

probationary period

profile

Qualification

Recruit

redundant

referee

reject

release

requirements

resource

résumé

roadshow

Sack

screen

search

select

shortlist

survivor

Take on

talent

test

testimonial

track record

Vacant

vet

Word-of-mouth

Resourcing

3

advertise (v)

/'ædvətaɪz/

advertisement (n)

ad (n, abbrev)

advertising (n)

When you advertise a job vacancy, you pay for information about the job to appear in newspapers or specialised magazines.

➡ a job advertisement, place

➡ advertise a vacancy

➡ advertise in the national press / advertise nationally

➡ advertise in the specialised press

Big companies normally advertise important vacancies both in the national and in the specialised press.

apply (v)

/ə'plaɪ/

applicant (n)

application (n)

consider an application (v ph)

turn down an application (v ph)

unsolicited application (n ph)

When you apply for a job, you tell the organisation formally that you would like the job. An **applicant** is someone who applies for a job.

A company considering an application is thinking about it and has not yet made a decision.

When a company turns down your application, it tells you that it is not going to give you a job.

When you make an unsolicited application, you write to a company asking for a job even though it has not advertised a vacancy. Also known as a **speculative application**.

➡ a completed application form, send ~ to

➡ a deadline for applications

➡ a job applicant

➡ a letter of application, write

➡ a written application, send

➡ an application form, fill in / complete

➡ an application procedure

➡ apply for a job

➡ apply for the post of

➡ consider an application

➡ invite applications from

➡ make / submit an application for the post of

➡ reject / turn down an application

➡ retain an application

➡ submit an application to

➡ the status of an application, inform a candidate of

appoint (v)

/ə'pɔɪnt/

appointee (n)

appointment (n)

When an organisation appoints someone to a post, it formally gives the job to that person. The **appointee** is the person appointed to a post.

➡ a first appointment

➡ announce an appointment

➡ make an appointment

Senior company appointments are announced in the business appointments sections of the national newspapers.

3

Resourcing

Resourcing

3

attract (v)
/ə'trækt/
attraction (n)
attractive (adj)

An organisation will attract the right people if it offers the kind of work and working conditions that they want. Companies with more interesting and enjoyable work to offer and with better pay and conditions will be more attractive than their competitors. See also **employee value proposition**.

biodata (n)
/'baɪəʊdeɪtə/

Your biodata are basic details about you and your background. See also **data**.
Biodata given on a CV or application form – including qualifications, years of experience, etc. – can be scored, and the score can then be used by the recruiter to shorten the list of applicants.

candidate (n)
/'kændɪdeɪt/
candidature (n)

When you apply for a job, you become a candidate for the job.
➡ a successful / unsuccessful candidate
➡ a strong / weak candidate

CV (abbrev)
/'siː 'viː/

Your CV is a formal document giving details of your education and professional history which you can send to a company when you apply for a job. CV stands for **curriculum vitae** (Latin). Used in the UK rather than in the US. See also **résumé**.
➡ send a copy of your CV to
Send your CV together with a letter of application, a recent photograph, and the names and addresses of two referees.

degree (n)
/dɪ'griː/

A degree is a qualification which you get at the end of a successful course of study at a university. See also **diploma**, **graduate**, **qualification**.
➡ a Bachelor's degree
➡ a degree-awarding institution
➡ a first degree
➡ a higher degree
➡ a Master's degree
➡ an honours degree
➡ an ordinary degree
➡ award a degree
➡ have a degree in (a subject)
➡ read for / study for a degree in (a subject)

diploma (n)
/dɪ'pləʊmə/

A diploma is a qualification, usually obtained after an examination. There are big differences in value and status among the large number of diplomas which are available.
See also **degree**, **graduate**, **qualification**.
➡ a professional diploma
➡ gain / obtain a diploma
➡ study for a diploma

employee value proposition (n ph)
/ɪmplɔɪ'iː 'væljuː prɒpə'zɪʃən/

An organisation with an employee value proposition communicates clearly to job applicants the reasons why they should want to join, and communicates the same message to all staff and agencies involved in recruitment, and other staff. See also **attract**.

employer branding (n ph)
/ɪmˈplɔɪə ˈbrændɪŋ/
employer brand (n ph)

Employer branding is a marketing strategy used by companies which want to improve their image as employers. It should also involve the organisation's thinking about what kind of employer it needs to be to attract the workforce which will help it realize its targets, about the HR policy which will help it deliver this, and about whether perceptions of the brand – internally and externally – match the brand the employer wants.
➡ employer brand management
McDonald's employer branding in the UK involved its HR, communications, training and marketing departments working together on special recruitment drives and new training schemes.

employment agency (n)
/ɪmˈplɔɪmənt ˈeɪdʒənsi/

An employment agency – also known as a **staff agency** or simply as an **agency** – finds new staff for organisations and provides them with temporary staff. See also **executive search**.
➡ an agency worker

engage (v)
/ɪnˈgeɪdʒ/
engagement (n)
re-engage (v)
re-engagement (n)

An organisation engages someone when it gives that person a job. When it **re-engages** someone, it gives a job to someone who used to work for the organisation and who has returned, although it is not necessarily the same job. See also **engaged**, **returner**.
➡ negotiate the terms of engagement / re-engagement

executive search (n ph)
/ɪgˈzɛkjətɪv sɜːtʃ/

Executive search is the process of finding (usually senior) managers for vacant positions. An **executive search agency** is a consultancy which helps companies to recruit them. See also **employment agency**, **head hunter**, **search**.
➡ carry out an executive search
➡ an executive search consultant
Companies sometimes complain that executive search agencies are expensive but they sometimes have to use them, for example when they are trying to recruit managers in another country where they have no local staff.

experience (n)
/ɪkˈspɪərɪəns/

The experience you have is the knowledge and skill you have got from your present and previous jobs. See also **track record**.
➡ a wealth of experience
➡ acquire / gain / get experience
➡ first-hand experience
➡ job experience
➡ previous experience
➡ professional experience
➡ wide / limited experience, have / possess

fire (v, informal)
/ˈfaɪə/

If your employer fires you, you are told that you no longer have a job and that you must leave the company. See also **discharge**, **dismiss**, **fire** (chapter 6), **hire and fire**, **sack**, **termination**.

3

Resourcing

Resourcing

3

gatekeeping (n)
/'geɪtkiːpɪŋ/

Gatekeeping is pre-employment health screening. When a company uses gatekeeping, it screens job applicants to check their physical or psychological fitness for a job. Gatekeeping is a way of reducing sickness absenteeism. See also **medical examination, screen.**

graduate (n,v)
/'grædjʊət/ (n)
/'grædjʊeɪt/ (v)

A graduate is someone with a university degree.
➡ a graduate recruit
➡ a graduate recruitment fair / scheme
➡ a postgraduate, ~ degree
➡ graduate recruitment
The recruitment officers of many big companies travel round their country's universities once a year to meet future graduates who could be potential recruits.

grande école
(n ph, French)
/'grɒnd ɛ'kɒl/

Grandes écoles offer an alternative to university for students in France and some of them have very high status. They include the country's top business and engineering schools. Entry is by competitive examination which can take up to two years to prepare for at post-secondary level.
➡ a top grande école
➡ the French grande école system
French executives sometimes have problems applying for jobs in international companies because non-French recruiters are not always aware of the high status of the grande école that they may have attended.

graphology (n)
/græf'ɒlədʒi/
graphologist (n)

Graphology is the study of the shape, size and style of handwriting in order to learn about the personality of the writer. Graphology tests are also known as **handwriting tests.**

halo effect (n ph)
/'heɪləʊ ɪ'fɛkt/

The halo effect makes a recruiter believe that because an applicant has some good points, most other things about the applicant must be good as well.

headhunter
(n ph, informal)
/'hɛd hʌntə/
head hunter (v ph)

Executive search consultants are informally known as headhunters. Their job is to identify managers for vacant posts at the companies which are paying them to carry out the search. Headhunters are often commissioned to find people for quite senior posts and for posts requiring candidates with skills which are in short supply. See also **employment agency, executive search, search.**
In France, head hunters can begin their searches by using data bases of names of graduates of the top business and engineering schools.

high potential
(adj ph, adv ph, n ph)
/'haɪ pə'tɛnʃəl/

A high potential is a young manager who is expected to rise to a high position in the company. Also known as a **high flyer** and informally as a **high pot.** High potentials are on the **fast track** or in the **fast stream.**
High potentials recruited to British companies are often put onto a special training programme which gives them experience in several different departments.
➡ a graduate high flier

hire (n, v)
/ˈhaɪə/

When a company hires someone, it finds and employs someone to do a job. 'Hire' is a less formal word than 'recruit' and is more often used with lower level or temporary staff. A new hire is a new recruit. See also **recruit**.

hire and fire
(v ph, adj ph, informal)
/ˈhaɪə rən ˈfaɪə/

When a company hires and fires people, it recruits and dismisses staff frequently. See also **hire**.
➡ a hire and fire approach / policy

intake (n)
/ˈɪnteɪk/

An intake is a group of people all recruited at the same time. See also **recruit**.
➡ a graduate intake
➡ an annual intake
Because of the economic situation, our annual intake of new recruits is smaller than usual.

intern (n)
/ˈɪntɜːn/
internship (n)

An intern is someone doing on-the-job training or work experience. Interns are often students. See also **work** (chapter 5), **work experience**.

interview (n,v)
/ˈɪntəvjuː/
interviewee (n)
interviewer (n)

An interview is a meeting between a job applicant and someone in the company who will decide or help to decide whether to give a job to this person. See also **panel**.

attend an interview
(v ph)

When candidates attend an interview, they go to and are present at the interview.

hold an interview (v ph)

When an organisation holds an interview, it organises an interview to which it invites shortlisted candidates.

competency-based interview (n ph)

In a competency-based interview, the interviewer tries to get information about the candidate's past behaviour in certain situations, based on the idea that past behaviour is the best way of predicting future behaviour. Competency-based interviews are structured, with questions that relate directly to the essential competencies required for the post. Questions are likely to start with: "Please give me an example when…" or "Please describe an occasion" etc. Also known as a **behavioural interview**. See also **competence**.

behavioural event interview (n ph)

In a behavioural event interview, interviewees are scored on their answers to questions about what they would do in a number of different professional situations. All the candidates are given the same situations. Also known as a **situational interview**.
➡ a group interview
➡ a non-directed interview
➡ a preliminary interview
➡ call a candidate for / to interview
➡ conduct / hold an interview
➡ interview performance, a good / bad / poor
➡ invite the candidate to attend an interview
➡ the final interview, reach ~ stage
Although he was invited to attend a preliminary interview for the vacant post, he did not reach the final interview stage.

3

Resourcing

job (n)
/'dʒɒb/
occupational.
job prospects (n ph)

A job is a position of regular paid work in a company. See also
occupation, half-time, job (chapters 1 and 5), **occupation,**
If you have a good chance of future promotion, your job prospects are
good.

⟶ a job advertisement
⟶ a job application
⟶ a job application form
⟶ a job description
⟶ a job interview, invite someone to attend
⟶ a job offer
⟶ a job specification
⟶ a job vacancy
⟶ apply for a job
⟶ offer a job to

*Job applicants are normally sent a job description or job specification
and a job application form.*

last in, first out (adj ph)
/lɑːst 'ɪn fɜːst aʊt/

A company which operates a last in, first out or **LIFO** policy chooses
for redundancy first the person who it recruited the most recently.

lay off (v)
/leɪ 'ɒf/
lay-off (n)

When a company lays off employees, they stop working temporarily
because there is not enough work for them to do. In the USA, lay off
means dismissal. See also **dismiss.**
*We have to lay off a certain number of workers due to a fall in sales
but we hope to take them all on again as soon as the economic
situation improves.*

leapfrog (v)
/'liːpfrɒg/

You leapfrog over the head of your immediate superior when you are
promoted to a position over him or her.

let go (v)
/lɛt 'gəʊ/

When an organisation says that it is letting someone go, it makes them
redundant. People managers should avoid this expression: it suggests
that employees are being allowed to leave because they want to when
in fact they are being sacked. See also **release.**

**medical
examination** (n phr)
/'mɛdɪkəl
ɪg'zæmɪneɪʃən/

When you have a medical examination, a doctor or nurse checks that
your physical and mental condition is good enough for the job you
have applied for. See also **check-up, gatekeeping, medical record,
screen.**

milk round
(n ph, informal)
/'mɪlk 'raʊnd/

The milk round is the annual tour of British universities made by the
recruitment officers of major companies in search of talented future
graduates. See also **roadshow, talent.**

offer (n, v)
/'ɒfə/

When someone offers you a job or makes you a job offer, they ask you
if you would like a job.

⟶ an offer letter
⟶ make a job offer to

old boy network
(n ph informal)
/'əʊld 'bɔɪ 'nɛtwɜːk/

An old boy network is a set of informal contacts among former students of certain high status schools and universities which can give members unfair advantages at work.
➟ belong to an old boy network
➟ operate an old boy network
The former students of some private schools in the UK as well as of the universities of Oxford and Cambridge are criticised for operating old boy (and old girl) networks while in France some of the best-known grandes écoles receive similar criticism.

panel (n)
/'pænəl/

A panel is a small group of interviewers. See also **interview**, **panel** (chapter 8).
➟ an interview panel, sit on / serve on / be a member of
➟ a panel interview
➟ a selection panel
Some selection procedures involve several stages including interviews with a single interviewer and panel interviews.

pick (v)
/'pɪk/

When someone is picked to do something, it means they have been chosen or selected to do something.
We always aim to pick the best person for the job.

pre-select (v)
/prɪsɪ'lɛkt/
pre-selection (n)

When an organisation receives a lot of applications for a post, it may make a pre-selection of a certain number of applicants as a first step in the recruitment process. See also **select**, **shortlist**.
When the company received more than 2,000 applications for six vacancies, it pre-selected 400 to go on to the next stage.

probationary period (n ph)
/prə'beɪʃənəri 'pɪərɪəd/

A probationary period is a period of a few weeks or months after you start a new job during which you or your employer can still decide not to make the appointment permanent. Also known as a **trial period**.
➟ an extension of the probationary period, decide on

profile (n, v)
/'prəʊfaɪl/

A profile is a short written summary giving the main features of something.
➟ a career profile
➟ a job profile
➟ an individual profile
Companies get information about job applicants from their CVs, from a completed application form, or from a letter written by candidates which contain profiles of their previous job experience.

qualification (n)
/kwɒlɪfɪ'keɪʃən/
qualify (v)
qualified (adj)
practical qualifications (n ph)

A qualification is an official recognition, often received after passing an examination, that you have successfully completed a course of education or training. See also **degree**, **diploma**.

If you have good practical qualifications, you have a lot of experience in a particular area, even if you do not have any formal qualifications for the job.

3

Resourcing

➠ a professional qualification
➠ a recognised qualification
➠ an academic qualification
➠ check someone's qualifications
➠ formal / no formal qualifications
➠ well / poorly qualified

For many managerial jobs, you need either an academic qualification like a degree or a professional qualification from a professional body or both.

recruit (v, n)
/rɪˈkruːt/
recruitment (n)

When a company recruits someone, it finds and employs someone to do a particular job.

recruitment channel (n ph)

A recruitment channel is a way an organisation can use to inform people of vacancies and to invite applications. Notices on notice boards, advertising, the internet and intranet are all channels which can be used in recruitment.

recruitment drive (n ph)

When a company needs to recruit a lot of people at the same time, it organises a recruitment drive.

recruitment freeze (n ph)

When a company freezes recruitment, it stops taking on new people completely.

volume recruitment (n ph)

An organisation has a volume recruitment requirement when it needs to recruit a large number of people in a short period.

➠ a graduate recruit, graduate recruitment
➠ a recruitment agency
➠ a recruitment brief
➠ a recruitment drive, launch / mount
➠ a recruitment officer
➠ a recruitment procedure
➠ an internal recruitment process
➠ an online recruitment site
➠ competency-based recruitment
➠ internal / external recruitment
➠ online recruitment
➠ recruitment advertising
➠ the recruitment process, stages in

The recruitment process can range from a few minutes of basic questions to several weeks of different stages of interviews and tests.

redundant (adj)
/rɪˈdʌndənt/
redundancy (n)

If you are made redundant, you lose your job. See also **termination**.

redundancy package (n ph)

You get a redundancy package from your employer when you lose your job and receive both money and training to help you find another job. Also known as a **severance package**. See also **severance pay**.

➠ a compulsory redundancy
➠ a redundancy agreement
➠ a redundancy notice, serve ~ on
➠ a redundancy procedure
➠ a voluntary redundancy
➠ collective redundancy

Resourcing

3

➡ make someone redundant
➡ mass redundancies, announce
➡ redundancy consultation
➡ redundancy counselling
➡ redundancy pay
➡ redundancy selection criteria
➡ redundancy terms, generous

We have to reduce the workforce and so we have served redundancy notices on 100 employees, informing them that their jobs will be cut as from 1 January.

referee (n)
/ˌrɛfəˈriː/
reference (n)
character reference (n ph)
follow up a reference (v ph)

A referee is a person who agrees to tell a company about a job applicant's professional or personal abilities and capacities. The company then contacts the applicant's referees to ask for a reference. A character reference talks more about someone's personal qualities than their professional ones.
When you follow up a reference, you request a reference from a referee.

➡ a character / personal reference, provide
➡ a professional reference, request
➡ a written reference
➡ act as a referee, agree to
➡ approach a referee
➡ ask for a reference, ask for references
➡ ask the candidate's permission to follow up references
➡ grant permission to follow up references

If a company is interested in an application, it will follow up the applicant's references by approaching his or her referees before the interview.

reject (v)
/rɪˈdʒɛkt/
rejection (n)

A company rejects an application when it tells the applicant that it does not want to give him or her the job.
Companies should always send letters of rejection to unsuccessful applicants so that they are clear about the status of their application.

release (n, v)
/rɪˈliːs/

An employee is released from his or her contract when the employer decides or agrees to end the employment contract early. Early release may therefore happen with or without the agreement of the employee. Since the word can have both meanings, some employers use it as a euphemism for redundancy. See also **dismiss**, **let go**, **redundancy**, **release** (chapter 5), **termination**.

signed release (n ph)

A signed release is a document that an employee agrees to sign at the time of the termination of his or her employment, for example, because of redundancy, early retirement, etc. When the employee signs the release, he or she gives up the right to take legal action against the employer in exchange for the terms of a severance agreement between them. See also **severance pay**.

➡ agree to an early release
➡ early release, release someone early

Resourcing

3

requirements (n)
/rɪˈkwaɪəmənts/
require (v)

Requirements are the abilities, qualifications and experience that you must have for a particular job.
➡ job requirements
➡ fulfil the requirements of the post
The requirements for this post include a university degree, three years' experience, and the ability to speak two foreign languages.

resource (n, v)
/rɪˈzɔːs/

Resourcing the organisation is the process of getting the right number of the right people to do the work needed to make the organisation successful. Resourcing is mainly about recruitment and selection practices. Also known as **sourcing**. See also **human resources**.
A company's resourcing strategy needs to be ready to deal with recruitment and selection in periods both of economic growth and of recession.

résumé (n)
/ˈrɛzjuːmeɪ/

A résumé is a written summary of your career up to now. Used in the US rather than in the UK. See also **CV**.
➡ a (short) career résumé, send

roadshow (n)
/ˈrəʊdʃəʊ/

A roadshow is a travelling recruitment fair with company stands designed to attract new recruits. See also **milk round**.

sack (n, v, informal)
/ˈsæk/
sackable (adj)

If your employer sacks you, you are told that you no longer have a job and that you must leave the company. See also **discharge, dismiss, hire and fire, termination**.
➡ a sackable offence, commit
➡ get the sack
The supervisor warned him that smoking in the production area was a sackable offence.

screen (v)
/ˈskriːn/
screening (n)

When a company screens an application, it checks it to make sure that the candidate has the right qualifications for the job or is really the kind of person that the company wants to employ. See also **screen** (chapter 6), **select**.
➡ an initial screening, do / carry out
➡ telephone screening, an automated ~ interview
➡ the screening process
Some companies use automatic telephone screening interviews to select new staff, with telephone lines open 24 hours a day, seven days a week.

search (v, n)
/ˈsɜːtʃ/

When a company or an agency carries out a search, it actively looks for and invites applications for a vacant post instead of waiting for candidates to apply in the normal way. See also **assignment, executive search, head hunter**.
➡ a search assignment
➡ a search consultant, commission
➡ an exhaustive / extensive search
➡ carry out a search

select (v)
/sɪ'lɛkt/
selection (n)

When a company selects a job applicant, it chooses the person who, in the opinion of the recruiter, is the best for the job. See also **screen**.
➥ a final selection
➥ a selection panel, face
➥ a selection procedure / process, undergo
➥ an initial selection
➥ make a selection
The selection process can take several months for senior positions in large companies.

shortlist (n, v)
/'ʃɔːtlɪst/

When a company receives a lot of applications for a job, it usually draws up a shortlist of, say, six people, who go on to the next stage in the selection process.
➥ a shortlist of candidates, draw up
➥ a shortlisted candidate

survivor (n)
/sə'vaɪvə/

Survivors are the employees who are left after a company has made a lot of others redundant.
After a company has made large-scale redundancies, survivors often have to overcome feelings of decreased motivation and morale and increased levels of stress.

take on (v)
/teɪk 'ɒn/

When a company takes on staff, it recruits new employees.
➥ take on (new) staff
Companies which have to take on large numbers of new staff rapidly need good induction programmes.

talent (n)
talent retention fund (n ph)

war for talent (n ph)

A talented person is someone with natural ability.
A talent retention fund is a special budget which human resources managers spend on trying to make sure that talented employees do not leave the company.
There is a war for talent when organisations have to compete a lot with each other to recruit people with particular skills. See also **skill** (chapter 1).
➥ talent management
In the UK, there is a war for talent in several sectors, particularly IT, due to the national shortage of people with advanced computing skills.

test (n,v)
/'tɛst/
tester (n)
testing (n)
testee (n)
aptitude test (n ph)

diagnostic test (n ph)

A test is a short or informal examination to measure someone's ability or capacity in some area. A tester is someone who gives you a test. A testee is someone who takes a test.

An aptitude test measures your potential to develop knowledge or skill in a particular area.
A diagnostic test is one which tests what testees do and do not know or can and cannot do. The results of diagnostic tests are important for training course design.

3

Resourcing

psychometric test (n ph)   A psychometric test tries to measure psychological aspects of the candidate such as personality and motivation.
→ a handwriting test
→ a personality test
→ a test battery / a battery of tests
→ a verbal aptitude test
→ administer / give a test
→ an achievement test
→ an attainment test
→ emotional competence testing
→ fail a test
→ get through / pass a test
→ occupational testing
→ sit / take / do a test

testimonial (n)   A testimonial is a statement about candidates' professional or personal
/tɛstɪˈməʊnɪəl/   qualities written by someone who knows them well, which candidates send to a company with their job applications or CVs.
→ submit a testimonial
Testimonials are an essential part of the application process in Switzerland but are rarely used now in the UK.

track record (n ph)   Your track record is your professional performance up to the present.
/ˈtræk rɛkɔːd/   See also **experience**.
→ a good / successful / proven track record

vacant (adj)   A vacant position is a job with no-one to do it. A vacancy is an empty
/ˈveɪkənt/   post. See **position, post**.
vacancy (n)   → a vacant position
→ advertise a vacancy
→ fill a vacancy
→ post a vacancy on the intranet / internet

vet (v)   When an organisation vets applications, it checks candidates carefully
/ˈvɛt/   to make sure of their suitability for the job. Vetting is often done for jobs with a high security risk or in the case where the candidate has a criminal record.
→ a vetting procedure, undergo / be subject to

word of mouth (adv phr)   When you hear about a vacancy by word of mouth, you learn about it
/ˈwɜːd əv ˈmaʊθ/   directly from a friend or acquaintance and not from an advertisement.
word-of-mouth (adj ph)   → by word of mouth
→ word-of-mouth recruitment

Exercises

Exercise 1

Match the definitions (1-10) with the terms in the balloon.

1   a group of interviewers
2   the abilities, qualifications and experience needed
    for the job
3   to employ
4   not to select
5   an empty post
6   to officially give a job to someone
7   first step in the recruitment process
8   search for senior executives
9   a group of people all recruited at the same time
10 a job applicant

take on
head hunt   appoint
requirements   pre-select
panel   intake   reject
vacancy   candidate

3

Resourcing

Exercise 2

Complete each sentence with terms from the box.

degrees	apply	executive search	profile	vet
agency	advertised	word of mouth	graduates	
track record		diplomas	trial period	

1   The candidate decided to _____ for the post after hearing about it by
    _____ from a colleague.
2   The European recruitment manager has to compare candidates' various national
    _____and _____ using an EU education guide.
3   Many service companies working in the banking sector _____ applicants for
    reasons of security.
4   Given the _____ required for the post of senior financial director, it was
    decided to carry out an _____ through an _____ .
5   The normal duration of a _____ is three months for
    executives and one month for manual workers.
6   The vacancy was _____ both in the in-house magazine and on the
    company intranet.
7   The recruitment and mobility department attempt to attract young _____
    by visiting their universities.
8   During the interview, she was asked to talk about her strengths and weaknesses and
    about her _____ in her previous company.

Exercise 3

Choose the best term (A, B, C or D) to complete each sentence.

1   After a series of initial interviews, a _____ of candidates was
    drawn up.
    A test   B pre-select   C shortlist   D screen

2   Many of the CVs we get are sent in answer to job ads. Others are _____,
    usually sent by people who would like to work for us because of our good reputation.
    A unsolicited applications   B referees   C qualifications   D testimonials

3   Before being accepted for the post, he was asked to undertake a _____
    to check he was in good health.
    A record   B biodata   C medical examination   D recording

4   After completing a _____ of three months, it was decided not to retain him.
    A term   B probationary period   C job   D time

5   During the training session, recruitment managers studied the _____ during
    interviews and ways to avoid being over-influenced by a candidate's strong points.
    A influencing effect   B secondary effect   C halo effect   D graphology

6   Some companies organise _____ which travel from university to
    university to reach potential graduate recruits.
    A agency   B coaches   C road shows   D newspaper

7   If we want to maintain the current quality of our senior management, we need to
    recruit several more young _____ now.
    A survivors   B high potentials   . C leapfrogs   D interns

8   He was the first to go after they announced the downsizing because of the
    _____ policy they operate in that company.
    A last in, first out   B let go   C release   D re-engagement

9 . The _____ is so intense in his sector that salaries have gone up
    by more than 10% in some areas.
    A employee value proposition   B executive search   C milk round D war for talent

10 American _____ differ from British CVs in that they often give
    detailed information about past successes and give strong reasons why the candidate
    is well suited to fill the vacancy.
    A interview   B summary   C presentation   D résumés

Exercise 4

Match a word (1-10) with another (a-j) to make ten HR expressions in this chapter.

1	selection	a	period
2	medical	b	test
3	handwriting	c	drive
4	job	d	position
5	recruitment	e	offer
6	job	f	examination
7	trial	g	panel
8	career	h	advertisement
9	vacant	i	profile
10	annual	j	intake

Exercise 5

Which verb goes with each of the key terms on the right?

1	draw up	a	word-of-mouth
2	hear by	b	a job
3	attend	c	a reference
4	apply for	d	a shortlist
5	carry out	e	a CV
6	be made	f	an executive search
7	send	g	experience
8	gain	h	an interview
9	turn down	i	redundant
10	ask for	j	an application

For discussion

1   How does your organisation recruit? How would you like to improve recruitment procedures?
2   How is technology changing recruitment? How will technology affect recruitment in the future?
3   What makes a good CV?
4   What advice do you give to interviewers?
5   What advice do you give to interviewees?
6   Are you a good interviewer? What makes you that good? How can you be even better?

3

Resourcing

Resourcing

3

Case studies

Mobility

You work for a large, international manufacturer of aeronautical equipment which operates ten sites in and around Paris, France. The sites are organised in three business units: radar, navigation systems and optronics. The company has now decided to close three sites at the beginning of next year. Historically, there has been an active policy of caring for employees, a policy which is encouraged and supported by strong union representation. There is also pressure from national and local government to maintain current headcount.

Management has decided to introduce a first phase in the reorganisation which aims at encouraging employees to apply for other vacancies within the group. The three sites to close (with a total of 2,300 employees) are located in the south of the city, meaning that staff will have to redeploy to two other sites in the south (340-post capacity), to two large sites in the north or to one in the eastern suburbs. Management is aware that:

- most employees have bought houses close to their original places of work
- employees' children attend the local schools in the area
- travel time to the northern and eastern suburbs is two hours' minimum during rush hours
- employees have not traditionally had to face major changes at work
- moving from one area to another involves the people concerned in a lot of administrative work which requires a lot of time to deal with and which can also be stressful.

Consider:

- how your company can promote mobility within the group
- what incentives you should offer
- what criteria you should apply to those transferring to other sites, and
- what policy to adopt for those employees refusing to make the move.

Recruitment media

You and your HR colleagues want to review the recruitment channels your company uses. Prepare for and then hold a meeting to brainstorm the advantages and drawbacks of:

- internal advertisements posted on notice boards
- lists of vacancies posted outside the company's premises
- advertising in the local, national and specialist press
- intranet and internet advertising on your company's website
- promotional films to accompany road shows
- others – ?

Reward

Key terms to talk about pay
and other forms of
remuneration.

**These are the key terms in this chapter.
Which of them do you understand?
Which of them can you use?**

Across-the-board increase
advance
allowance
arrears
assisted passage
assurance
average
award
Backdate
basic
benefit
bonus
broadbanding
Cafeteria plan
cash
childcare
commission
compensation
contribution
cover
crèche
Deduction
differential
double time
Earn
eldercare
Fat cat
fee
fleet
freebie
Golden handcuffs
golden handshake
golden hello
golden offering
golden parachute
guarantee
Hay
Incentive
income
increment

indemnity
index
inducement
insurance
Lump sum
Merit
Overtime
Pay
payment
payroll
pension
perk
piecework
portable
profit-sharing scheme
protection
Qualifying period
Rate
remuneration
reward
rise
royalty
Salary
severance pay
share plan
social charges
stock option plan
subsidise
Tax
time and a half
trustee
Underpaid
Voucher
Wage
weighting
wind down
wind up
workholder
Zonal system

4

Reward

across-the-board increase (n ph)
/əˈkrɒs ðə ˈbɔːd ˈɪŋkriːs/

When a company gives an across-the-board increase to a group of employees, all the employees get the same total or percentage increase in pay.

➡ a percentage across-the-board increase
➡ award / grant an across-the-board increase
➡ negotiate an across-the board increase

advance (n, v)
/ədˈvɑːns/

If you ask for an advance, you ask for prepayment of some or all of your pay before the normal payment date. The amount of any advance is then subtracted from your next wage or salary payment.

➡ a salary advance
➡ agree to an advance
➡ make an advance
➡ refuse an advance
➡ request an advance

allowance (n)
/əˈlaʊəns/
cost-of-living allowance (n ph)

hardship allowance (n ph)

subsistence allowance (n ph)

An allowance is extra pay for something special in your working conditions. See also **weighting**, **zonal system**.
You may get a cost-of-living allowance if you live in a part of the country where life is more expensive.
Your employer may pay you a hardship allowance if you have to live and work in a region or a country which is more difficult to live in than your own.
A subsistence allowance is a daily amount of money you receive from your company to buy food and accommodation when you are travelling away from home on company business.

➡ a car allowance
➡ a currency allowance
➡ a fixed allowance
➡ a generous allowance
➡ a living allowance
➡ a shift allowance
➡ a travel allowance
➡ an age allowance
➡ an attendance allowance
➡ an entertainment allowance
➡ an overseas allowance
➡ be entitled to an allowance
➡ pay an allowance

arrears (n pl)
/əˈrɪəz/

Arrears is money owed to you. See also **pay**.

➡ be in arrears
➡ fall into arrears
➡ pay arrears
➡ wage arrears

The employer was taken to the employment tribunal by an employee who claimed that his pay had fallen into arrears on several occasions.

4

Reward

assisted passage (n)
/ə'sɪstɪd 'pæsɪdʒ/

You receive assisted passage when a company helps you to pay for a move from one country to another. See also **relocate**.
➡ receive assisted passage
➡ take assisted passage to

assurance (n) **assure** (v)
/ə'ʃʊərəns/

An assurance policy pays you a sum of money when something which is certain to happen does happen. Also often known as **insurance**. See also **insurance**.

life assurance policy (n ph)

A life assurance policy pays your family a sum of money when you die.
➡ adopt a life assurance scheme
➡ cancel a life assurance policy
➡ take out a life assurance policy

average (adj)
/'ævərɪdʒ/

The average of a list of numbers is the total of the numbers added together and then divided by the number of numbers in the list.
➡ an average income, receive / earn
➡ an average wage, average wages
➡ average earnings, average weekly earnings
➡ on average

award (n, v)
/ə'wɔːd/

When someone – an employer or a tribunal in settlement of a dispute - makes a financial award, it takes a formal decision to give some kind of benefit to someone. See also **award** (chapter 8), **backdate**.
➡ a pay award
➡ a tribunal award
➡ award a bonus
➡ make an award

backdate (v)
/'bæk'deɪt/

When an organisation backdates a pay award, it pays its employees the extra money from a date before the date of the decision to make the increase. See also **pay**.
➡ backdate a pay award
As from 1 June, all their employees received a 2% increase backdated to the previous January.

basic (adj)
/'beɪsɪk/

Your basic pay is your standard salary or wage, not including any extra payments like bonuses, commission, overtime pay or other non-standard earnings.
➡ basic income
➡ basic pay
➡ basic salary / wage
➡ be on the basic (pay) rate
➡ start at the basic rate
Sales people can have low basic pay but have the chance to earn more from commission on sales.

benefit (n, v)
/'bɛnɪfɪt/
beneficiary (n)

Benefits are:

1 advantages, like, for example, extra money, a company car and a pension plan, which you get from your company in addition to your basic wage or salary. See also **cafeteria plan**, **compensation**, **pension**, **remuneration**.

2 payments you get from an insurance scheme.

A **beneficiary** is someone who receives a benefit, for example, from a pension plan.

accident benefit (n ph)

Accident benefit is the money that an employer or an insurance company pays to you or to your family when you belong to an employee benefit plan and you have an accident which results in your death or permanent disability.

employee benefit plan
(n ph)

An employee benefit plan is a plan that gives you insurance against accident, sickness, disability or death.

flexible benefits (n ph)

A flexible benefits plan is one which allows employees to choose between different forms of remuneration. Flexible benefits can be informally referred to as **flex**.

fringe benefits (n ph)

Fringe benefits are other advantages offered to employees, usually managers, as well as their salary. A company car or help with housing are examples of fringe benefits.

mix-and-match benefits
(n ph, v ph)

A mix-and-match plan is a system of flexible benefits which lets you choose the benefits you want from a range available. Also called **pick-and-mix benefits**. See also **cafeteria plan**.

relocation benefits (n ph)

A company pays you relocation benefits when it pays for some or all of what it costs you to move house. See also **relocate**.

unemployment benefit
(n ph)

Unemployment benefit is money you get from the government when you do not have a job.

within-benefit flexibility
(n ph)

Within-benefit flexibility is a form of flexible benefits which allows employees to decide whether they want more benefits and less salary or vice-versa.

- a benefits package, a generous benefits package
- a defined benefit pension plan
- a salary and benefits package
- apply for a benefit
- death benefit
- death-after-retirement benefit
- death-in-service benefit
- dependents' benefit
- disability benefit
- earnings-related benefit
- enjoy a benefit
- family benefit
- flexible retirement benefit
- funeral benefit
- incapacity benefit
- injury benefit
- join an employee benefit plan
- receive a benefit

4

Reward

➡ retirement benefit
➡ sickness benefit
➡ survivor's benefit
➡ short-term / medium-term / long-term benefit

A system of flexible benefits allows employees to choose the benefits which suit their own lifestyle and can therefore improve motivation and morale. Flexible benefits can help with the management of diversity, with retention and with employees' understanding of their total compensation.

bonus (n)
/'bəʊnəs/

A bonus is:
1 an extra payment made to an employee for special work;
2 a present.
See also **award, payment**.

loyalty bonus (n ph)

You get a loyalty bonus when the company pays you extra money for staying with the company for a certain period of time.

➡ a bonus payment
➡ a bonus scheme
➡ a Christmas bonus
➡ a cost-of-living bonus
➡ a one-off bonus
➡ ·a performance-related bonus
➡ a piecework bonus
➡ a productivity bonus
➡ an attendance bonus
➡ an expatriate bonus
➡ an incentive bonus
➡ award / pay a bonus
➡ qualify for a bonus
➡ receive / get a bonus

broadbanding (n)
/'brɔːdbændɪŋ/

Broadbanding (or broad banding) is the practice of reducing the number of salary levels to a smaller number of grades with broader pay ranges.
One survey found that the average number of bands used by broadbanding companies was five.

cafeteria plan (n ph)
/kæfɪ'tɪərɪə 'plæn/

A cafeteria plan is a system of flexible benefits in which employees can choose from a range of benefits using a sum of money or a certain number of points awarded by the employer. Also known as **across-benefit flexibility, cafeteria package** or **cafeteria benefits**. See **benefits**.

➡ implement / introduce a cafeteria plan

The Price Waterhouse cafeteria plan calculated the total reward figure for each employee who had to take 80% of the figure as salary and then mix and match a range of other benefits, including the option of a company car for all employees.

cash (n)
/'kæʃ/

If you are paid in cash, you receive your wages in the form of coins and bank notes.
➡ cash in hand
➡ payment in cash
➡ pay someone in cash
It is more difficult for the tax authorities to know how much self-employed people earn when they are paid in cash.

childcare (n ph)
/'tʃaɪldkɛə/

Organisations which help their employees with childcare provide different kinds of help to employees with young children. See also **crèche, eldercare, portable**.

childcare facilities (n ph)

Childcare facilities are the services provided by the company or the state for looking after children of pre-school age while parents are at work.
➡ childcare help, offer / provide
Providing childcare facilities for a company's employees is expensive, but the results – lower absenteeism, lower turnover and higher rates of women returning to work after maternity leave – can be very positive.

commission (n)
/kə'mɪʃən/

Sales people can be paid commission in relation to how much they sell. The commission is usually a percentage of the sale price.
➡ pay commission
Successful sales representatives sometimes earn more than the people who manage them because of the amount of commission they earn.

compensation (n)
/kɒmpən'seɪʃən/
compensate (v)

Your compensation is the reward your receive from your employer for the work you do. Your compensation package is the total of all the money and benefits that your employer gives you. Also referred to informally as **comp and ben**. See also **benefit, compensation** (chapter 8), **remuneration, reward**.

deferred compensation (n ph)

Deferred compensation refers to payments that you will receive in the future, for example, from a pension or stock option plan or from a profit sharing scheme. See also **pay**.
➡ a (generous) compensation package
➡ a compensation evaluation
➡ a compensation policy
➡ a compensation scheme
➡ a compensation survey
➡ a compensation system
➡ offer compensation
➡ receive compensation

contribution (n)
/kɒntrɪ'bjuːʃən/
contribute (v)
contributor (n)
contributory (adj)

When you contribute to an insurance or pension scheme, you make regular payments to the scheme. The contribution is the sum of money that you pay. See also **insurance, pension**.

4

Reward

contribution holiday (n ph) When an employer decided to take a contributions holiday, it stops paying money into its pension fund because it believes the fund is already large enough to make all the payments it has to. Also known as a **pension holiday**.
- a weekly / monthly / regular contribution, make
- additional voluntary contribution
- a contribution rate
- a contribution period
- a defined contribution pension plan
- contribution-linked

cover (n, v) Insurance cover is the protection you get from an insurance policy. It
/'kʌvə/ gives you financial protection against damage or injury. See **cover** (chapter 2), **insurance**.
- take out (additional) cover
You need to be sure that you are covered against accident when you travel on business abroad.

crèche When a company provides crèche facilities, it pays for a room with
(or creche) (n ph) equipment and trained personnel where employees can leave their
/'krɛʃ/ pre-school age children during working hours. See also **childcare**, **eldercare**, **portable**.

granny crèche A granny crèche is a place where employees can leave elderly
(n ph informal) relatives during working hours.

deduction (n) A deduction is money taken away from your wages or salary before
/diˈdʌkʃən/ you receive it. Deductions are also known informally in British English
deductible (adj) as **stoppages**. See also **check off**, **social charges**.
- an automatic deduction
- make a deduction
- tax-deductible
Deductions can include tax, social security and national insurance contributions, and insurance premiums.

differential (n) A differential is the difference in the pay rate between two different
/dɪfəˈrɛnʃəl/ kinds of work or between two pay grades.
erosion of differentials Differentials become eroded when the rates of pay of lower paid
(n ph) workers increase faster than the rates of pay of higher paid workers.
- maintain differentials
- narrow differentials
- remove differentials
- wage differentials

double time (n ph) You get double time when you are paid twice the standard rate per
/'dʌbəl 'taɪm/ hour. See also **overtime**, **time and a half**.

earn (v) The money that you earn is the money you get for your work. Your
/'ɜːn/ employer pays you your **earnings** for the work you have done. See
earnings (n) also **pay**, **salary**, **wage**.

➡ average earnings, above / below
➡ earnings-related, an ~ plan
➡ gross earnings
➡ increase earnings
➡ net earnings, a ~ calculation
➡ overtime earnings
➡ total earnings

Companies often tell their employees that increased earnings are possible only through increased productivity.

eldercare (adj, n)
/'ɛldəkɛə/

As the populations of many industrialised countries become older, more companies will become involved in eldercare by offering facilities for the care of employees' ageing relatives during working hours. See also **childcare facilities**, **crèche**.
➡ eldercare insurance
➡ provide eldercare

In the future, in some Western countries at least, more people will be involved in eldercare than in the care of children.

fat cat (n ph, informal)
/'fæt kæt/

Fat cats are company directors who have made a lot of money - unjustifiably in the eyes of their critics – from stock option plans, privatisation or other windfall payment.

fee (n)
/'fiː/
hefty fee (n ph)

You pay fees to professional people like architects and accountants for the work they do for you.
A hefty fee is a surprisingly or unacceptably large one.
➡ to charge a fee / fees

fleet (n)
/'fliːt/

The company's fleet is the collection of vehicles (cars, lorries, vans, etc.) which it owns or leases for the use of its employees. Fleet administration can include servicing and maintenance, buying and replacing vehicles, and measuring driver performance. HR people may have to match grades of employee with grades of company car.
➡ a car fleet
➡ fleet administration
➡ fleet management

freebie (n, informal)
/'friːbiː/

A freebie is something you get free. See also **perk**.

golden handcuffs (n ph)
/'gəʊldən 'hændkʌfs/

Senior managers agree to let their employers put golden handcuffs on them when they accept a major benefit in exchange for a promise not to leave the organisation. An example of golden handcuffs could be a share option scheme which becomes effective after a certain period of service.

golden handshake (n ph)
/'gəʊldən 'hændʃeɪk/

A golden handshake is a large amount of money paid to a senior manager when his/her employment is ended before the end of the contract of employment.
➡ receive a golden handshake

4

Reward

golden hello (n ph)
/'gəʊldən hə'ləʊ/

A golden hello is a large amount of money paid to a senior manager when s/he joins a company as a way of encouraging him/her to stay.

golden offering (n ph)
/'gəʊldən 'ɒfərɪŋ/

When a company makes a senior manager a golden offering, it asks him/her to agree to take early retirement in exchange for an improved pension and/or other financial incentives. Golden offerings are often made after takeovers.

➡ accept a golden offering

golden parachute (n ph)
/'gəʊldən 'pærəʃuːt/

A golden parachute is a guarantee of a certain level of benefit so that senior managers do not lose income if their company is taken over by another and their employment contract is ended.

guarantee (n, v)
/gærən'tiː/
guaranteed (adj)

When employers give guarantees, they make employees a promise about something.

➡ an income guarantee
➡ a guaranteed minimum rate
➡ a guaranteed (annual) minimum wage
➡ make / provide a guarantee
➡ offer a guarantee

Many Japanese companies no longer provide guarantees of employment during periods of economic difficulty.

Hay (n)
/'heɪ/

The Hay system is a popular system sold by Hay Management Consultants which evaluates jobs and, when used together with a salary survey, can help employers fix salaries in relation to levels of responsibility and what competitors pay people in equivalent positions.

incentive (n)
/ɪn'sɛntɪv/

An incentive is anything which encourages or motivates an employee to be more productive. See also **inducement**, **motivate**, **voucher**.

➡ a financial / non-financial incentive
➡ a share incentive scheme
➡ a tailor-made incentive
➡ act as an incentive
➡ an incentive bonus
➡ an incentive salary
➡ an incentive system
➡ an incentive voucher
➡ an incentive wage
➡ an incentives scheme
➡ incentive pay
➡ incentive travel
➡ offer / provide an incentive

Incentive vouchers, which can be exchanged for goods or services such as free hotel weekends for employees and their families, are one way of motivating staff.

4

Reward

income (n)
/ˈɪŋkəm/
disposable income (n ph)

Your income is the money you get from your work, your pension or from investments. See also **pay**, **remuneration**, **reward**, **salary**, **wage**. Your disposable income is the money you have left to spend after tax, social security payments and other essential expenditure is taken away.

➡ annual income
➡ average income
➡ enjoy a rise in income
➡ fixed income
➡ gross income
➡ income tax
➡ make a good income
➡ net income
➡ real income
➡ suffer a drop in income
➡ taxable income

increment (n)
/ˈɪŋkrəmənt/
incremental (adj)

An increment is a regular automatic increase in your salary.
➡ an annual increment
Annual increments are less common nowadays as more and more pay agreements are linked to performance and productivity.

indemnity (n)
/ɪnˈdɛmnɪti/

An indemnity is a payment made to compensate for something, often an unpredicted loss. See **compensation** (chapter 8).
➡ end-of-career indemnity
➡ redundancy indemnity
If an employee has a fatal accident while at work, the company may pay an indemnity to the employee's family.

index (n, v)
/ˈɪndɛks/
indexation (n)

An index is a measure of the level of something, for example prices. When an organisation indexes salaries, it increases them at the same rate as, for example, the general price level.
➡ a consumer price index
➡ a share index
➡ index-linked
➡ the cost of living index

inducement (n)
/ɪnˈdjuːsmənt/

An inducement is something that encourages you to work more. See also **incentive**, **motivate**.
➡ a financial / non-financial inducement, receive
➡ offer an inducement
An organisation can offer a range of inducements to its staff but it is not always easy to measure the return on investment in terms of increased productivity or sales.

insurance (n)
/ɪnˈʃʊərəns/
insure (v)
insured (n)
insurer (n)

An insurance policy pays you a sum of money when an accident which could happen does happen. The **insured** is the person covered by the insurance. See also **assurance**, **contribution**, **cover**, **wind down**, **wind up**.

4

Reward

4

Reward

contributory insurance scheme (n ph)

A contributory insurance scheme or plan is one into which both the employer and the employee make payments.

non-contributory insurance scheme (n ph)

In a non-contributory insurance scheme or plan, only the employer makes payments to the scheme, not the employee.

insurance claim (n ph)

When you want to get money from an insurance scheme, you make a claim to the insurance company. See also **claim**.

insurance policy (n ph)

An insurance policy is a contract between an insurance company and the insured person.

insurance premium (n ph)

The insurance premium is the amount of money you pay to be insured.

permanent health insurance (n ph)

A permanent health insurance policy pays you a percentage of your normal income when you are absent from work through illness for a long time. See also **benefit**.

➡ accident insurance
➡ adequate insurance cover, have
➡ an insurance claim, make
➡ an insurance policy, take out
➡ an insurance policyholder
➡ an insurance premium, pay
➡ be covered by insurance / be covered by an insurance policy
➡ cancel an insurance policy
➡ critical illness insurance
➡ dental insurance
➡ life insurance / life assurance
➡ long-term sickness insurance
➡ medical insurance
➡ private medical insurance
➡ take out insurance against

In recent years, employee health insurance cover has become a major cost for companies in the United States.

lump sum (n ph)
/'lʌmp 'sʌm/

A lump sum is an amount of money which is paid to an employee all at the same time rather than at regular intervals.

➡ make a lump sum payment to

Some pension schemes pay both a lump sum on retirement and a monthly sum after that.

merit (n, Am Eng)
/'mɛrɪt/

A merit raise is a wage or salary increase given to an employee as a reward for good individual performance. See **award**, **bonus**, **reward**, **rise**.

➡ a merit appraisal
➡ a merit award
➡ a merit increase
➡ a merit plan
➡ a merit raise
➡ a merit rating
➡ merit pay

Merit awards in the USA are more often made to white-collar managerial staff than to blue-collar employees.

overtime (n)
/'əʊvətaɪm/

When you do overtime, you work extra hours. See also **double time**, **time and a half**.
➡ do overtime
➡ overtime pay
➡ paid / unpaid overtime
➡ work overtime
In some countries, for example in Norway and Sweden, there are strict controls on the amount of overtime that can be worked in many jobs.

pay (n, v)
/'peɪ/
paid (adj)

Your pay is the money you get for doing your job. Your company pays you for doing your job and at certain times when you are not actually at work or are not able to work. See also **earn**, **salary**, **severance**, **underpaid**, **wage**.

back pay (n ph)

Back pay is money which the company owes you for work which you did in the past and for which you have not been paid. See also arrears.

competency-based pay (n ph)

Competency-based pay (CBP) is a system which links how much you earn to an assessment of your performance compared with a set of competencies. Also known as **competence-related pay** and **skills-based pay.**

deferred pay (n ph)

Deferred pay is income you receive some time after you do the work. Under European equality law, occupational pensions are a form of deferred pay. See also **compensation**.

equal pay (n ph)

Men and women receive equal pay when they get the same money for the same or similar work.

pay anomaly (n ph)

There is a pay anomaly between different groups of employee when they do not receive the same amount of money for the same kind of work.

Pay As You Earn (adj ph, n ph)

Some countries operate a Pay-As-You-Earn (PAYE) system in which employers take tax from salaries before the employees receive them, and then pay the tax directly to the government. See also **deduction**.

pay devolution (n ph)

Pay devolution happens when pay negotiations start to take place at local rather than at national level.

pay gap (n ph)

A pay gap is the difference in pay between two groups of employees. For example a gender pay gap is a difference in earnings between men and women.

pay in lieu (n ph)

You get pay in lieu when you are paid in exchange for something else, for example if you leave your job and take money instead of unspent holiday.

pay parity (n ph)

There is pay parity between different groups of employee when they receive the same amount of money for the same kind of work.

pay statement (n ph)

A pay statement is a piece of paper with details of your earnings written on it. Also known as a **pay slip** or **wage slip**.

itemised pay statement (n ph)

An itemised pay statement is one with the details of each payment and deduction written down separately.

performance-related pay (n ph)

Performance-related pay (PRP) is a system which links how much you earn to an assessment of how well you do your job.

rolled up holiday pay (n ph)

An employee receives rolled-up holiday pay when the employer adds a certain percentage (for example, about 8%, representing 4 weeks out of 52) to the employee's weekly wage so that the holiday pay is spread

4

Reward

out over the year rather than paid at the time of leave. This practice is illegal in a number of countries.

sick pay (n ph)

Sick pay is money you receive when you are away from work because you are ill.

➡ a pay agreement
➡ a pay code
➡ a pay cut, make
➡ a pay cut, accept / take
➡ a pay differential
➡ a pay floor
➡ a pay freeze
➡ a pay increase, award
➡ a pay level
➡ a pay philosophy
➡ a pay plan
➡ a pay range
➡ a pay rate
➡ a pay rise
➡ a pay scale
➡ a pay structure, a unified
➡ a pay system, ~ design
➡ a performance-related pay scheme
➡ an annual pay review
➡ an equal pay audit / survey
➡ basic pay
➡ equal work for equal pay
➡ gross pay
➡ highly paid
➡ holiday pay / paid holiday
➡ low pay, the low paid
➡ maternity pay
➡ merit pay
➡ net pay
➡ pay day
➡ pay in lieu of notice
➡ profit-related pay
➡ sick pay, ~ entitlement
➡ sick pay, draw
➡ strike pay
➡ take-home pay
➡ team-based pay

Supporters of competency-based pay say that it is a better measure of performance than performance-related pay because it looks at the totality of the employee's performance, taking into account know-how, skills, attitudes and behaviour.

payment (n)
/ˈpeɪmənt/
discretionary payment (n ph)

A payment is an amount of money paid or the act of paying something.

Discretionary payments are ones which employers choose to make when there is no contractual obligation for them to do so. Also known as an **ex-gratia payment**. See also **bonus**.

Reward

4

➡ a cash payment
➡ a lump sum payment
➡ a one-off payment
➡ a payment system
➡ a social insurance payment
➡ a termination payment
➡ make a payment to
➡ payment in cash

payroll (n)
/'peɪrəʊl/

The company's payroll is:
1 the list of its paid employees;
2 the money paid out by the company in salaries

payroll giving (n ph)

Payroll giving happens when employees have money which they want to give to charities deducted directly from their salaries.
➡ manage a company's payroll
➡ on the payroll
➡ payroll administration
➡ payroll management
➡ payroll software
25% of US employees and 35% of firms participate in payroll giving compared with 2% and 1% respectively in the UK.

pension (n)
/'pɛnʃən/
pensionable (adj)
pensioner (n)

Your pension is the money you receive regularly from the government or from your employer or from a private insurance scheme after your retirement. See also **portable**, **trustee**, **wind down**, **wind up**.

bridging pension (n ph)

A bridging pension is a pension which members of a pension scheme can receive between the time they retire and the time when they become old enough to receive the state pension.

career average pension scheme (n ph)

With a career average scheme, each year's benefit is linked to the salary in that year so that the pension is worth the sum of the target percentage (for example, 50%) for each year.

career average revalued earnings pension scheme (n ph)

With a career average revalued earnings (or CARE) scheme, each year's benefit is linked to the salary in that year so that the pension is worth the sum of the target percentage (for example, 50%) for each year, revalued according to retail price inflation or another indicator and averaged over the whole career.

closed pension scheme (n ph)

A closed pension scheme is one that is not open to new members or that is being wound up. See also **wind up**.

defined benefit pension (n ph)

With a defined benefit pension plan or scheme, or **defined benefit occupational pension plan**, the size of your contributions to the plan can be decided in relation to how much you want to receive when you retire. A defined benefit plan then pays you a fixed annual amount during your retirement. A defined benefit pension can provide a fixed sum for each year of your pensionable service, generally a fraction – for example, one sixtieth – of your final salary at retirement.

defined contribution pension scheme (n ph)

A defined contribution scheme or plan defines how much you, and perhaps your employer, will contribute to the plan, without saying exactly how much you will receive in benefits when you retire. The

4

Reward

contributions are not based on your expected retirement benefit, but rather on a percentage of your income, a percentage that is specified in the plan.

final salary pension scheme (n ph)
A final salary scheme calculates the size of the pension from how much employees are earning when they retire or on the average during the last few years of their service.

money purchase pension scheme (n ph)
A money purchase pension plan has contributions that are fixed, are based upon the employee's compensation, and are not affected by employer's profits. The size of the pension then depends on the size of the contributions and how far the fund has grown through investment. This kind of scheme offers no guarantee of a particular level of revenue after you retire.

profit-sharing pension plan (n ph)
A profit-sharing plan is one kind of defined contribution plan for sharing the profits of the business with employees.

top-up pension (n ph)
If you need extra pension cover in addition to the cover you already have, you can take out a top-up pension to bring your pension up to the level you want.

- a company pension
- a disability pension
- a final salary defined benefits scheme
- a pension fund
- a pension holiday
- a pension package
- a pension plan
- a personal pension
- a portable pension
- a private pension
- a stakeholder pension
- a state pension
- a supplementary pension
- an individual pension
- an occupational pension, ~ scheme
- contribute towards
- draw a pension
- pay into a pension fund
- pension adjustment
- pension entitlement
- pension provision
- pensionable age, be of / reach
- provide for your pension
- retire on a pension

In Britain, many companies are closing defined benefits pension schemes to new recruits because they say they are too expensive, and adopting defined contribution or CARE schemes in their place. At the same time, responsibility for pensions and communication to employees about pensions has moved increasingly from the finance department to HR.

4

Reward

perk (n, abbrev of perquisite, informal) /'pɜːk/

A perk is any kind of advantage - like a company car - from the company which is extra to the financial and non-financial benefits agreed in the terms of your employment. See also **benefit**, **freebie**.
➡ enjoy a perk / perks

piecework (n ph) /'piːs wɜːk/ piece worker (n ph) piece working (n ph)

When you do piecework, you are paid per unit produced. The **piece rate** is the money you get per unit produced when you do piece work.
➡ piece rate working

portable (adj) /'pɔːtəbəl/ portability (n)

Something which is portable is something which you can take with you from one organisation to another when you change your job. See also **childcare**, **pension**.
➡ a portable pension
➡ portable childcare
As job mobility increases, more and more people want to have portable pensions which they can take with them when they move from one company to another.

profit-sharing scheme (n) /'prɒfɪt ʃɛərɪŋ 'skiːm/

A profit-sharing scheme is a company plan to share the company's profits with some or all of its employees.
Profit-sharing schemes can be a way not only of increasing employees' incomes but also of motivating them and encouraging them to identify more with the company's future.

protection (n) /prə'tɛkʃən/ protect (v)

When you buy protection against long-term disability or loss of income, then you buy insurance to cover yourself against serious health problems, unemployment, etc.; or your employer may provide some kinds of protection for you. See also **cover**, **disability**, **insurance**, **protect**.
➡ (group) disability protection
➡ income protection

qualifying period (n ph) /'kwɒlɪfaɪɪŋ pɪərɪəd/

The qualifying period is the time you have to wait before you can join your employer's pension scheme. Also called a **waiting period**.

rate (n) /'reɪt/ **flat rate** (n ph) **going rate** (n ph)

The rate of pay for a job is the amount of money paid per hour or per unit of production. See also **rate** (chapter 5).
The flat rate for a job is the standard rate which everyone gets.
The going rate for the job is the average rate of pay for that work across a large group of workers.

sick rate (n ph)

The sick rate is the rate at which you are paid when you are absent from work because of illness.

rating drift (n ph)

Rating drift happens when the people responsible for making performance ratings of employees give too many of them the top rating so that they receive more money in a performance-related pay scheme.
➡ a flat rate
➡ the basic rate, start at
➡ a pay rate

4

Reward

➠ a piecework rate
➠ an hourly rate
One solution to the problem of rating drift may be to increase the number of ratings in the middle of the ratings range.

remuneration (n)
/rɪmjuːnəˈreɪʃən/

Your remuneration is the total of all the financial and non-financial benefits that you receive from the company. See also **benefit, compensation, reward**.

remuneration committee (n ph)

A remuneration committee is a committee of members of the board of directors of a company, often including non-executive directors, which decides the pay of the company's top managers. See also **director**.
➠ a (total) remuneration package
➠ executive remuneration
A manager's total remuneration package can include not only salary but also a generous pension plan, a company car, an entertainment allowance and so on.

reward (n, v)
/rɪˈwɔːd/

Reward is what you get from the company in exchange for your work. Reward includes money and benefits; and other returns which are more difficult to measure such as job satisfaction. See also **benefit, compensation, motivation, remuneration**.

extrinsic reward (n ph)

An extrinsic reward is one which comes from outside yourself, like money.

intrinsic reward (n ph)

An intrinsic reward is one which comes from inside yourself, like the satisfaction that you get from doing a job well.
➠ a reward audit
➠ a reward system
➠ an employee reward survey
Reward is normally based on skill level, qualifications, competencies and responsibilities.

rise (n, v)
/ˈraɪz/

If you get a rise at work, you get an increase in pay. In American English, this is called a **raise**. See also **merit**.

royalty (n)
/ˈrɔɪəlti/
royalties (n pl)

A royalty is a payment made to someone like a writer or a musician each time a piece of their work is sold or performed. The royalty is often a percentage of the money received by the producer or publisher of the work.

salary (n)
/ˈsæləri/
salaried (adj)

Your salary is the money that you are paid for doing a regular job. Salaries are usually paid monthly. See also **earn, pay, wages**.

salary capping (n ph)

Salary capping happens when there is an upper limit to how much any employee can be paid. Salary capping schemes have been used by groups of football clubs in financial difficulties.
➠ a competitive salary
➠ a salaried employee
➠ a salary adjustment, make

➡ a salary advance, ask for / request a
➡ a salary payment
➡ a salary policy
➡ a salary proposal
➡ a salary range
➡ a salary review, undertake
➡ a salary scale
➡ a salary scheme
➡ a salary structure
➡ a salary survey
➡ an attractive salary
➡ an increase in salary / a salary increase
➡ basic salary
➡ gross salary
➡ net salary
➡ salary progression
➡ the initial / starting salary

severance pay (n ph)
/'sɛvərəns peɪ/

If you lose your job with a company, you may receive severance pay as compensation for being made redundant. See also **redundant**.
➡ a severance package
➡ offer (generous) severance terms
➡ receive severance pay
A manager's severance package might include not only a lump sum payment but also advice about how to get another job.

share plan (n ph)
/'ʃɛə plæn/

A share plan or scheme is a scheme to allow employees to buy shares in their company. Some schemes help employees save for the future purchase of shares at a subsidised price. Also known as **employee share ownership plan** or **ESOP**. See also **stock option plan**.
➡ an employee share plan
➡ an executive share plan
➡ a deferred bonus share plan
A US study carried out between 1952 and 1969 showed that the share price of companies with well-developed share plans grew almost twice as fast as similar companies without share plans.

social charges (n ph)
/'səʊʃəl 'tʃɑːdʒɪz/

Social charges are payments made usually by both employers and employees to funds to pay for employees' pensions, sick pay and other benefits. See also **deductions**.

stock option plan (n ph)
/'stɒk 'ɒpʃən 'plæn/

A stock option plan or scheme gives managers the right to buy a certain number of their company's shares at a fixed price during a stated period of time so that if the price of the shares rises, the shares will be worth more than the manager had to pay for them. Also known as a **share option plan** or scheme.

**Save-As-You-Earn
share option scheme**
(n ph)

In the Save-As-You-Earn share option schemes operated by some British companies, all employees can choose to pay part of their salaries into a savings plan which they can then use to buy shares in

4

Reward

the company at a pre-agreed price.
Stock option plans can be criticised in the press if they help senior managers to increase their earnings in a way unrelated to the performance of the company.

subsidise (v)
/'sʌbsɪdaɪz/
subsidy (n)

When a company subsidises the cost of something for its employees, it pays part of the cost for them. See also **voucher**.
➡ subsidised accommodation
➡ subsidised holidays
➡ subsidised meals
➡ subsidised transport
Some companies buy property in seaside or ski resorts in order to be able to provide staff with subsidised holiday accommodation.

tax (n)
/'tæks/
taxation (n)
taxable (adj)
taxation (n)
tax code (n ph)

Tax is the money you pay to the government on your earnings, on the things that you buy, etc.

In Britain, people have different tax codes depending, for example, on whether they are married or not, and so pay different amounts of tax.
➡ a (business-friendly) tax regime
➡ a child tax credit
➡ a tax advantage
➡ a tax allowance
➡ a tax deduction
➡ a tax disincentive
➡ a tax incentive
➡ a working tax credit
➡ income tax
➡ liable to (pay) tax
➡ tax efficiency
➡ tax-deductible
➡ tax-free

time and a half (n ph)
/'taɪm ənd ə 'hɑːf/

You are on time and a half when you get paid 50% more than the standard rate per hour. See also **double time**, **overtime**, **rate**.

trustee (n)
/trʌs'tiː/

A trustee is someone who is responsible for managing a fund, for example, a pension fund. In Britain, one third of the trustees of an occupational pension scheme must be elected by the scheme's members. See also **pension**.

underpaid (adj)
/ʌndə'peɪd/

Someone who is underpaid is not paid enough. The opposite of underpaid is **overpaid**. See also **pay**.

voucher (n)
/'vaʊtʃə/

A voucher is a kind of ticket with a money value, provided or subsidised by the employer, which an employee can exchange for certain kinds of goods or services. See also **incentive**.

4

Reward

luncheon voucher (n ph) A luncheon voucher is a ticket with a certain money value, paid for by the employer or by the employer and the employee together, which can be used to buy lunch in cafés and restaurants on workdays.

merchandise voucher (n ph) A merchandise voucher can be exchanged for consumer goods in shops. Also known as a **retail voucher** or an **incentive voucher**.

➡ a childcare voucher

wage (n)
/'weɪdʒ/ A wage is the money that the company pays you for the work that you do. Wages are usually paid weekly. See also **earn**, **pay**, **salary**.

wages council (n ph) A wages council is a national committee of employers and employee representatives which meets to negotiate pay and conditions for an industry, particularly one where there is low trade union representation because there is a large number of workplaces with small numbers of employees.

wage freeze (n ph) When a government or company imposes a wage freeze, there is no pay increase for anyone.

➡ a decent wage, earn
➡ a (national) minimum wage
➡ a wage ceiling, impose
➡ a wage differential
➡ a wage earner
➡ a wage floor
➡ a (retroactive) wage increase
➡ a wage index
➡ a wage level
➡ a wage rate
➡ a wage review
➡ a wage scale
➡ a wage structure
➡ a wage table
➡ accept a wage claim
➡ an hourly wage
➡ impose a wage freeze
➡ reject a wage claim
➡ the average wage
➡ the basic wage
➡ wage costs

The union submitted a wage claim of 2.5% on behalf of its members but this was rejected by management since it did not include a commitment to increase productivity.

weighting (n)
/'weɪtɪŋ/
weight (v) A weighting is an extra payment which you receive, because, for example, you live in a place where the cost of living is higher. See also **allowance**, **zonal system**.

➡ a London weighting

The union wanted an increase in the weighting because it said that the cost of living was much higher in the capital city.

4

Reward

wind down (v)
/'waɪnd 'daʊn/

When an organisation winds down a scheme, for example a defined benefit pension scheme, it slowly brings it to an end.

wind up (v)
/'waɪnd 'ʌp/

When an organisation winds up a scheme, for example a defined benefit pension scheme, it brings it to an end.

workholder (n)
/'wɜːkhəʊldə/

Workholders are employees who receive part of their wages in time shares – a certain number of working hours – which the employees can re-invest in the company, and save up for early retirement or extra holiday. See also **stakeholder**, **work**.

Workholder value has been developed by a number of German companies, such as Volkswagen, in part as a way of developing better industrial relations.

zonal system (n ph)
/'zəʊnəl 'sɪstəm/

A company may operate a zonal system of pay when the cost of living varies from one part of the country to another. Employees living in a more expensive zone get more money than those living in a cheaper area. Zonal systems can also be based on other criteria like staff turnover and local employment rates. Also known as the **zonal approach**. See also **allowance**, **weighting**.

One London-based company created a zonal system based on the distance of offices from the centre of London. Offices outside London with staffing problems due to low unemployment could then apply to move into a higher zone to help them attract and retain staff.

4

Reward

Exercises

Exercise 1

Choose the best term (A, B, C or D) to complete each sentence.

1   Most employees receive a combination of basic pay and other _____.
    A awards   B cash   C benefits   D contributions

2   The total of everything you receive from your employer is your
    _____ package.
    A payroll   B remuneration   C payment   D salary

3   Most sales representatives receive a fixed salary plus a _____ on
    sales.
    A reward   B commission   C revenue   D royalty

4   Some companies offer private _____ schemes to their white-collar
    employees.
    A tax   B compensation   C bonus   D pension

5   Professional people like architects and accountants charge their clients
    _____ for the work they carry out.
    A fees   B royalties   C commission   D payment

6   Employees subject to PBR (Payment By Results) receive _____ for
    good performance.
    A cash   B vouchers   C bonuses   D fees

7   People in _____ are responsible for the administration of employee
    salaries.
    A arrears   B piecework   C weighting   D payroll

8   When an organisation fixes the pay of a new employee, it also calculates the
    _____ it must pay to the state for national health and social security.
    A compensation   B insurance   C assurance   D social charges

4

Reward

Exercise 2

Match each key term (1 - 10) with a definition (a - j).

1	fat cat	a	Money taken from your salary before you get it
2	share plan	b	An overpaid business person
3	broadbanding	c	An encouragement to boost productivity or results, usually in the form of money
4	deduction	d	A salary increase
5	time and a half	e	A pay increase which is the same for all employees in the organisation
6	across-the-board increase	f	When an employee receives 50% more than the standard hourly working rate
7	weighting	g	Reducing the number of pay grades so that more employees go into each category
8	incentive	h	An additional payment made to employees because, for example, they live in a capital city where the cost of living is higher
9	rise	i	A person responsible for the management of a pension fund
10	trustee	j	When employees are offered the opportunity to buy a stake in the company

Exercise 3

Read the company welfare policy and put the right term from the box into each space (1 – 8).

cover	childcare facilities	crèche	vouchers
eldercare	insurance	index	subsidised

The aim of our welfare policy is to provide our employees with a range of
(1)_____ services and provisions. And because we employ a large number of
women, we also offer a range of (2)_____ such as the company
(3) _____ and a minibus service operating to and from local schools.
Insurance (4)_____ for these services is also paid by the company and salaries are
linked to the cost of living (5) _____ . Since many employees care for ageing
relatives, we offer (6)_____ facilities in cooperation with the local senior
citizens' association and the local council. The company further contributes to family
welfare by providing free (7) _____ policies, ensuring indemnity for accident or
loss of life. Lastly, employees benefit from our staff canteen, which provides low-cost
quality meals and snacks. (8)_____ for this can be obtained on a monthly
basis from the personnel department information office.

Exercise 4

All the terms 1 - 10 refer to money in some way. For each one:
- first write a definition for it
- then insert it into the right sentence, (a - j)
- then check your own definitions against the ones in the glossary.

1   advance: _____

2   allowance: _____

3   awarded:_____

4   cash:_____

5   double time: _,_____

6   earn:_____

7   increment:_____

8   severance pay:_____

9   lump sum:_____

10 inducement:_____

a   When employees have financial problems, they sometimes ask their employer for an _____ on salary.

b   Some organisations offer _____ to employees whom they are going to make redundant.

c   In addition to his basic pay, he was _____ a bonus for good performance.

d   In some industries, for example construction, some workers are paid in _____ rather than by bank transfer.

e   When she retired, she chose to receive a _____ from the pension scheme so that she could pay off the rest of the money she had borrowed to buy her house.

f   In certain circumstances, such as night shift work, employees can be paid _____ for working under difficult conditions.

g   Blue-collar workers _____ wages; white-collar employees _____ salaries. (The same term is used twice)

h   If one part of the country, for example the capital city, is more expensive than others, employees may receive an extra cost-of-living _____ .

i   Companies sometimes offer free holidays to their sales teams as an _____ to obtain better results.

j   Organisations can add an annual _____ to their employees' salaries as well as increasing them through performance results.

4

Reward

Exercise 5

Which terms in the box apply to the three employee categories? Some of them apply to more than one.

salary	wage	stock option plan		paid overtime
piecework	golden handshake		perks	profit-sharing scheme

Blue-collar workers	White-collar employees	Senior management

Exercise 6

Match each golden term in the box with one of the clues, then write your own definition of the term. Then check your definitions against the ones in the glossary.

golden parachute	golden handshake	golden hello
golden offering	golden handcuffs	

1   A shining greeting between friends?

_____

2   Good to know that if the company falls quickly, you will fall slowly.

_____

3   A welcome or unwelcome present at the end of a career?

_____

4   Your hands were trapped with money, not like the police.

_____

5   A friendly and enriching manual gesture.

_____

For discussion

1   How is pay decided in your organisation?
2   How should pay be decided? Do you think employee benefit should be based on competence, service, individual performance, team performance, effort, added value, profit, other factors, or some mixture of these?
3   How can a company integrate its reward strategy into its business strategy?
4   What incentives motivate people most?
5   How should pensions be managed?

Case studies

The pay scale paradox

The GEME Group, a large, multinational group dealing in services to the oil, gas, electricity and nuclear energy sectors, has a number of companies in Germany as well as subsidiaries in ten countries abroad. Corporate headquarters are based in Frankfurt and are home to four hundred employees, mainly in management positions.

In addition to a group-wide profit-sharing scheme, the headquarters has operated an incremental pay scale for over fifteen years, with seven steps in each ladder for each category of employee: clerical and administrative employees, technical and specialist, middle, general and senior management. Typically, new employees will begin their career at level one and finish at level seven, after which they either remain in their post or are promoted to a higher employee category.

The system used to work well. While some employees moved up the scale, others retired, resigned or were replaced by new recruits at the bottom of the scale. However, the last six years have seen a change in the job market. Due to the increasing difficulty in finding employment, employees have been reluctant to change company and recruitment has been low. Staff turnover is also low at the headquarters. The pay scale has therefore stopped being self-financing through lack of labour market movement.

Both senior management and senior employee representatives have been invited to meet in order to discuss the advantages of keeping the system in place or finding an alternative solution. As an attendee, what are your views on the situation?

4

Reward

The remuneration package under attack

NELLEC, an engineering studies firm based in the Netherlands, operates a remuneration package comprising four elements:

- basic pay
- PRP (performance-related pay)
- a company profit-sharing scheme
- an end-of-year bonus.

Since its implementation three years ago, the system has worked well, providing employees with incentives to produce concrete results; and rewarding employees with what has been seen as a good return on personal investment.

However, there has been a major setback to this year's financial forecast on results because of the bankruptcy of an important customer and a general slowing down in European business. Suddenly, as the end of the year approaches, NELLEC is confronted, for the first time, with little cash in hand to reward its employees' efforts.

After the annual appraisal interviews in November, the HR function recognises that all employees have reached or surpassed their personal objectives. The sales team, however, have seen their results diminished by nearly 35% due to the external factors mentioned above. The situation is therefore as follows:

- There is no cash available for the end-of-year bonus.
- Profits are zero for this year, so there will be no return from the profit-sharing scheme.
- Individual performance is high throughout the workforce.
- The sales department has seen its results plummet.

HR and top management are aware that the impact on the workforce will be highly negative. They fear loss of motivation, a feeling of unfairness among employees, a loss of belief in the system in place, employee representative disapproval and eventual resignations on the part of employees.

Consider:

- How should the situation be approached?
- Who should receive an increase in pay?
- How should management communicate its new message on pay?
- How should management deal with the 'losers' in this situation?

5

Developing people

Key terms to talk about raising
people's performance through
training, development and
appraisal.

**These are the key terms in this chapter.
Which of them do you understand?
Which of them can you use?**

Accredit
action plan
appraise
apprentice
aptitude
assess
away day
Behaviour
buddy system
Career
cascade
case
coach
comfort zone
competence
competency
continuing education
course
Development
Evaluate
Facilitator
false beginner
feedback
Gap year
graveyard slot
Happy sheet
In-company
in-house
in-service
in-tray exercise
indenture
induction
instruct
Job
Learn
Materials
mentor
methodology
mind map
mindset
model

module
multiple intelligences
multi-skilling
Myers Briggs
Needs analysis
neurolinguistic programming
Off-the-peg
one-to-one
orientation
Pace
pre-experience
programme
protégé
Ranking and rating
rate
release
reskilling
resources
retrain
role play
Sabbatical
second
self access
seminar
simulation
skills
SMART objectives
suggestopedia
Tailor
train
tutor
Unit
VAK
visual aid
vocational
Work experience
work placement
work sampling
workshadowing
workshop

Developing people

5

accredit (v)
/ə'krɛdɪt/
accreditation (n)
accrediting (adj)

An accredited organisation has the power to give official recognition to a person or to another organisation. It can, for example, decide who shall be a member of a professional group.

➡ get / receive accreditation from an accrediting body

British companies must have their quality assurance systems approved by an organisation accredited by the government before they can use an international quality standard logo.

action plan (n ph)
/'ækʃən 'plæn/

An action plan is a list of things you decide to do with the dates by which you plan to do them. Action plans are essential parts of training and coaching.

appraise (v)
/ə'preɪz/
appraisal (n)
appraiser (n)
appraisee (n)

When you appraise employees, you measure or evaluate their job performance. See also **assess**, **evaluate**, **feedback**.

360 degree appraisal
(n ph)

360 degree appraisal takes place when people below you in the organisation, colleagues at the same level as you, and people above you all have the opportunity to assess your performance. Sometimes people outside the organisation take part in 360 degree appraisals. A 360 degree appraisal can be referred to informally as a **360**.

peer appraisal (n ph)

Your peers are your colleagues. Peer appraisal happens when people at the same level as you in the organisation appraise you rather than people above you in the organisation. See also **peer**.

upward appraisal (n ph)

Upward appraisal takes place when people below you in the organisation have the opportunity to assess your performance.

➡ an appraisal interview
➡ an appraisal system
➡ a group appraisal
➡ carry out / do an appraisal
➡ performance appraisal
➡ self appraisal

Appraisal interviews have less chance of being successful if the manager and the employee do not communicate very often outside the interview.

apprentice (n, v)
/ə'prɛntɪs/
apprenticeship (n)

An apprentice is someone who works with a qualified person for a period of time, usually several years, in order to learn a particular skill and gain a qualification. See also **indenture**.

➡ an apprentice mechanic / an apprentice electrician, etc.
➡ run an apprenticeship scheme
➡ do / serve an apprenticeship
➡ sign up as an apprentice / for an apprenticeship

In Britain, apprenticeships are usually taken up by young people learning manual skills but elsewhere, for example in Switzerland, white-collar apprenticeships are common.

5

Developing people

aptitude (n)
/'æptɪtjuːd/
apt (adj)

When you show aptitude for something, then you show a natural skill or ability or at least the potential to do that thing well. See also **talent**.
⇒ an aptitude test
⇒ have / possess a natural aptitude for
⇒ show aptitude for
He has a natural aptitude for learning languages.

assess (v)
/ə'sɛs/
assessment (n)
assessor (n)

When you assess someone or something , you make a judgement about the quality of the person or the thing. See also **appraise, evaluate, feedback**.

assessment centre (n ph)

An assessment centre is a detailed programme, which can last several days, designed to measure the competence of external applicants or the competence or performance of employees. Assessment centres may aim not only to appraise staff but also to develop them. Some aim to identify candidates for management development programmes.

online assessment (n ph)

Online assessment is a way of measuring the performance of a person doing an examination via the internet.
⇒ a balanced assessment
⇒ continuous assessment
⇒ self-assessment, engage in a process of continuous
⇒ staff assessment
⇒ make / carry out a rapid / detailed assessment of
⇒ design an assessment centre
⇒ run an assessment centre

away day (n ph)
/ə'weɪ deɪ/

When you and the people you work with have an away day, you all go to somewhere different from the place where you normally work as a reward, to discuss work in a different environment, for team development, training, etc.
⇒ go on an away day

behaviour (n)
/bɪ'heɪvjə/
behave (v)
behavioural (adj)
behaviourist (adj n)

Your behaviour is the way you typically do and say things. Your behaviour is the expression of your personality.
⇒ a pattern of behaviour
⇒ change the behaviour of
The objective of all training is to change employees' behaviour.

buddy system (n ph, Am Eng)
/'bʌdi sɪstəm/

A buddy system is an on-the-job training system where a trainee works with an experienced employee. See also **workshadowing**.

career (n)
/kə'rɪə/
careerist (n)

Your career is the process of moving from one job to another with increasing money or responsibility or both during your professional life. **Careerists** are ambitious people whose careers are very important to them.

career break (n ph)

You take a career break when you stop working for a time – possibly for up to several years – and then return to work. Many women take career breaks in order to care for young children. See also **returner**.

lateral career move (n ph)   A lateral career move is a move to another job at the same level in the organisation. Also known as a **lateral transfer**. See also **sideways move**.

portfolio career (n ph)   A portfolio career is built not on an upward rise through an organisation but on the development of a range of varied skills and experiences. Self-employed people in particular may see their careers in portfolio terms.
- a career block
- a career change
- a career plateau
- a careers adviser
- a careers counsellor
- a promising career
- an internal career path
- career counselling
- career development
- career expectations
- career management
- career opportunities
- career planning
- career prospects, have good / poor
- career-minded, be very
- careers advice, a ~ centre
- careers guidance
- climb a career ladder
- follow a career path / track
- give up a career
- interrupt a career

cascade (n, v)
/kæs'keɪd/   A cascade system of training is one where a company first trains senior managers who then use the same programme to train middle managers who in turn train their subordinates so that the training passes down the line from top to bottom. Organisations can also cascade important internal messages from top to bottom in the same way.
- cascade down

case (n)
/'keɪs/   A case is a (usually) detailed description of a business situation or business or organisational problem used in teaching business and professional subjects. See also **case** (chapter 8).

case building (n ph)   Case building is when trainees themselves write their own cases rather than analyse cases presented by the teacher.
- case analysis
- case study
- the case method

In case study, students read a report of a business situation and then present their analysis of it to the teacher.

coach (n, v)
/'kəʊtʃ/   When you coach someone, you teach them how to do something better. Coaches help sports people, in particular, to improve their

5

Developing people

coaching (n)
coachee (n)

performances. You can also receive coaching before an examination or to improve your job performance. Some coaches place most emphasis on helping coachees find their own solutions to the problems they raise during coaching sessions. See also **mentor, protégé**.

coaching approach (n ph)

In the coaching approach, managers who are going to change their jobs coach the people who are going to replace them until they are ready to take over.
➡ a coaching session
➡ executive coaching
➡ life coaching
➡ peer coaching
➡ performance coaching
➡ self-coaching
➡ skills coaching
➡ team coaching
While mentors give advice which is usually career-oriented and future-focused, coaching is more about behavioural change – improving current performance and specific skills.

comfort zone (n ph)
/ˈkʌmfət zəʊn/

When you go outside your comfort zone, you put yourself in an unfamiliar and challenging situation which may well cause you stress and discomfort but which will help you to learn and to develop. See also **mindset**.
➡ go / move outside your comfort zone
➡ stay within / inside your comfort zone

competence (n)
/ˈkɒmpətəns/
competent (adj)
competently (adv)

1 When you are competent at a job, you do it well because you have the skills you need for it. Competence (uncountable noun) is the overall ability to do a job. The opposite of competent is **incompetent**.
➡ gross incompetence, be guilty of gross incompetence
2 Competence (countable noun) can be used in the same way as competency. See also **competency**.

competency
(n, countable)
/ˈkɒmpətənsi/

A competency is a mix of skills, attitudes and knowledge applied within a particular cultural context to achieve a specific objective. See also **competence, pay, skills**.
➡ a competency framework, derive
➡ a competency-based approach
➡ competency assessment
➡ competency-based performance
➡ competency development
➡ competency management
➡ identify competencies
➡ measure competencies
One HRM consultant distinguishes between input competencies – the personal characteristics and knowledge you put into the job; process competencies – what you do to get things done; and outcome competencies – the results for the organisation. Others simply distinguish between behaviour-based and work-based competencies.

Developing people

5

continuing education (n ph)
/kən'tɪnjuːɪŋ ɛdjə'keɪʃən/

Continuing education is a policy of providing learning opportunities for people throughout their working lives. Continuing education is also known as **ongoing education**. See also **training**.
The difference between continuing education and training is one of emphasis: education is concerned more with the general learning needs of the individual and training with the job-related learning needs of the individual.

course (n)
/'kɔːs/

A course is a set of training lessons. See also **programme**, **materials**, **module**, **unit**.

course participant (n ph)

A course participant is someone who follows a course.

crash course (n ph)

A crash course teaches you a lot about something in a short period of time.

extensive course (n ph)

In an extensive course, the lessons take place regularly on, say, a weekly basis, over a longer period of time.

in-plant course (n ph)

An in-plant course takes place in the company, probably for people directly involved in the production process.

intensive course (n ph)

In an intensive course, all the lessons take place one after the other. A week's intensive course, for example, lasts full-time for one week. Also known as an **immersion course**.

sandwich course (n ph)

A sandwich course is a college or university course where a period of work experience comes in between periods of study.

⟹ a correspondence course
⟹ a one-to-one course
⟹ a refresher course
⟹ a short course
⟹ a total immersion course
⟹ an after-hours course
⟹ attend a course
⟹ complete a course
⟹ course attendance
⟹ course fees
⟹ course registration
⟹ design a course
⟹ deliver a course
⟹ drop out of a course
⟹ enrol / register for / sign up for a course
⟹ follow / go on a training course
⟹ run a training course
⟹ send someone on a training course
Companies should send their export sales personnel on language training courses to give them at least a basic knowledge of the language of the countries where they are trying to sell.

development (n)
/dɪ'vɛləpmənt/
develop (v)
developmental (adj)

A development programme is one which aims to improve the competencies of the participants. See also **competence**, **competency**, **skills**.

5

Developing people

self development (n ph)

Self development is an approach which encourages employees to take responsibility for their own learning and for choosing the best way to do it.
➠ a development centre
➠ competence development
➠ continuing professional development (CPD)
➠ management development
➠ organisational development
➠ personal development
➠ staff development
Talking about management development rather than management training stresses longer-term results over process.

evaluate (v)
/ɪ'væljueɪt/
evaluation (n)

When you evaluate something, you measure how useful or effective it is. See also **appraise**, **assess**, **feedback**, **rate**.

course evaluation (n ph)

At the end of training courses, trainees are asked to evaluate the course they have followed by answering questions or by filling in a questionnaire. See also **happy sheet**.

student evaluation (n ph)

A student evaluation can be:
1 an evaluation of a student by a trainer, or
2 an evaluation by a student of a course or of a trainer.
➠ a job evaluation
➠ a programme evaluation
➠ do / carry out an evaluation of
➠ performance evaluation
Good training organisations use the results of evaluations to make improvements to future courses.

facilitator (n)
/fə'sɪlɪteɪtə/
facilitate (v)
facilitation (n)

When you facilitate something, you make it easier for groups of people to do. Facilitators can be trainers who try to make it easier for their students to learn; or others whose job is to help people make decisions, solve problems or achieve results in meetings or other group events.
➠ a workshop facilitator
➠ develop facilitation skills
Some trainers call themselves facilitators to underline the importance to them of helping trainees to learn and to become independent learners.

false beginner (n ph)
/'fɒls bi'gɪnə/

False beginners are language learners who never knew very much of the language they are learning and who have forgotten quite a lot of what they used to know.
False beginners need to be given the confidence to communicate as much as they can in the language they are learning.

feedback (n)
/'fiːdbæk/

You get feedback from people when they tell you what they thought of your performance or of a service, for example a training course, which you provided. See also **appraise**, **assess**, **evaluate**, **rate**.

5

Developing people

180 degree feedback (n ph)   You get 180 degree feedback from colleagues at the same level as you and from people below you in the organisation.

360 degree feedback (n ph)   You get 360 degree feedback from people below, above and at the same level as you in the organisation.

➡ a feedback questionnaire, complete / fill in
➡ accept feedback
➡ constructive feedback
➡ give feedback
➡ ignore feedback
➡ positive / negative feedback
➡ receive feedback
➡ reject feedback

There is no such thing as failure, only feedback.

gap year (n ph, Br Eng)   In Britain, about 10% of students who have gained a university place
/'gæp jɪə/   decide to wait for a year after leaving school before starting their university studies. Examples of gap year activities are working for money and then travelling, gaining work experience, studying abroad, and doing charitable work.

graveyard slot   A graveyard slot is a session in a conference or course programme
(n ph, informal)   when the energy level or level of interest of the participants may be
/'greɪvjɑːd 'slɒt/   lower than usual, for example straight after lunch.

happy sheet   A happy sheet is a feedback questionnaire given to participants at the
(n ph, informal)   end of a course or a conference to find out their level of satisfaction
/'hæpi ʃiːt/   with the event. See also **evaluate, feedback**.

in-company   In-company training is provided by the company itself rather than by
(adj ph, adv ph)   an outside agency. See also **in-house, course**.
/'ɪn 'kʌmpəni/
➡ an in-company training course
➡ an in-company training operation
➡ an in-company training programme
The advantage of in-company training operations is that the trainers know the company and its products or services well.

in-house (adj ph, adv ph)   An in-house training course is a course which takes place physically
/ɪn 'haʊs/   inside the company, not at an outside location like a hotel or conference centre. See also **in-company, course**.
Some companies prefer to have in-house training facilities for their staff so that trainees do not lose time travelling to and from distant training centres.

in-service (adj ph, adv ph)   In-service training is given to people who already have jobs. See also
/ɪn 'sɜːvɪs/   **pre-experience**.

in-tray exercise (n ph)   An in-tray is the metal or plastic tray on your desk in which incoming
/'ɪntreɪ 'ɛksəsaɪz/   documents are placed. In-tray exercises are used in training, recruitment and in assessment centres. In an in-tray exercise, you are

5

Developing people

given a number of documents – letters, memos, press cuttings, agendas, and so on, all relating to a professional problem or to the work of a particular manager – and a task to complete within a certain period of time. Also known as an **in-basket exercise**.

The candidates for the job were all given an in-tray exercise and two hours to read the documents and to prepare to say what action they would recommend.

indenture (v)
/ɪnˈdɛntʃə/
indentures (n pl)

Indentures are the employment contract between an apprentice and the employer. See also **apprentice**.

induction (n)
/ɪnˈdʌkʃən/

Your induction period in a new organisation is the time that you spend being told about your new organisation and the job. See also **orientation**.

⇒ induction training

Induction programmes for new managers should include a lot of information about the culture and objectives of the organisation.

instruct (v)
/ɪnˈstrʌkt/
instructor (n)
instructional (adj)
instruction (n)

When you instruct people, you teach them something practical, like how to operate a machine, in a formal, structured and teacher-centred way.

Safety rules are an essential component in any course of instruction in machine operation.

job (n)
/ˈdʒɒb/
job enlargement (n ph)
job enrichment (n ph)

job rotation (n ph)

See also **job** (chapters 1 and 3), **occupation**.

Job enlargement gives a job more variety or responsibility.

A job enrichment plan aims to make the job more satisfying to the person doing it.

Job rotation happens when people change from one job to another (and back) quite regularly. Job rotation for routine jobs on the shop floor can happen as often as every thirty minutes. A job rotation programme for trainee managers moves them from one department to another over a period of months so that they get to know all the different parts of the business.

Good executive job rotation plans are not standard programmes: they are adapted to the needs of individual trainee managers.

learn (v)
/ˈlɜːn/
learning (n)

You learn something when you know or understand something that you did not know before. When trainers teach you, they hope that you are learning what they are teaching you. See also **learning representative**, **train**.

accelerated learning (n ph)

Accelerated learning, a development from suggestopedia, involves a number of techniques including an emphasis on motivation, the learning environment, movement, team learning and the power of stories, to make learning more effective. See also **suggestopedia**.

action learning (n ph)

Action learning is a method of helping managers to develop their abilities by exposing them to real problems. Action learning is learning by doing.

5

Developing people

asynchronous e-learning (n ph)
Asynchronous e-learning happens when learner and trainer communicate with each other via the internet or an intranet but not directly. Trainer and learner can therefore be online at different times.

blended learning (n ph)
Blended learning is a mix of face-to face learning and e-learning. Some companies favour blended learning solutions because they believe it is an effective way to deliver training. Many others favour it because they think it can be cheaper than traditional face-to-face training.

distance learning (n ph)
Distance learning programmes are courses which people can follow in their own time and at their own pace using self-access materials, TV and radio, while communicating with tutors by telephone and the internet.

individual learning account (n ph)
An individual learning account (ILA) is an account into which both an individual and an employer or the government pays money for the individual to buy training with. ILA schemes encourage people to take more responsibility for their own learning by giving them more control over their own programmes.

learner autonomy (n ph)
The aim of learner training is learner autonomy – the development of learners who take responsibility for their own learning, and who learn effectively because they set targets, work towards them successfully and who are aware of their own learning styles and the way they learn best. Also known as **learner independence**.

learner training (n ph)
Learner training aims to help trainees become more effective learners and to take more responsibility for their learning by encouraging them to think about how they learn and about what learning strategies suit them best.

learner-centred training (n ph)
A learner-centred training programme is one which encourages the learner as far as possible to decide the objectives, content, methodology and pace of the programme. See also **train**.

learning curve (n ph)
Your learning curve shows the time you have to learn something new, and the amount and level of difficulty of what you have to learn. If you face a steep learning curve, it means that you have to learn a lot in a short period of time.

learning organisation (n ph)
A learning organisation is a company which aims to make its employees able to adapt to continuing change.

learning style (n ph)
Your learning style is the way you prefer to learn. Honey and Mumford have identified four different learning styles profiles: the activist, who likes to learn by doing; the theorist, who wants to know the rules first; the pragmatist, who wants to practise applying the rules; and the reflector, who likes to learn by watching others doing. Trainees can have a wide variety of learning styles and preferences.

open learning (n ph)
Open learning is learning which takes place at the time, place and pace which suits you best.

synchronous e-learning (n ph)
Synchronous e-learning happens when learner and trainer are online at the same time and communicate with each other directly via the internet or an intranet.

⇒ a learning and development strategy
⇒ a learning culture, create
⇒ a learning resource centre

5

Developing people

➡ a learning solution
➡ a steep learning curve
➡ an open learning centre
➡ an open learning programme, set up
➡ flexible learning
➡ informal learning
➡ learning by doing
➡ learning difficulties, a person with
➡ learning from your mistakes
➡ lifelong learning
➡ on-the-job learning
➡ open learning materials
➡ work-based learning

The objectives of a learner-centred approach are to achieve higher levels of motivation and learning through involving the learner much more in the learning process.

materials (n)
/məˈtɪərɪəlz/

Training materials are the books, video and audio cassettes, films, computer programmes and so on that you learn from during a training course. See also **resources**, **tailor**, **unit**.

self-study materials (n ph)

Self-study materials are materials which you can use on your own, without a trainer. See also **self access**.
➡ authentic materials
➡ design / develop / write materials
➡ learning materials
➡ materials development
➡ tailor-made materials
➡ up-to-date / out-of-date materials

The design and writing of materials can sometimes be the most expensive part of a training course.

mentor (n)
/ˈmɛntɔː/
mentee (n)
mentoring (n)

A mentor is an experienced professional person – usually a non-line manager from within your organisation or a senior manager from outside – who agrees to help you with your professional development. Mentors meet their mentees regularly, giving them advice and telling them what they have learnt about the job during their own careers. See also **coach**, **protégé**.
➡ a mentoring programme
➡ a mentoring scheme
➡ take someone on as a mentee

The name 'Mentor' comes from the man whom Ulysses asked to educate his son while he was away on his odyssey.

methodology (n)
/mɛθəˈdɒlədʒi/
methodological (adj)

The methodology of a training course is the way the content is taught.
Good trainers adapt their methodology to suit the learning styles of the individuals they are training.
➡ adapt the methodology to

mind map (n ph, v)
/'maɪnd mæp/
mind mapping (n)

A mind map ® is a way of representing information visually with lines, pictures and different colours so that you can see the big picture, make new connections and identify key ideas quickly. Mind mapping was invented by Tony Buzan.
Mind maps are a useful learning tool: they can help people organise their learning, understand complex information, and plan and present better.

mindset (n)
/'maɪndsɛt/

Your mindset is the way you typically see the world and the way you typically react to it. Human resources managers are often keen to change the mindsets of employees. See also **comfort zone**.
➡ change the mindset of
➡ an entrepreneurial mindset
➡ develop a successful mindset

model (n, v)
/'mɒdəl/
modelling (n)

When you model your behaviour on someone else's, you try to copy their behaviour. In neurolinguistic programming, learners are encouraged to model by copying as well as they can the behaviour of people who are very good at whatever it is that the trainee wants to learn to do. See also **neurolinguistic programming**.

module (n)
/'mɒdjuːl/
modular (adj)
modularisation (n)

A module is one part of a training programme. See also **programme**, **unit**.
A training programme for HR staff might contain modules on policy and planning, health and safety, benefits, and employee relations.

multiple intelligences (n ph)
/'mʌltɪpəl ɪn'tɛlɪdʒənsɪs/

Howard Gardner's theory of multiple intelligences argues that we should think of intelligence as involving more than logical-mathematical and verbal-linguistic thinking, the traditional measures of IQ (intelligence quotient). Gardner has identified eight different kinds of intelligence including the musical, the visual-spatial, the intrapersonal (knowledge of self) and the interpersonal (awareness of others). See also **emotional intelligence**.
Trainers who are aware of the unique make-up of multiple intelligences within each learner they work with can then try to adapt their training style to suit the learning style of the learner in order to make their learning more effective.

multi-skilling (n)
/'mʌlti skɪlɪŋ/
multi-skill (v)

Multi-skilling is training individual employees and groups of employees to be able to perform a variety of different jobs. See also **reskilling, skill, skills**.
Multi-skilling the workforce goes hand in hand with the development of a team building approach to production.

Myers Briggs (n)
/'maɪəz 'brɪgz/

The Myers Briggs Type Indicator ® is a popular psychometric instrument, derived from Carl Jung's theory of psychological types, for assessing the personalities of individuals. It helps people understand

5

Developing people

themselves generally, their motivations and their (learning) preferences. It is based on eight behavioural characteristics on four scales: extraversion – introversion, sensing – intuition, thinking and feeling, and judging and perceiving. Myers Briggs has a variety of applications including recruitment, team development and conflict resolution.

needs analysis (n ph)
/'niːdz ə'næatlɪsɪs/

The needs analysis is the stage before the training course begins when the trainer questions the trainees to find out what their training objectives and their needs are for the course that they are going to follow.

➠ carry out / do a (detailed) needs analysis

Once the needs analysis has been carried out, the training department can design the course and then write or collect together the training materials.

neurolinguistic programming (n ph)
/njʊərəʊ'lɪŋgwɪstɪk 'prəʊgræmɪŋ/

Neurolinguistic programming (NLP) is a training method which aims at improved performance in an activity by analysing excellent performance and breaking it down into small components; and by encouraging trainees to understand how their thinking processes affect their performance. See also **model**.

off-the-peg (adj ph)
/ɒf ðə 'pɛg/

An off-the-peg training course is a course with a fixed content, not one designed to fit an individual trainee or group of trainees. See also **tailor**.

Many training organisations advertise a range of off-the-peg courses with brief descriptions of the objectives, duration and content of each one.

one-to-one
(adj ph, adv ph, n ph)
/'wʌn tə 'wʌn/

One-to-one training is training involving a single learner with one trainer at any one time.

➠ have a one-to-one (meeting) with
➠ one-to-one training
➠ a one-to-one meeting / interview

orientation (n)
/ɔːrɪən'teɪʃən/
orientate (v)

An orientation course or programme trains you to understand a new activity or to do a new job. See also **induction**.

Some people still receive little or no orientation when they start a new job: this can lead to inefficiency and loss of time and money later.

pace (n)
/'peɪs/
pacing (n)

If a training course moves at a fast pace, then it moves along quickly. Trainers can also move through their material at a fast or at a slow pace.

The main feedback on the course was that sometimes the pace had been too slow.

pre-experience (adj ph)
/priː ɪk'spɪərɪəns/

Pre-experience or **pre-service** training is the training people receive before they start a job. See also **in-service**.

5

Developing people

programme (n, v)
/'prəʊɡræm/

A training programme is a training plan for an individual or a group. A programme may include one or several courses or modules. See also **course**, **module**, **unit**.
⟹ a development programme
⟹ adopt a programme
⟹ follow a programme
The aim of the company's range of training programmes is to increase the level of performance of the whole workforce.

protégé (n)
/'prəʊtɪʒeɪ/

A protégé is the less experienced person whom a mentor agrees to help with his or her professional development. See also **mentor**.
The success of mentoring depends very much on how far a relationship of trust and respect can be established between the mentor and the protégé.

ranking and rating
(n ph, v ph)
/'ræŋkɪŋ ən 'reɪtɪŋ/

Ranking and rating is an assessment system, used in particular by some companies in the US computer industry, which benchmarks your performance against the performance of colleagues.
Intel's ranking and rating scheme required any employee rated slower than colleagues in more than one area to be put on a corrective action programme.

rate (n, v)
/'reɪt/
rating (n)

When you rate a thing or a person, you measure how good they are. See also **evaluation**, **feeback**, **rate** (chapter 4).
⟹ a rating scale
⟹ give a rating to
Employees were asked to rate their job satisfaction using a rating scale of 1 – 10.

release (n, v)
/rɪ'liːs/

If your company releases you for training, it agrees to let you go on a training course rather than go to work. See also **course**, **release** (chapter 3).

block release (n ph)

Apprentices and other employees on block release attend courses for periods of up to several weeks as part of their overall training.

day release (n ph)

Someone on day release is officially absent from work for one day per week in order to go to a local school or college to study.
⟹ operate a day release scheme
⟹ paid release
It can be difficult for small firms to release individual members of staff for training because there is no-one to replace them while they are absent.

reskilling (n)
/ri'skɪlɪŋ/
reskill (v)

Reskilling is teaching people new skills. Also known as **upskilling**. See also **multi-skilling**, **skill**, **skills**, **retrain**.
One principle of any company training programme should be to reskill employees whose current skills are out of date and no longer needed.

resources (n pl)
/rɪ'zɔːsɪz/
resource (n, v)

A resource is any piece of material or input which helps trainers to train and learners to learn. See also **human resources**, **materials**, **resource** (chapter 3).

5

Developing people

resources centre (n ph)

A resources (or resource) centre is the place where an organisation's training and learning materials are kept. See also **self access**.
➡ a learning resource centre
The trainer's best resource is the learners themselves.

retrain (v)
/riˈtreɪn/
retraining (n)

When you retrain, you learn how to do a new job. See also **reskilling**.
➡ a retraining programme

role play (n ph)
/ˈrəʊl pleɪ/

A role play is a learning method in which you take part in a short improvised drama in which you and each of the other participants play the parts of other (usually imaginary) people. See also **simulation**.
➡ a role play exercise
➡ do / act out / take part in a role play
On our health and safety training course, we did a pairwork role play: one of us played the role of the safety officer and the other took the part of someone caught breaking a safety rule.

sabbatical (n)
/səˈbætɪkəl/

When you take a sabbatical, your organisation gives you permission to take some time off – usually between three months and a year – from your normal job for a special project, for example to do research, write a book or travel.
➡ a sabbatical term / year
➡ be on sabbatical / be on sabbatical leave
➡ grant a sabbatical
➡ take a sabbatical year
➡ take sabbatical leave

second (v)
/sɛˈkɒnd/
secondment (n)
secondee (n)

When a company seconds employees, it transfers them temporarily to another part of the company or lends them to another organisation for a certain period of time. A **secondee** is an employee who is on secondment. See also **corporate social responsibility**.
➡ be on secondment to
Although she normally works in the HR department of a large company, she is currently on secondment to a charity dealing with homeless people.

self access (n ph)
/sɛlf ˈæksɛs/

Self access learning or **self study** is learning on your own, without a trainer. See also **materials**.
➡ a self access learning centre
➡ a self access resources centre
➡ self access / self study materials

seminar (n)
/ˈsɛmɪnɑː/

A training seminar is a meeting led by a trainer or outside speaker. In management training seminars, the leader often does a lot of the talking. In others, for example university seminars where the number of participants may be smaller, the students have plenty of opportunity for questions and discussion.
➡ lead a seminar
➡ take part in a seminar on

5

Developing people

simulation (n)
/sɪmjə'leɪʃən/
simulate (v)

In a simulation, you invent and take part in a short improvised drama in which you play yourself, not someone else. See also **role play**.
Simulations of meetings and negotiations followed by analysis and feedback is one technique for improving people's abilities in these areas.

skills (n pl)
/'skɪlz/

Your skills are the abilities that you have to do different things. See also **competence, competency, multi-skilling, reskilling, skill** (chapter 1).

core skills (n ph)

Core skills are the essential or basic skills which you need to do a job properly.

hard skills (n ph)

You have hard management skills when you have knowledge and experience of a business area such as finance, accountancy or logistics.

interpersonal skills (n ph)

If you have good interpersonal skills, you are able to communicate successfully with a variety of people.

soft skills (n ph)

People with good soft skills have good communication, social and people management skills. See also **emotional intelligence**.

skills gap (n ph)

The skills gap is the difference between the number of people in the job market who have the skills which employers want to use and the number of people with these skills that employers want to recruit. Also known as a **skills deficit**.

➡ a skill(s) set
➡ a skills shortage
➡ communication skills
➡ develop skills
➡ language skills
➡ life skills
➡ management skills
➡ marketable skills, possess
➡ narrow / reduce the skills gap
➡ people skills
➡ practise skills
➡ supervisory skills
➡ upgrade skills

Employers today are looking for employees with skills in a wide range of areas including communication, team working, problem-solving, adaptability and critical thinking.

SMART objectives
(n ph, abbrev)
/'smɑːt əb'dʒɛktɪvz/

SMART objectives are objectives which are Specific, Measurable, Agreed, Realistic and Time-bound (although there are a number of variations on this version). Getting people to think in SMART terms can help them both to define and to realise their objectives.

suggestopedia (n)
/sədʒɛstə'piːdɪə/
suggestopedic (adj)

Suggestopedia is a teaching method (originally for learning languages) developed by Georgi Lozanov, a Bulgarian psychologist, which stresses the importance of non-conscious learning in the learning process. See also **learn**.

5

Developing people

Learners in a suggestopedic classroom are encouraged to relax in an attractive and comfortable learning environment so that their minds become more open to the information presented to them.

tailor (v)
/'teɪlə/
tailored (adj)

When you tailor a training course, you design it to fit the student's needs as closely as possible. Tailor-made training is also known as **customised training**. See also **off-the-peg**, **materials**, **needs analysis**.
➡ a tailored training course / training programme
➡ a tailor-made course / programme
Before clients come to our training centre, they first of all undergo a detailed needs analysis so that we can tailor the training precisely to their needs.

train (v)
/'treɪn/
training (n)
trainer (n)
trainee (n)
traineeship (n)

When you train someone, you teach them how to do something specific and usually job-related.

assertiveness training (n ph) Assertiveness training aims to help you to speak and behave in a stronger, more confident way.

continuing training (n ph) Continuing training is a policy of providing job-orientated training opportunities for people throughout their working lives. See also **continuing education**.

outdoor training (n ph) Outdoor training courses can include activities such as hill walking, sailing, climbing and canoeing. Also known as **adventure training** or **outward bound training**.

self-managed training (n ph) A self-managed training programme is one you organise yourself without a trainer or with a trainer playing a less important role in your training.

survival training (n ph) A survival training course places the participants in an unfamiliar, difficult and possibly dangerous situation – on a boat at sea or in difficult countryside – where they must work together to solve problems set by the trainer.

training levy (n ph) A training levy is a tax on companies, so that they have to spend a certain proportion of, for example, profits or of the salaries budget, on training.
➡ a training budget
➡ a training centre
➡ a training course, do / follow
➡ a training course, run
➡ a training department
➡ a training manual
➡ a training method
➡ a training pack
➡ a training package
➡ a training period
➡ a training policy, implement
➡ a training programme
➡ a training provider, select

Developing people

5

➡ a training session
➡ analyse training needs
➡ basic training
➡ communication skills training
➡ deliver training
➡ design training
➡ do training
➡ evaluate training
➡ face-to-face training
➡ further training
➡ hands-on training, receive
➡ in-house training
➡ intensive training
➡ management training
➡ off-the-job training
➡ on-the-job training
➡ one-to-one training
➡ performance-related training
➡ supervisory training
➡ trainee potential
➡ trainer training
➡ training administration
➡ training costs
➡ training facilities
➡ training materials
➡ training measures
➡ training needs
➡ training needs assessment
➡ training requirements
➡ training resources
➡ undertake training

Among the most common kinds of training organised by companies are courses to improve language, computer and communication skills.

tutor (n, v)
/ˈtjuːtə/
tutee (n)
tutorial (n)
tuition (n)

A tutor is a teacher or trainer, often for only one student or for a small group of students.

unit (n)
/ˈjuːnɪt/

A unit is one piece of training material, designed to take just one or two lessons to work through. See also **course**, **materials**, **module**, **programme**.

VAK (n ph, abbrev)
/ˈvæk/

VAK stands for Visual (sight), Auditory (hearing) and Kinesthetic (touch and movement), a term used in neurolinguistic programming to stress how different one person's sensory perception of the world can be from another's. Trainers who are aware of VAK will try to adapt their teaching style to suit the different VAKs and hence the different learning styles of the different learners in the group.

5

Developing people

visual aid (n ph)
/'vɪʒʊəl 'eɪd/

A visual aid is a technical support involving pictures which you can use to help you to communicate your message to your audience in a presentation or in training. A transparency projected by an overhead projector is an example of a visual aid.

vocational (adj)
/vəʊ'keɪʃənəl/
vocation (n)

Vocational training gives you the skills you need to do a particular job.
➡ vocational education
➡ vocational qualification, obtain
➡ vocational training
➡ vocational guidance, need, give
➡ pre-vocational training
There is a general need to increase the number of young people with vocational qualifications in Western countries because the shortage of skills is growing.

work experience (n ph)
/'wɜːk ɪk'spɪərɪəns/

School pupils and college students get work experience when they work in an organisation for a short time to get an idea of what working there is like. See also **intern**, **work placement**, **work sampling**.
➡ a work experience scheme

work placement (n ph)
/'wɜːk 'pleɪsmənt/

A work placement or work experience placement is a pupil or student working in a company for a short time; or the job that the student is doing. Placements are often arranged between the company and the student's educational institution. See also **intern**, **work experience**.
➡ offer a work (experience) placement
➡ take up a work (experience) placement

work sampling (n ph)
/'wɜːk 'sɑːmplɪŋ/

Work sampling is when you try different jobs in a company either to help you decide which job you would like to do or to help you know the company better. See also **work experience**.
This company runs a work sampling scheme which enables teenagers in their last year at school to try out different jobs for a short period.

workshadowing (n)
/'wɜːk ʃædəʊɪŋ/

Workshadowing is when you learn a job from someone by following them around and watching what they do over a period of time. Workshadowing is also known as **shadowing**. See also **buddy system**.
Workshadowing, like mentoring, is a new name for an old induction and training technique.

workshop (n)
/'wɜːkʃɒp/

A workshop is a practical form of training session with a high level of participation. Workshops often involve participants working in pairs or small groups and then reporting back to the whole group.
➡ a workshop facilitator
➡ a workshop leader

Exercises

Exercise 1

Choose the best term (A, B, C or D) to complete each sentence.

1   The organisation evaluates employees' job performance by _____ them twice a year.
    A inducting   B training   C appraising   D testing

2   The company regularly organises _____ for its engineers in which technical experts are invited to speak and lead workshops.
    A courses   B lessons   C meetings   D seminars

3   The company manages change by having senior managers train middle managers, who then train lower grades so that the message _____ from top to bottom of the organisation.
    A falls down   B cascades   C careers   D feeds back

4   When companies have to adapt to changing market conditions, they often have to _____ their employees to do new jobs.
    A recruit   B retain   C retrain   D re-invent

5   Many companies which have recognised the importance of employee development, have increased their budget for _____.
    A extended learning   B continuing education   C competence   D programmes

6   An important part of employees' _____ development is the continuing need to improve their skills and competences.
    A job   B life   C career   D experience

7   The company organises regular _____ to develop creative thinking and communication techniques.
    A workshops   B topics   C guidelines   D trainings

8   We need to change the _____ of more of our employees so that they are more willing to think in new ways and take on new challenges.
    A mindset   B feedback   C skills   D resources

9   Many organisations now have a _____ where trainees can use a variety of study media such as books, CD-ROMs and the internet for learning both outside and during working hours.
    A library   B workshop   C resources centre   D seminar

10   People can only improve the way they do things if they get good _____ on their performance.
    A kick back   B payback   C come back   D feedback

Exercise 2

These terms (1 – 8) all describe types or methods of training. Match each term with the right definition (a - h).

1	simulation	a	A kind of improvised play for learning or practising a skill in which you pretend to be someone else
2	outdoor training	b	A kind of improvised play for learning or practising a skill in which you are yourself
3	induction	c	What you should do between training sessions
4	mind mapping	d	When recently recruited employees are welcomed to the organisation and are given information about it, its vision, their jobs, their colleagues, etc.
5	modelling	e	A way of showing information which helps people to visualise clearly the elements of an issue, subject or situation
6	role play	f	An NLP tool for studying the way experts do well the thing you want to learn, and then trying to learn how to do it as well as them
7	self study	g	When an employee closely follows the working methods of a peer
8	workshadowing	h	When teams of trainees take part in open air activities such as trekking, climbing and orienteering

Exercise 3

Insert a key term from the box, which all refer to different kinds of people involved in training, into each sentence (1 - 8).

apprentice	coach	facilitator	false beginner	trainer
	mentor	mentee	tutor	

1   Generally speaking a teacher is concerned with the general education of students while the job of the _____ is to help students to learn things relating to their work.

2   He has signed up as an _____ and will spend the next five years working and studying before he finally becomes a master plumber.

3   She has just started in a new job and the managing director has agreed to take her on as his _____ .

4   To improve his performance, the manager decided to employ the services of a _____ skilled in personal and professional development techniques.

5   With only two years of study of the language from her school days, the trainee was assessed as a _____ after testing.

6   In addition to sessions with the teacher, each trainee was assigned a personal _____ who closely followed and commented on their progress during their time on the course.

7   In order to create better rapport in business meetings, a _____ was hired to help improve communication among the participants.

8   Due to her long career and experience in the company, she was asked to become a _____, transferring her knowledge and advice to younger managers and helping with their professional development.

Exercise 4

Match the terms in the box, which all refer to different types of training, with their definitions (1 – 5), then insert them in the appropriate gaps (a - e) in the text.

in-house	vocational	tailored	in-company	off-the-peg

1   customised training, designed to fit with a trainee's specific needs
2   training provided by people in the organisation and not an external provider
3   training which takes place physically inside the company and not at an outside location
4   a training course with a fixed content and not personalised for individual trainees or groups
5   training which gives you the skills you need for a particular job

The HR department is starting the New Year with a new approach to (a) _____ training, to provide all our skilled shopfloor people with the skills they need for their jobs today. All training will now take place completely (b) _____, thus reducing time lost through travelling to outside providers. In addition, it is our belief that our organisation already possesses the necessary knowledge and skills without referring to external agencies and we therefore plan to introduce an (c)_____ training policy, proposing
(d)_____ training to suit individual, customised needs as well as
(e)_____ fixed-content solutions for group training in areas such as IT.

Exercise 5

Combine each word in the box with one of the four development words below to create word pairs. Then try and define each term you have made.

adventure	distance	organisation	continuing	participant
crash	core	extensive	interpersonal	intensive
levy	survival	gap	sandwich	hard	style
	blended	curve	assertiveness	soft	

course	learning	skills	training

For discussion

1   How is the training budget determined in your organisation? How is it spent?
2   How can you evaluate return on training investment? Do you get a good ROI on the training your organisation buys?
3   How does your company's appraisal system work? What is it for?
4   What is a learning organisation? Can your organisation become one?
5   Can coaching change your organisation?

Case studies

Training for change

After a long period of speculation, DelSilba, a Spanish firm employing 5,000 people and with a solid image and culture built up over thirty years in business, was acquired by an American corporation in July of last year. A two-week period followed in which company life continued as usual.

Then, on the Monday morning of the third week in July, employees discovered that the DelSilba company logo had been changed and that all signs previously displaying the traditional colours of yellow and white had been replaced by a new colour scheme. Departmental managers found instructions on their desks about the new formatting of company business correspondence, words to avoid using and a pamphlet outlining a new set of guidelines for corporate ethics.

After its traditional closing period in August, employees were issued with a firm reminder from US headquarters of the importance of good results, and that in order to satisfy shareholders' investment, the company would do whatever necessary to achieve profit. Americans were placed in charge of the finance and treasury departments; many employees found it challenging to have to report to their US counterparts in English.

In late September, it was decided to turn each site throughout Spain into an independent legal entity, while retaining a reduced head office in Madrid. Staff at head office thought that a redundancy scheme would be put in place, but none came. Instead, employees were invited to move to one of the subsidiaries or to negotiate an individual leaving package. In addition, in late December, Spanish management had still not received any statement of vision or other information about the future of the Spanish organisation. Motivation among employees fell and rumours began to circulate that part of the company would be sold off to a competitor.

Consider:
- How could the new owners have worked differently with their Spanish employees regarding the change?
- How can the HR department help employees to deal better with this period of crisis?

How to keep potential

You have been hired by Hake International, a small, specialised services company developing software for a number of sectors and customers throughout Europe. The company has a partnership with a local technical high school and regularly recruits intakes of young employees who, after two years' experience, tend to move on to larger engineering companies. Part of your function is to strengthen the link between the appraisal system (currently used as a tool for bonuses and additional pay increases) and career development among the young employees in an attempt to retain a skilled and motivated workforce. Senior management recognises that training is a key factor in maintaining and developing skills and this is something which is highly appreciated by the staff.

Consider:
- How can you improve the appraisal system to identify potential high performers? Which criteria should you use?
- What key competences do you believe your employees should acquire? What is the framework for a continuous training policy which will help them acquire these?

5

Developing people

6

Health, safety, welfare and environment

Key terms to talk about ensuring and improving the physical and psychological well-being of employees.

Health, safety, welfare and environment

6

**These are the key terms in this chapter.
Which of them do you understand?
Which of them can you use?**

Abuse
accident
agent
asbestos
assembly point
asthma
Body odour
breathing apparatus
bully
burn out
Carcinogen
check-up
contaminate
convalesce
corporate manslaughter
counselling
Discharge
Emergency
employee assistance programme
environmental audit
ergonomics
evacuate
Fatal
fire
first aid
Goggles
Harass
hazard
health
health and safety
hot-desking
hygiene
Incapacity
industrial
injure
inspect
intimidate
Machine guard
manual handling
medical record
Near miss

neglect
noise
notice
Occupational
open day
overwork
Pollute
preventive
prohibit
protect
Recreation
rehabilitate
repetitive strain injury
respiratory
rest break
risk assessment
Safe
screen
security
sedentary
self esteem
sick
silicosis
slips, trips and falls
smoking
solvent
spillage
stress
sunlight-deprivation syndrome
Toxic
trauma
Upper limb disorder
user-friendly
Ventilate
vibration
visual display unit
Warning
welfare
wellness
working environment

abuse (n, v)
/ə'bjuːs/

1 If you abuse alcohol or drugs, you use them in a way which is dangerous for your health. See also **solvent**.
➡ alcohol abuse, engage in
➡ drug abuse
➡ solvent abuse
Millions of working days are lost every year in the industrialised world as a result of alcohol and drug abuse.
2 You abuse someone when you treat them in a way that hurts them physically or emotionally. You abuse someone verbally when you say things to them which hurt them physically or emotionally. See also **bully**, **harass**.
➡ child abuse
➡ physical abuse
➡ sexual abuse, abuse sexually
➡ verbal abuse

accident (n)
/'æksɪdənt/
accidental (adj)

accident log (n ph)

avert an accident (v ph)

When someone has an accident, they hurt or injure themselves in some way. See also **fatal**, **injure**, **near miss**.

The accident log is the book in which details of all accidents in the workplace are written.

If you avert an accident, you stop it from happening.
➡ a minor accident
➡ a serious accident
➡ accident benefit
➡ accident insurance
➡ accident prevention
➡ accident prevention regulations
➡ accident statistics
➡ an accident black spot
➡ an accident book
➡ an accident frequency rate
➡ an accident rate
➡ an accident record
➡ an accident report
➡ an accidental death
➡ an industrial accident
➡ cause an accident
➡ prevent an accident
➡ report an accident
➡ suffer an accident
➡ witness an accident
Almost 30% of fatal accidents in the industrial sector in Britain occur in the construction industry.

agent (n)
/'eɪdʒənt/

An agent is a substance which can cause a chemical change or a reaction. Agents are often dangerous and so need careful handling. See also **carcinogen**.
➡ a biological agent

Health, safety, welfare and environment

6

➡ a chemical agent
➡ a physical agent
➡ exposure to an agent
British companies have to label all the chemical agents in their factories clearly so that people can decide what to do quickly if there is an accident.

asbestos (n)
/æz'bɛstɒs/

Asbestos is a material used in many products and processes, for example in fire protection materials. People who have breathed in asbestos dust can get cancer.
➡ a dangerous level of asbestos
➡ asbestos levels / levels of asbestos
➡ asbestos particles / particles of asbestos
➡ exposure to asbestos, exposed to asbestos.
There are a number of different kinds of asbestos including white asbestos (chrysotile), and the more dangerous blue (crocidolite) and brown (amosite) asbestos.

assembly point (n ph)
/ə'sɛmbli 'pɔɪnt/

An assembly point is a place in or outside a building where people must go when the alarm sounds for an emergency. On a ship or oil platform, an assembly point can also be called a **muster station**.

asthma (n)
/'æsmə/
asthmatic (adj, n)

Asthma is an illness which makes breathing difficult. See also **respiratory**.
➡ acute / severe asthma
➡ an asthma sufferer
➡ an asthmatic attack, have / experience / suffer

body odour (n ph)
/'bɒdi 'əʊdə/

People with body odour (BO) smell strongly because they do not wash themselves or their clothes enough. In some cases, body odour is the result of a medical problem. See also **hygiene**.

breathing apparatus
/'briːðɪŋ æpə'reɪtəs/
(n ph)

Breathing apparatus is equipment with portable oxygen which you can use when the air is dangerous to breathe.

bully (v, n)
/'bʊli/
bullying (n)

A bully is someone who dominates another person physically, verbally or emotionally or who causes another person physical or mental harm so as to cause unhappiness and stress to that person. See also **abuse, harass, intimidate, victimise**.
➡ a workplace bully
➡ an anti-bullying policy
➡ be the victim of bullying behaviour
Research into bullying at work tells us that around a quarter of the workforce in Britain has been bullied in the last five years, with similar figures for the USA and Australia.

burn out (v)
/'bɜːn 'aʊt/
burn-out (n)
burnt-out (adj)

Employees can burn out if they put so much energy into their work that suddenly they have none left.
➡ experience / suffer (total) burn-out

carcinogen (n)
/kɑːˈsɪnədʒən/
carcinogenic (adj)

A carcinogen is an agent which can cause cancer. See also **agent**.
➠ a carcinogenic agent

check-up (n)
/ˈtʃɛk ʌp/
check up (v)

A check-up is a quick, general medical examination. See also **medical examination**.
➠ have / get a check-up

contaminate (v)
/kənˈtæmɪneɪt/
contamination (n)
contaminated (adj)

When an agent contaminates a working area, it makes the office or factory dangerous from the health point of view. See also **agent**, **pollute**.
➠ contaminated water
➠ contamination of the air
The company closed off the plant to check that radiation had not contaminated the area.

convalesce (v)
/kɒnvəˈlɛs/
convalescent (adj, n)
convalescence (n)

When you convalesce, you spend time resting and getting better after an accident or an illness. See also **rehabilitate**.
➠ a convalescent home
➠ a period of convalescence

corporate manslaughter (n ph)
/ˈkɔːpərɪt ˈmænslɔːtə/

An organisation can be found guilty of corporate manslaughter in some countries if the court finds that it is responsible for the death of an employee, customer or member of the public. Also known as **corporate killing**. See also **neglect**.

counselling (n)
/ˈkaʊnsəlɪŋ/
counsellor (n)
counsel (n, v)
bereavement counselling (n ph)

Counsel is advice. Counselling is giving advice and a counsellor is someone who gives advice professionally. Organisations can employ **counsellors** to listen to employees' problems and to give advice or offer help. See also **employee assistance programme, stress, trauma**. People may receive bereavement counselling after someone close to them dies.
➠ a careers counsellor
➠ career counselling
➠ crisis counselling
➠ debt counselling
➠ employee counselling
➠ financial counselling
➠ give / provide counselling
➠ outplacement counselling
➠ pre-retirement counselling
➠ receive counselling
➠ stress counselling
➠ trauma counselling
➠ workplace counselling

discharge (n, v)
/ˈdɪstʃɑːdʒ/ (n)
/dɪsˈtʃɑːdʒ/ (v)

A factory discharges something when it puts a gas, liquid or other waste substance into, for example, the air or a nearby river. A discharge is also known as an **emission**. See also **discharge** (chapter 2), **pollute, spillage**.

Health, safety, welfare and environment

6

Health, safety, welfare and environment

6

emergency (n)
/i'mɜːdʒənsi/
emergency service
(n ph)

An emergency is a very dangerous situation where you need to take immediate action.
The emergency services are the police, ambulance and fire services, and, on the coast, the coastguard.

➡ an emergency exit
➡ an emergency procedure, review
➡ call out an emergency service
➡ emergency lighting
➡ in an emergency
➡ in the event of an emergency

In the event of an emergency, the alarm bell will sound and all employees must leave the building by the emergency exits as soon as possible.

employee assistance programme (n ph)
/ɛmplɔɪ'iː ə'sɪstəns 'prəʊgræm/

Employee assistance programmes (EAPs) offer advice to employees on balancing work and family life, dealing with stress, and counselling for alcohol or financial or other kinds of problem. See also **counselling**.
In the UK, more employees ask to join EAPs while in the USA, more people are referred by their managers.

environmental audit (n ph)
/ɪnvaɪrən'mɛntəl 'ɔːdɪt/

An environmental audit is a detailed measure of the balance between the positive and negative effects a company has on the natural environment of land, air and water.

➡ carry out an environmental audit

Deutsche Telekom's annual sustainability report contains full details of the environmental audit which the company carries out every year.

ergonomics (n)
/ɜːgə'nɒmɪks/
ergonomist (n)
ergonomical (adj)

Ergonomics is the study of the relationship between employees and their working environment. The aim of ergonomics is to make machines, processes and products as comfortable, convenient, safe and healthy as possible for the user. Ergonomics aims to provide compatibility between the user, the environment and the equipment. See also **user-friendly**.

➡ an ergonomic design
➡ ergonomically designed

Ergonomics can be used to make improvements in office layout, lighting, ventilation and the design of office furniture.

evacuate (v)
/i'vækjueɪt/
evacuation (n)

When an expatriate manager has to leave a country suddenly, for example because of the political situation, the company organises an emergency evacuation. When you evacuate a building, you empty it of people because there is a fire or some other kind of emergency. See also **emergency**, **relocate**.

➡ an emergency evacuation

fatal (adj)
/'feɪtəl/
fatality (n)

A fatal accident is one that results in death. A **fatality** refers to the death of the person in an accident or to the person who dies. See also **accident**, **injure**.

➡ a fatal accident
➡ a fatal injury

fire (n)
/'faɪə/

There is a fire when something burns. See also **fire** (chapter 2).

fire drill (n ph)

When there is a fire drill, the people in a workplace practise what they would do if there were a real fire.

fire extinguisher (n ph)

A fire extinguisher is a standard piece of equipment to put out a fire, using foam, water or carbon dioxide.

tackle a fire (v ph)

When you tackle a fire, you try to put it out.

- ➡ a breakout of fire
- ➡ a fire alarm
- ➡ a fire certificate, issue
- ➡ a fire door
- ➡ a fire engine
- ➡ a fire escape
- ➡ a fire exit
- ➡ a fire fighter
- ➡ a fire marshal
- ➡ a fire safety notice, display
- ➡ a fire warden
- ➡ extinguish a fire
- ➡ fight a fire
- ➡ fire detection
- ➡ fire fighting equipment
- ➡ fire practice, a fire practice
- ➡ fire precautions
- ➡ fire prevention, a ~ officer
- ➡ fire safety
- ➡ put out a fire
- ➡ set something on fire
- ➡ the fire service / brigade, call

All employees should take part in regular fire drills so that they know how to leave the building if there is a fire.

first aid (n ph)
/'fɜːst 'eɪd/
first aider (n ph)

First aid is emergency medical treatment. A **first aider** is someone who knows how to give basic medical treatment to an injured person after an accident.

first aid box (n ph)

A first aid box is a box containing items for basic medical treatment like bandages, ointment to treat burns, disinfectant, and so on.

- ➡ a first aid kit
- ➡ a first aid post
- ➡ a first aid room
- ➡ administer first aid
- ➡ first aid treatment
- ➡ receive first aid

goggles (n pl)
/'gɒgəlz/

Goggles are heavy duty safety glasses to protect your eyes. See also **protect**.

harass (v)
/hə'ræs/ or /'hærəs/
harassment (n)
harasser (n)

When someone harasses you, they annoy or worry you by causing trouble for you on repeated occasions. See also **abuse**, **bully**, **intimidate**, **victimise**.

Health, safety, welfare and environment

6

Health, safety, welfare and environment

6

personal harrasment (n ph)

Personal harassment is another term for bullying.

sexual harassment (n ph)

Employees suffer sexual harassment when a colleague makes unwelcome sexual remarks or behaves sexually towards them in an unwelcome way.

➡ a victim of harassment

➡ an anti-harassment policy

➡ complain about harassment

➡ experience / suffer harassment

Forms of sexual harassment include unwelcome physical contact, questions about your private life, persistent invitations to social activities, and unwanted phone calls and emails.

hazard (n)
/'hæzəd/
hazardous (adj)

A hazard is any kind of substance or equipment which can be dangerous in the workplace.

➡ a biological hazard

➡ a dust hazard

➡ a hazard identification statement

➡ a hazardous substance, handle

➡ a health hazard

➡ a maintenance hazard

➡ a skin hazard

➡ a welding hazard

health (n)
/'hɛlθ/

An employee who is in good health is physically and mentally well.

➡ a health hazard

➡ a health risk / a risk to health

➡ a private health (insurance) scheme, join

➡ a regular health check, undergo / have

➡ be bad / good for your health

➡ be in good / bad health

➡ health protection

➡ health surveillance

health and safety (n ph)
/'hɛlθ ən 'seɪfti/

Health and safety is the area of human resources work which is concerned with keeping employees physically and mentally well and protecting them from workplace hazards. See also **safe**, **welfare**.

health and safety representative (n ph)

A health and safety representative or rep is a union or employee representative, usually elected in western industrialised countries, who has a special responsibility for health and safety. Also known as a **safety representative** or safety rep. See also **learning representative**, **shop steward**.

➡ a health and safety code

➡ a health and safety inspector

➡ a health and safety policy

➡ a health and safety procedure

➡ a health and safety regulation

➡ a health and safety requirement

➡ health and safety enforcement

➡ health and safety legislation

⟶ health and safety rights
⟶ occupational health and safety

hot-desking (n)
/ˈhɒt ˈdɛskɪŋ/

When there is a system of hot-desking in your office, you and your colleagues do not have your own desks but take whichever desk is free when you arrive. Hot-desking is often done by people who work away from their offices a lot.

hygiene (n)
/ˈhaɪdʒiːn/
hygienic (adj)

A hygienic workplace is a clean workplace. The opposite of hygienic is **unhygienic**.

personal hygiene (n ph)

People with a good standard of personal hygiene wash regularly. People with a poor standard of personal hygiene do not. See also **body odour**.
⟶ high / low hygiene standards
⟶ maintain a good standard of hygiene
⟶ observe strict rules of hygiene
⟶ occupational hygiene
⟶ rules of hygiene, observe the (basic)

incapacity (n)
/ɪŋkəˈpæsɪti/
incapacitate (v)
incapacitation (n)
incapacitated (adj)

An incapacity is any kind of physical or mental condition which stops you from working.
⟶ a temporary / permanent incapacity
⟶ temporarily / permanently incapacitated
⟶ total incapacitation
The fall incapacitated him for several weeks but he was able to claim sickness benefit and did not lose too much money as a result of the accident.

industrial (adj)
/ɪnˈdʌstrɪəl/
industry (n)
industrialise (v)
industrialist (n)

Industrial, in the context of health and safety, usually means work-related. See also **occupational**, **industrial action**, **industrial relations**.
⟶ an industrial accident
⟶ an industrial disease
⟶ an industrial injury
⟶ industrial medicine
⟶ industrial safety
Industrial injuries can be reduced by enforcing health and safety rules and by giving all employees health and safety training.

injure (v)
/ˈɪndʒə/
injury (n)
injured (adj)

When employees are injured in an accident, they are physically hurt. See also **accident**, **fatal**, **injury to feelings**.
⟶ a minor injury
⟶ a serious injury
⟶ a slight injury
⟶ receive / sustain an injury
⟶ seriously injured
Workers can suffer serious injuries if health and safety rules are not strictly observed.

Health, safety, welfare and environment

6

6

inspect (v)
/ɪnˈspɛkt/
inspection (n)
inspector (n)
inspectorate (n)
spot inspection (n ph)

When you inspect something, you look at it in detail or check it formally to make sure that it is as it should be.

A spot inspection is an inspection which no-one knows about in advance.
➡ a close / detailed inspection
➡ a factories inspector
➡ a health and safety inspector
➡ a routine inspection
➡ a weights and measures inspector
➡ carry out / conduct / make an inspection

intimidate (v)
/ɪnˈtɪmɪdeɪt/
intimidating (adj)
intimidation (n)
intimidatory (adj)

Employees are being intimidated when they are being frightened in order to make them do something. See also **bully**, **harass**, **victimise**.
➡ blatant / serious intimidation
➡ be subjected to / suffer intimidation
➡ display intimidatory behaviour

machine guard (n ph)
/məˈʃiːn ˈɡɑːd/
machinery guarding (n ph)

A machine guard is a barrier, usually made of metal, which is placed round a dangerous machine or piece of equipment to protect the user from injury. Also known as a **fence**. See also **protect**.
Fixed machine guards must be properly fitted and inspected regularly.

manual handling (n ph)
/ˈmænjʊəl ˈhændlɪŋ/

When factory goods are handled manually, they are picked up and moved about by employees, not by machines. See also **manual**.
➡ manual handling techniques
➡ manually handle heavy loads
Incorrect manual handling leads to thousands of back injuries every year.

medical record (n ph)
/ˈmɛdɪkəl ˈrɛkɔːd/

Your medical record is the file containing the history of your health. See also **data**, **medical examination**.

near miss (adj ph, n ph)
/ˈnɪə ˈmɪs/

A near miss is an accident which almost happens.
The company has had no accidents at all this year although there have been three near misses.

neglect (v)
/nɪˈɡlɛkt/
negligence (n)
negligent (adj)

If you neglect to do something and are therefore **negligent**, you fail to do something which you should have done. If you are guilty of **negligence**, then you do not take care of something or do something that you should have done, with the result that someone or something is harmed or damaged. See also **liable**.
➡ a case of negligence
➡ be guilty of negligence
➡ criminal negligence
➡ gross / serious negligence
➡ neglect to do your duty
➡ negligent behaviour

*An employee who has been the victim of an industrial accident may
claim compensation on the grounds of the employer's negligence.*

noise (n)
/'nɔɪz/
noisy (adj)

Noise is sound which is loud or unpleasant.
- a noise barrier
- a noise certificate
- a noise level
- excessive noise
- experience / suffer exposure to noise
- noise pollution
- noise prevention
- noise protection
- noise standards

notice (n)
/'nəʊtɪs/
notice board (n ph)

A notice is a piece of paper with information which is displayed in a
place where employees can read it. See also **notice** (chapter 2).
You attach notices to a notice board. You can also post notices on
electronic notice boards on the internet.
- an electronic noticeboard, post a notice on
- display a notice on a notice board
- pin up a notice

occupational (adj)
/ɒkjə'peɪʃənəl/
occupation (n)

Occupational means job-related. See also **industrial**, **job**, **occupation**.

**occupational health
practitioner** (n ph)

An occupational health practitioner (OHP) is a medically qualified
person who works in a company or who advises on occupational
health questions.

**occupational health
unit** (n ph)

An occupational health unit is a department of a company which
looks after employee health issues and which can have responsibility
for a range of health-related functions including lifestyle screening,
absence monitoring, and the prevention of work-related diseases. See
also **preventive**, **screen**.
- an occupational disability
- an occupational disease, suffer from
- an occupational hazard, deal with
- an occupational health service
- an occupational illness
- an occupational injury, suffer
- occupational medicine
- occupational safety
- occupational stress

open day (n ph)
/'əʊpən 'deɪ/

When a company or institution organises an open day, it invites
members of the public in to look round the workplace and organises
events to inform the visitors of the work being carried out there. See
also **corporate social responsibility**.
*Open days can help with recruitment and can also be a valuable
public relations tool for organisations which want to improve their
image and build better links with the local community.*

Health, safety, welfare and environment

6

overwork (n, v)
/'əʊvə 'wɜːk/

You overwork when you work too hard. See also **overtime**, **stress**.
➡ be overworked
➡ suffer from overwork
Many road accidents are caused by overworked drivers.

pollute (v)
/pə'luːt/
pollutant (n)
pollution (n)

If you pollute something, for example the air or a river near a factory, you make it dirty. A **pollutant** – for example, smoke from a factory – is something which pollutes. See also **contaminate**, **discharge**, **spillage**.

preventive (adj)
/pri'ventɪv/
preventative (adj)
prevention (n)
preventable (adj)
preventive health policy (n ph)

When you take preventive or **preventative** action, you do something to stop something else from happening.

A preventive or preventative health policy is a company policy designed to keep employees in good health and to stop them from falling ill. See also **occupational**.
➡ noise prevention
➡ preventive health / preventative health
➡ preventive measures / preventative measures, take
➡ preventive medicine

prohibit (v)
/prə'hɪbɪt/
prohibition (n)
prohibitive (adj)
prohibition sign (n ph)

When something is prohibited it means you must not do it.

A prohibition sign, for example a no smoking sign, tells you that you must not do something. See also **safety**.

protect (v)
/prə'tɛkt/
protective (adj)
protection (n)
protector (n)

Something that protects you keeps you safe from injury. See also **goggles**, **machine guard**, **protection**.
➡ ear protector
➡ eye protector
➡ personal protective equipment
➡ protective clothing
➡ protective headgear
➡ protective materials
➡ protective measures, take
People who work near noisy machines should always wear ear protectors.

recreation (n)
/rɛkri'eɪʃən/
recreational (adj)

Recreational activities are things you do for pleasure when you are not working. Many organisations provide facilities and support for recreational activities for their employees. See also **welfare**.
➡ a recreation area
➡ a recreation centre
➡ a recreation facility
➡ a recreational programme, organise
➡ recreational facilities, provide

6

rehabilitate (v)
/riːəˈbɪlɪteɪt/
rehabilitation (n)
rehabilitative (adj)

A company rehabilitates employees by helping them back to full-time employment after an accident. See also **convalesce**.
➡ a long period of rehabilitation

repetitive strain injury (n ph)
/rɪˈpɛtətɪv ˈstreɪn ˈɪndʒəri/

You can get repetitive strain injury (RSI) if you have to use the same parts of the body to do the same thing again and again. See also **injure**, **vibration**.
One of the commonest examples of RSI is the pain that secretaries, journalists and other people who type a lot, get in their wrists and arm muscles when they work for too long at the keyboard without proper breaks.

respiratory (adj)
/ˈrɛspərətri/ or
/rɛsˈpɪrətri/
respiration (n)

A respiratory problem is a breathing problem. See also **asthma**, **silicosis**.

rest break (n ph)
/ˈrɛst ˈbreɪk/

A rest break or **rest period** gives an employee the chance to stop working for a certain length of time.
European Union rules give workers in EU countries a rest break of twenty minutes every six hours and eleven hours in any one 24-hour period.

risk assessment (n ph)
/ˈrɪsk əˈsɛsmənt/

Risk assessment involves making a list of workplace tasks and then measuring the degree of risk or danger involved in each one.
The idea behind risk assessment is that if you can first of all identify the major hazards in the workplace, you can then go on to reduce the size and number of hazards which exist.

safe (adj, adv)
/ˈseɪf/
safety (n)

A safe workplace is one where employees are properly protected from danger. See also **health and safety**, **security**.

safety harness (n ph)

A harness is a set of straps which you wear when you are working in a difficult or dangerous place, for example on the outside of a tall building, on a cliff face, or when being transferred from ship to shore.

safety helmet (n ph)

A safety helmet is a kind of protective headware. It is compulsory to wear one in some kinds of workplace like construction sites and on oil platforms. Also known as a **hard hat**.

safety sign (n ph)

A safety sign, often showing a symbol, is a sign in the workplace which gives information, instructions or a warning to an employee. See also **prohibit**.
➡ a safety audit, carry out
➡ a safety committee
➡ a safety officer
➡ a safety representative
➡ electrical safety
➡ follow / observe / respect safety procedures
➡ office safety
➡ safety measures, take adequate / inadequate

Health, safety, welfare and environment

6

➟ safety precautions, take
➟ safety procedures, adequate / inadequate
➟ safety record, a good / bad
➟ safety regulations, call for tighter
➟ safety rules, enforce

Companies with active safety committees tend to have good safety records and fewer industrial accidents.

screen (n, v) `
/'skriːn/
screening (n)
lifestyle screening (n ph)

When a doctor screens you, he or she checks your general physical condition. See also **medical examination, screen** (chapter 3).

Lifestyle screening looks at your health in relation to the way you live, for example what you eat, how much you drink, and how much physical exercise you take.
➟ health screening assessment
➟ medical screening
➟ screening for drug abuse

security (n)
/sɪ'kjʊərɪti/
secure (adj)

If your company has good security, it means that it is well protected from people who may wish to enter the buildings to steal or to cause physical damage or do some other kind of harm. See also **safe**.
➟ security arrangements, adequate / inadequate
➟ security measures
➟ tight security
➟ tighten security

Security is especially important for companies which think that competitors may try to steal their industrial secrets.

sedentary (adj)
/'sɛdəntri/

People with sedentary jobs spend most of their time at work sitting down.
➟ a sedentary job / occupation
➟ remain in a sedentary position

People who remain in a sedentary position for long periods during the working day should make special efforts to take some physical exercise outside working hours and also to do exercises while sitting down at work.

self esteem (n ph)
/sɛlf ɪs'tiːm/

Self esteem is how you feel about yourself and about knowing and accepting who you are. People with high self esteem have a positive view of themselves. People with low self esteem have a negative view of themselves.
➟ build / develop a sense of self esteem
➟ high / low self esteem
➟ raise self esteem

Your level of self esteem has a fundamental impact on how you learn and often on how well you learn.

sick (adj, adv)
/'sɪk/
sickness (n)
sickie (n, Br Eng informal)

'Sick' is another word for 'ill'. A **sickie**, in informal British English, is a day you take off work when you are ill or claim to be ill.

off sick (adv ph)

If you are off sick, you are away from work because you are ill. See also **day off**.

sick building syndrome (n ph)

People who suffer from sick building syndrome can have any of a range of illnesses including headaches, and eye, nose and throat problems. These may be caused by features of the building where they work such as the lighting, heating, ventilation and so on.

sick note (n ph)

A doctor writes a sick note for you to give to your employer to show that you are or were ill.

➡ a sick day
➡ a sick room
➡ a sickness allowance
➡ fall sick
➡ long-term sickness
➡ sick leave
➡ sick pay
➡ sick pay, statutory sick pay
➡ sickness benefit

Around 166 million sick days are lost in Britain every year, equivalent to 6.8 days per employee.

silicosis (n)
/sɪlɪ'kəʊsɪs/

Silicosis is a respiratory disease caused by breathing in silica dust. Miners have historically suffered from high levels of silicosis. See also **respiratory**.

slips, trips and falls (n ph)
/'slɪps 'trɪps ən 'fɔːlz/

These three kinds of accident are often grouped together in accident record books. Slips and trips are both kinds of fall: you can slip, for example, on a banana skin; you can trip on, for example, a computer cable or the edge of a carpet.

smoking (n)
/'sməʊkɪŋ/
smoke (n, v)
smoker (n)

Cigarette smoking causes cancer and death.

designated smoking area (n ph)

A designated smoking area is an area in a workplace where people may smoke: smoking anywhere else is prohibited.

passive smoking (n ph)

Someone who has to breathe in someone else's cigarette smoke is a victim of passive smoking.

➡ a heavy smoker
➡ a no-smoking policy
➡ a no-smoking zone
➡ a victim of passive smoking
➡ smoking ban, impose

34 million working days are lost in Britain each year through smoking. Smoking costs British industry £3 billion pounds per year.

Health, safety, welfare and environment

6

Health, safety, welfare and environment

6

solvent (n)
/'sɒlvənt/

Solvents are chemicals used to dissolve or dilute other substances or materials. See also **abuse**.
➡ an industrial solvent
➡ a victim of solvent abuse
➡ be over-exposed / suffer over-exposure to a solvent
When employees have too much contact with solvents, they can feel sick and get skin problems and headaches. Some solvents can kill.

spillage (n)
/'spɪlɪdʒ/
spill (n, v)

A spillage or spill happens when a liquid escapes from its container by accident. See also pollute, discharge.
➡ an oil spill

stress (n)
/'strɛs/
stressful (adj)
chronic stress (n ph)

Someone suffering from stress has feelings of anxiety or of mental and physical discomfort. Difficult situations are likely to create feelings of stress. See also **comfort zone, overwork**.
Chronic stress is extreme or very serious stress.
➡ a stress-related illness
➡ be / work under (a lot of) stress
➡ encounter stress
➡ occupational stress
➡ organisational stress
➡ relieve stress, stress relief
➡ stress symptoms / symptoms of stress
➡ suffer (from) stress
Stress can be caused, among other things, by overwork, bad work relationships, bad job design, a bad work environment and bad work conditions.

sunlight-deprivation syndrome (n ph)
/'sʌnlaɪt dɛprɪ'veɪʃən 'sɪndrəʊm/

Sunlight-deprivation syndrome is a form of depression caused by living or working in a place without enough natural light.

toxic (adj)
/'tɒksɪk/
toxicity (n)

A toxic substance is a solid, a liquid or a powder which is poisonous. The **toxicity** of a chemical is its potential to cause harm.
➡ a toxic hazard
➡ a toxic substance
➡ highly toxic
➡ toxic waste
All toxic substances used in the workplace should be clearly labelled with indications about how to handle them and what to do in an emergency.

trauma (n)
/'trɔːmə/ or /'traʊmə/
traumatic (adj)
traumatise (v)

Trauma is the shock you feel when something very bad happens to you.

post-traumatic stress disorder (n ph)

Post-traumatic stress disorder (PTSD) is the effect you may feel some time after a dangerous or violent event happens to you or after you see such an event happen.

⇒ have a traumatic experience
⇒ experience trauma
⇒ trauma counselling, receive
London Underground employees who saw people die in a big fire, received treatment for PTSD from counsellors at a trauma centre.

upper limb disorder (n ph)
/'ʌpə 'lɪm dɪs'ɔːdə/

You have an upper limb disorder if you have a medical problem with your arms.

user-friendly (adj)
/'juːzə 'frɛndli/
user-friendliness (n)

A user-friendly piece of equipment is comfortable, easy and convenient to use. See also **ergonomics**.
⇒ user-friendly equipment

ventilate (v)
/'vɛntɪleɪt/
ventilation (n)

A ventilated room has a proper supply of fresh air, or air circulated by an air conditioning system.
⇒ poorly / well ventilated
Poor ventilation in the workplace can lead to headaches and breathing problems among employees.

vibration (n)
/vaɪ'breɪʃən/
vibrate (adj)

A machine which vibrates is one which shakes and moves continuously. Employees who use equipment which vibrates a lot, for example drills, often suffer from vibration-related injuries and diseases. Two common problems are **hand-arm vibration syndrome** and **vibration white finger**.

visual display unit (n ph)
/'vɪʒʊəl dɪs'pleɪ 'juːnɪt/

The visual display unit (VDU) of a computer is the screen on which the user can read text or figures. VDUs are also known as **display screen equipment** (DSE).
Regular VDU users should get frequent breaks from working on the screen and should also get regular eye tests.

warning (n)
/'wɔːnɪŋ/
warn (v)

A warning tells you to be very careful because something is dangerous. See also **warning** (chapter 7).
⇒ a warning notice / sign
Cigarette packets in many countries now carry warning notices about the dangers of smoking to health.

welfare (n)
/'wɛlfɛə/

Welfare is:
1 your general well-being. See also **recreation**, **wellness**.
⇒ a welfare policy
⇒ general welfare
⇒ promote welfare
⇒ welfare facilities
⇒ welfare provision
2 government benefits.
See also **welfare to work**.
⇒ the welfare state

Health, safety, welfare and environment

6

Health, safety, welfare and environment

6

➡ welfare benefits, receive
Company welfare policies are usually concerned with improving physical working conditions, for example, washing, canteen and rest facilities but welfare is also about managing stress levels and looking after people in general.

wellness (n)
/'wɛlnəs/

Wellness can refer to a general feeling of well-being or, more specifically, to a human resources programme designed to keep an ageing workforce healthier for longer. Wellness programmes can therefore also be a way of dealing with the costs of sickness and absence.
➡ a wellness initiative, take
➡ a wellness manager
➡ a wellness programme / scheme
An important current goal for Nestlé is to transform itself from a food company into a "food, nutrition, health and wellness" company.

working environment (n ph)
/'wɜːkɪŋ ɪn'vaɪrənmənt/

The working environment is the set of physical and psychological conditions which together define the situation in which an employee works.
Companies can improve productivity and reduce staff turnover by improving the employees' working environment.

Exercises

Exercise 1

Write the verb forms of these key nouns for health, safety and welfare.

1	inspection:	2	rehabilitation: ....
3	convalescence:	4	bullying : ....
5	harassment :	6	protection: ....
7	injury:	8	evacuation: ....
9	contamination:	10	prohibition: ....
11	ventilation:	12	intimidation: ....
13	pollution:	14	counselling : ....
15	abuse :	16	discharge: ....

Exercise 2

Match the definitions (1 – 10) with verbs from exercise 1.

1 Use something in a way which is dangerous to your health
2 Repeatedly cause someone trouble, worry and bother
3 Look at in detail or formally check something
4 Help someone back to full-time employment after an accident
5 Physically hurt or be hurt following an accident
6 Empty a building of people when the fire alarm sounds
7 Keep employees safe from accident and injury
8 Listen to employees' problems and give professional advice
9 Physically or mentally cause harm to another person
10 Emit gas, liquid or waste substance into the environment

Exercise 3

Separate the key terms in the box into one group of terms describing danger or potential danger in the workplace and another group for safety measures.

accident	assembly point	solvent	hazard	asbestos
goggles	breathing apparatus	smoking	fire	check-up
machine guard	warning	ergonomics		slips, trips and falls
security	screen	muster station	carcinogen	first aid	agent

Potential danger in the workplace	Safety measures

Exercise 4

Match the terms on the left (1 - 8) with nouns on the right (a - h) to make word pairs in chapter 6.

1	fatal	a	equipment
2	occupational	b	occupation
3	toxic	c	hazard
4	sedentary	d	standards
5	preventive	e	exit
6	emergency	f	waste
7	user-friendly	g	measures
8	hygiene	h	accident

Exercise 5

Put the terms in the box into the right gaps in sentences 1 - 8.

risk assessment	rest breaks	stress	fatality	
burn out	employee assistance programme		neglect	sick

1   Their safety record at home is good but levels of industrial injury and _____ are much higher abroad, with five deaths this year so far.

2   Many accidents were caused by simple _____ such as people not wearing the right safety clothing or not following equipment safety guidelines.

3   Thanks to our action on absence, the number of employees calling in _____ and taking days off work decreased last year.

4   When there are delays in the work schedule and people don't get proper _____ , absence can start to go up again.

5   Increased workloads and shorter deadlines also lead to higher levels of physical and psychological _____ .

6   She puts such a lot of effort into her work and has been working long hours for so many months now, that we're worried that one day soon she's just going to _____ .

7   We must give the health and safety manager a detailed checklist of the potential hazards on the new site so that he can carry out a _____ before we start work there.

8   It has been decided to implement an _____ for our sites abroad, giving advice and assistance in areas such as family life, stress, alcohol abuse and financial problems.

Exercise 6

Sentences a - d refer to different types of work-related illness. Choose the most appropriate response (1 - 4) according to the circumstance.

1	post-traumatic stress syndrome	2	repetitive strain injury
3	upper limb disorder	4	sunlight deprivation syndrome

a   He spent three days carrying heavy building materials from the warehouse to the yard and then reported sick with severe muscular pains in his shoulders and arms.

b   After the explosion, a number of employees who escaped injury were treated for shock and were monitored for several months by doctors and psychiatrists.

c   The journalist, having spent long periods working at his computer in order to meet deadlines, started to get severe aches and pains in his arms and wrists.

d   These workers, tunnelling in shifts of up to ten hours at a time, were given prolonged sick leave after showing signs of depression.

For discussion

1   How good is your working environment?
2   Are there too many rules for health and safety?
3   What should organisations do for the general welfare of their employees?
4   What is your organisation's policy on the environment? How far is it committed to the notion of sustainability?

Health, safety, welfare and environment

6

Health, safety, welfare and environment

6

Case studies

Getting the environment to work for you

Place-Finn, a struggling Irish construction company, has recently been subject to a management-employee buyout. In order to turn the business round, the new owners feel that it must not only increase its sales activity, but accompany this with marketing a new image targeted at both the general public, and private and public contractors. As a member of the management board, suggest ways in which Place-Finn may improve its image through health, safety and environmental issues.

Think of the following factors:
- the company health and safety record
- company logo and colours
- employee behaviour
- company sponsorship
- site worker dress code
- the construction site itself and what it may communicate to the general public
- the impact of the company on the environment
- quality and sustainability.

When health and safety becomes an issue of conflict

A large manufacturer of office equipment, with good cooperation between HR and the unions on health and safety issues, recently called on an external consulting company to assess company policy in this area.

The consultants suggested that the company promote its excellent health and safety record to its potential customers by making it part of strategic policy. In order to do this, it also encouraged management to take greater interest in and control of health and safety within the company. When the consultants' report was discussed during a works council meeting, it caused heated debate between HR and the unions over who should have most influence over supervising health and safety.

Consider:
- How might the unions see management influence over health and safety as a threat?
- Is a clear separation of roles needed between HR and the unions or could they work together?

7

Employee relations and representation

Key terms to talk about
relations between the
management and employees of
an organisation and about the
work of trade unions.

**These are the key terms in this chapter.
Which of them do you understand?
Which of them can you use?**

Employees relations and representation

7

Accompany
activist
affiliate
agreement
amalgamate
arbitrate
Ballot
bargain
beauty contest
binding
black
block vote
branch
Chapel
check off
claim
closed shop
co-determination
collective
conciliate
consultation
contingency arrangements
convenor
cooling off period
craftsman
Deadlock
demarcation
discipline
disclose
dispute
down tools
Elect
employee
employers' association
Fudge
General secretary
go over the head of
go slow
grievance
Industrial action
industrial relations
Lay member
learning representative
lockout

Mediate
merge
militant
misconduct
misdemeanour
motion
National executive
negotiate
Organise
Parity
partnership
picket
poach
political fund
Ratify
recognise
reinstate
renege
repudiate
reserved seat
restrictive practice
Shop steward
show of hands
social dialogue
solidarity
staff association
stoppage
strike
subscription
supervisory board
suspend
sweetheart deal
'Them and us' mentality
trade union
tripartism
Union
Victimise
Walk-out
warning
whistle-blower
withdrawal of labour
work-to-rule
worker director
works council

accompany (v)
/ə'kʌmpəni/
accompaniment (n)

Employees have a right to accompaniment when they can ask another employee or union representative to go with them to a meeting or hearing called to deal with a grievance or disciplinary matter. See also **hearing**.

➡ the right to be accompanied

activist (n)
/'æktɪvɪst/
active (adj)

An activist is a member of a union or a political party who plays an active role in the organisation by attending meetings, organising campaigns, recruiting new members, etc. See also **lay member, militant**.

affiliate (n, v)
/ə'fɪlieɪt/
affiliation (n)
disaffiliate (v)
disaffiliation (n)

An organisation affiliates when it becomes a member of another (usually larger) organisation. Most unions affiliate to both a national and to an international trade union confederation. Unions and confederations may also be affiliated to political parties. When a union **disaffiliates** or is disaffiliated, it leaves the organisation to which it was affiliated and is no longer a member. See also **trade union, union**.

➡ become affiliated

agreement (n)
/ə'griːmənt/
agree (v)

The aim of negotiation between management and employee representatives is usually to reach an agreement on the details of pay or working conditions. Also known as a **deal** or a **settlement**. See also **collective, terms**.

blanket agreement (n ph)

A blanket agreement covers all the employees in a particular company, industry or other group.

dilution agreement (n ph)

A dilution agreement is one which allows unskilled labour to be used when skilled labour is unavailable.

framework agreement (n ph)

A framework agreement is a general agreement for an industry or sector which allows management and employee representatives within individual organisations to then negotiate and agree on the details.

interim agreement (n ph)

An interim agreement or settlement is a temporary one which is valid for a limited time and which holds until a final agreement is reached.

no-strike agreement (n ph)

When a union signs a no-strike agreement with a company's management, it agrees not to go on strike.

no-union agreement (n ph)

When the employees of a company sign a no-union agreement with the management, they agree not to join a trade union.

outline agreement (n ph)

An outline agreement is a general agreement which lacks detail.

single status agreement (n ph)

A single status agreement or deal is an agreement by management to treat blue and white collar workers the same.

single union agreement (n ph)

When the management of a company wants to deal with only one union and a union agrees to this condition, the two sides enter into a single union agreement. See also **beauty contest, sweetheart deal**.

threshold agreement (n ph)

A threshold agreement is one where employees receive an automatic pay increase if inflation goes up by a certain amount.

➡ a national agreement
➡ a partnership agreement
➡ a pay settlement
➡ an agreement on pay and conditions

Employee relations and representation

7

Employee relations and representation

➠ an industry-wide agreement
➠ complete / conclude / reach an agreement
➠ enter into an agreement
➠ honour / respect an agreement
➠ negotiate an agreement
➠ settle for
Governments hope that the national average level of pay settlement will be lower than the rate of inflation.

amalgamate (v)
/ə'mælgəmeɪt/
amalgamation (n)
amalgamated (adj)

When two or more unions joined together in the past, the result was often called an amalgamated union. Today, we usually talk about unions merging. See also **merge**.
➠ The Amalgamated Union of …
Britain's Amalgamated Engineering and Electrical Union merged in 2002 with another big union, MSF, to form Amicus, one of the country's biggest unions, with 1.2 million members.

arbitrate (v)
/'ɑːbɪtreɪt/
arbitrator (n)
arbitration (n)

When a negotiation between an employer and a union breaks down, the two sides can agree to ask a third party to make the final decision about the agreement for them. The arbitrator's decision is often a compromise between the positions of the two parties. See also **binding, conciliate, mediate, party**.

arbitration clause (n ph)

An arbitration clause is a part of a contract which says how two parties should use an arbitrator to deal with any disagreements they may have. See **clause**.

arbitration ruling (n ph)
pendulum arbitration (n ph)

The arbitration ruling is the decision of the arbitrator.
In pendulum arbitration, the arbitrator must decide 100% for one party and against the other. This is also known as **final offer arbitration**.
➠ an arbitration agreement
➠ an arbitration award
➠ an independent arbitrator
➠ compulsory arbitration
➠ go to arbitration
➠ refer a dispute to arbitration
➠ resort to arbitration
➠ submit / take a dispute to arbitration
➠ the arbitrator's ruling, accept / reject
Unlike mediation and conciliation, arbitration does not require cooperation between the parties to the conflict so arbitration can be useful in cases where the other two approaches have failed.

ballot (n, v)
/'bælət/

A ballot is a secret vote organised by a union to allow its members, for example, to elect union officers, or to decide whether to go on strike. A union ballots its members when it wants their opinion on an important question. See also **elect, show of hands**.

ballot rigging (n ph)

When someone rigs a ballot, they illegally influence the result of the vote.
➠ a ballot paper
➠ a postal ballot

➠ a secret ballot
➠ ballot members
➠ hold a ballot
➠ organise a ballot

bargain (v)
/'bɑːgɪn/
bargaining (n, adj)

Management and employee representatives bargain when they have formal discussions in order to solve a problem or reach an agreement on, for example, pay or conditions. Bargaining is also known as negotiation. See also **collective**, **negotiate**.

bargaining scope (n ph)

The scope of any bargaining is the range of issues which can be negotiated by the two sides. Anything which cannot be negotiated falls outside the scope of the bargaining.

bargaining unit (n ph)

A bargaining unit is a group of employees recognised by an employer as having negotiating rights. It can be, for example, a group of workers in the same workplace or a group of a particular type of employee.

➠ a bargaining session
➠ a round of bargaining
➠ a tough / weak bargaining position
➠ bargaining structure
➠ central / centralised bargaining
➠ fall inside / outside the scope of the bargaining
➠ industry-wide bargaining
➠ joint bargaining
➠ productivity bargaining
➠ tough bargaining, engage in

beauty contest
(n ph informal)
/'bjuːti 'kɒntɛst/

A beauty contest takes place when two or more unions compete for recognition by an employer, often in a new workplace or one which was not unionised before. See also **agreement**, **recognise**, **sweetheart deal**.

binding (adj)
/'baɪndɪŋ/
bind (v)
binding arbitration (n ph)

A binding agreement is one which both management and unions must accept. The opposite of binding is **non-binding**. See also **arbitrate**.

If both parties agree to binding arbitration, they cannot legally reject the arbitrator's decision.

➠ a binding agreement
➠ be bound to comply with an agreement
➠ legally bound by an agreement

black (v)
/'blæk/
blacking (n)

Workers may black a company or its products by refusing to deal with that company or its goods, for example because its employees are engaged in industrial action which the other workers support.
The union wants to black all goods delivered by that company's lorries because its drivers recently crossed a picket line.

block vote (n ph)
/'blɒk 'vəʊt/

When union leaders cast block votes at union or party conferences, they give the individual votes of the whole membership of the union in one go.

Employee relations and representation

7

Employee relations and representation

The block votes of big German and British unions can sometimes represent more than one million members.

branch (n)
/'brɑːntʃ/

A branch is a local section of a trade union's organisation.
➡ a local branch
➡ a workplace branch

chapel (n, Br Eng)
/'tʃæpəl/

A chapel is the workplace branch of a British union in the printing or media industries. Journalists and print workers therefore attend meetings of the union chapel.

father / mother of the chapel (n ph, Br Eng)

The father or mother of the chapel is the elected leader of the local branch of a British union of print workers or journalists.

check off (n)
/tʃɛk 'ɒf/

The check off is the automatic deduction by the employer of employees' union subscription payments from their weekly wage or monthly salary payment. See also **deduction, subscription**.

claim (n)
/'kleɪm/

A union makes or submits a **pay claim** or **wage claim** when it formally tells the management of a company how much more money it wants for its members. See also **claim** (chapter 8), **pay, wage**.
➡ accept a pay claim
➡ an annual pay claim
➡ make / submit a pay claim
➡ reject a pay claim

closed shop (n ph)
/'kləʊzd 'ʃɒp/

In a closed shop, all the employees in a workplace must be members of a union.
➡ a closed shop agreement, enforce a
An employer who agrees to a closed shop, agrees to give certain jobs only to union members or to employ only union members in certain sections of the company.

co-determination (n)
/kɛʊ dit'ɜːmɪn'eɪʃən/

Co-determination is the practice of management and employees working together to solve labour relations problems and cooperating in other areas of company business. See also **employee, partnership**.

collective (adj)
/kə'lɛktɪv/
collectivism (n)

Collectivism is the process of consultation and negotiation between management and employee representatives at a central company, industry, national or international level, the opposite of negotiation between management and individual employees. See also **collectivism**.

collective bargaining (n ph)

Collective bargaining is a form of central negotiation, for example at industry or national level, between employee representatives and management about wages and working conditions. See also **bargain, negotiate**.
➡ abide by a collective agreement
➡ free collective bargaining, engage in
➡ negotiate a collective (wage) agreement

7

conciliate (v)
/kən'sɪlɪeɪt/
conciliator (n)
conciliation (n)
conciliatory (adj)

Someone who conciliates in a dispute is usually a third party who tries to persuade the two parties to change their positions when there is a risk that the negotiation will break down. See also **arbitrate, mediate, party**.

➡ a conciliation board
➡ a conciliation committee
➡ call in a conciliator
➡ conciliation proceedings
➡ fixed-term conciliation
➡ resort to a conciliator

Conciliation is less formal than mediation and arbitration and involves an independent third party having discussions either separately or jointly with both sides in a dispute in order to help them understand each other's point of view and from there to move towards an agreement.

consultation (n)
/kɒnsəl'teɪʃən/
consult (v)
consultant (n)
consultative (adj)
consultation machinery
(n ph)

When you consult someone, you ask them for their opinion or advice about something. Consultation happens when management informs employee representatives of important business developments in the company. See also **co-determination, consultant, partnership, works council**.

Consultation machinery is the collection of formal structures - for example, consultative committees, works councils, etc. – through which communication between management and employee representatives takes place.

joint consultation (n ph)

Joint consultation takes place when channels exist for management and unions to discuss questions and problems frequently together.

➡ a consultative body, create / set up
➡ a consultative committee
➡ collective consultation
➡ employee consultation
➡ engage in consultation
➡ full consultation

Consultative committees can give employee representatives the chance to contribute to company policy on issues such as salary levels, equal opportunities and health and safety.

contingency arrangements (n ph)
/kən'tɪndʒənsi ə'reɪnʒmənts/

When an organisation makes or puts into place contingency arrangements, it takes action and checks emergency procedures before a planned strike takes place so that it has as few problems as possible during the strike.

When the British fire fighters union gave five weeks' notice of its plan to strike in 2004, the government announced that its contingency arrangements would take eight weeks to put into place.

convenor (n)
/kən'viːnə/

A convenor is a senior shop steward. See **shop steward**.

Employee relations and representation

7

cooling off period
(n ph)
/ˈkuːlɪŋ ˈɒf ˈpɪərɪəd/

A cooling off period is a time during an industrial dispute when both sides agree not to take action against the other so that someone, for example a third party, can try and find a solution.

craftsman (n, Br Eng)
/ˈkrɑːftsmən/

A craftsman is a skilled male manual worker. See also **skill, union**.

deadlock (n, v)
/ˈdɛdlɒk/

When negotiations reach deadlock, the two sides in a dispute are unable to reach any kind of agreement.
➡ break a deadlock
➡ reach deadlock
After a week of deadlock, the two sides at last agreed to submit the matter to arbitration.

demarcation (n)
/diːmɑːˈkeɪʃən/
demarcate (v)

Demarcation is the definition of a clear distinction between the duties and responsibilities of one employee or group of employees and another. See also **restrictive practice**.
➡ a demarcation dispute

discipline (n, v)
/ˈdɪsɪplɪn/
disciplinary (adj)

Keeping discipline means making sure that people in a company follow its rules. When employers discipline employees, they punish them in some way for not following the rules. See also **capability, contract, discipline, misconduct, misdemeanour, suspend, warning**.
➡ a (formal) disciplinary procedure, handle ~ well / badly
➡ a disciplinary appeal
➡ a disciplinary hearing
➡ a disciplinary interview, conduct
➡ a disciplinary investigation, conduct
➡ be the subject of disciplinary proceedings
➡ disciplinary rules
➡ impose discipline
➡ maintain discipline
➡ relax discipline
➡ take disciplinary action / measures against
➡ tighten discipline

disclose (v)
/dɪsˈkləʊz/
disclosure (n)

When you disclose information, you give new or secret information to someone. The management of an organisation can disclose financial or other information to employees or their representatives. See also **disclose** (chapter 8).
➡ disclosure of information
➡ make a disclosure

dispute (n, v)
/ˈdɪspjuːt/ (n)
/dɪsˈpjuːt/ (v)
alternative dispute resolution (n ph)

A dispute, sometimes called a **trade dispute** or **industrial dispute**, is a disagreement between an employer and a group of employees or between groups of employees. See also **demarcation**.
The process of dispute resolution or alternative dispute resolution is a way of dealing with disputes in the workplace, for example through mediation or conciliation, so that they do not go to the employment tribunal.

inter-union dispute (n ph)
mandatory dispute resolution (n ph)

An inter-union dispute is a disagreement between two or more unions. In mandatory dispute resolution, both sides to the dispute have to go through the resolution process.

➡ a demarcation dispute
➡ a disputes procedure / process, go through
➡ a labour dispute
➡ a pay dispute / a dispute over pay
➡ a wage dispute
➡ an industrial dispute, take part in
➡ an official dispute
➡ an unofficial dispute
➡ resolve a dispute
➡ statutory dispute resolution

The negotiation of single-union agreements in Britain led at first to a number of inter-union disputes.

down tools (v ph)
/'daʊn 'tuːlz/

When employees down tools, they stop working in protest against some part of their pay or working conditions. See also **industrial action**, **stoppage**, **strike**, **walk-out**, **withdrawal of labour**.

elect (v)
/ɪ'lɛkt/
election (n)
electoral (adj)
elected (adj)

An elected official of a union is one who has been voted into office by the members and not appointed by other officials. See also **ballot**, **show of hands**.

employee (n)
/ɛmplɔɪ'iː/
employee forum (n ph)

An employee is someone who has a contract of employment with an organisation. See also **employ**.

An employee forum is a consultative committee of management and employee representatives. Also known as a **workplace forum**. See also **consultation**, **works council**.

employee participation (n ph)

Employee participation is a policy or philosophy of encouraging employees to play an active part in the affairs of the company. Also known as **industrial democracy**. See also **co-determination**, **partnership**.

➡ achieve a low / high level of employee participation

employee relations (n ph)

Employee relations are the relations between a company's management and its employees. Also known as **employment relations** and **labour relations**. See also **industrial relations**.

employee representative (n ph)

An employee representative is someone who is asked by other employees to discuss and negotiate with management for them. An employee representative is not necessarily a member of a trade union. See also **health and safety**, **learning representative**, **shop steward**.

➡ a good / bad employee relations climate
➡ cultivate / develop good employee relations
➡ maintain good employee relations

Some companies and unions working together achieve a high level of employee participation in areas such as training, quality assurance and health and safety controls.

Employee relations and representation

7

employers' association
(n ph)
/ɪm'plɔɪəz ə'səʊsieɪʃən/

An employers' association is a group representing employers in a certain area or from a certain industry. Also known as an **employers' organisation**.
In collective bargaining, union representatives usually negotiate with representatives of the national employers' association for the industry or sector.

fudge (n, v)
/'fʌdʒ/

Management and unions fudge an agreement when one or both sides deliberately leaves unclear what has been agreed so that they can present different versions of the same agreement to their own sides.
➡ a fudged agreement, negotiate

general secretary
(n ph, Br Eng)
/'dʒɛnərəl 'sɛkrətəri/

Most full-time leaders of British trade unions have the title of general secretary. The **president** of a union is usually elected for a one-year term of office.

go over the head of
(v ph)
/gəʊ əʊvə ðə 'hɛd əv/

You go over the head of your boss when you talk about a problem to your boss's boss rather than to your boss.

go slow (n ph, v ph)
/'gɛʊ sləʊ/ (n ph)
/gəʊ 'sləʊ/ (v ph)

When workers go slow, they work more slowly to protest against some aspect of their pay or conditions. See also **industrial action, work-to-rule**.

grievance (n)
/'griːvəns/

A grievance is a formal complaint. When employees are unhappy about some part of their work, they may decide to initiate a grievance. See also **appeal**.

air a grievance (v ph)

When you air a grievance, you talk about the thing that is making you unhappy.

settle a grievance (v ph)

When someone settles a grievance, they find a way of solving the problem in a way that satisfies the employee who had the grievance.
➡ a deep-seated grievance
➡ a genuine grievance
➡ a grievance committee
➡ a grievance procedure
➡ a legitimate grievance
➡ articulate / voice a grievance
➡ grievance handling
➡ initiate a grievance
➡ pursue a grievance

industrial action (n ph)
/ɪn'dʌstrɪəl 'ækʃən/

When a group of employees decides to take industrial action, it decides on a way of protesting to the management about pay and / or conditions. See also **down tools, go slow, injunction, stoppage, strike, walk-out, work-to-rule, withdrawal of labour**.

secondary industrial action
(n ph)

Secondary industrial action happens when there are people involved in the industrial action who are not employees in the workplace where the dispute is taking place. See **picket**.

threaten industrial action
(v ph)

When workers threaten industrial action, they say they will take industrial action if their demands are not met. See also **militant**.

⟹ a form of industrial action
⟹ call for industrial action
⟹ resort to industrial action
⟹ take industrial action
Strikes, go slows, work-to-rules and overtime bans (a refusal to work overtime) are all examples of industrial action.

industrial relations
(n ph)
/ɪn'dʌstrɪəl rɪ'leɪʃənz/

Industrial relations are the relations between a company's management and its employees, in particular the unions representing the employees. See also **employee**.
⟹ achieve a good industrial relations record
⟹ maintain a good industrial relations record
⟹ build / develop good industrial relations
⟹ damage industrial relations

lay member (n ph)
/leɪ 'mɛmbə/
lay membership (n ph)

A lay member or **rank and file member** or **grass roots member** of a union is an ordinary member who is not an elected official or an officer.

learning representative (n ph)
/'lɜːnɪŋ rɛprɪ'zɛntətɪv/

Learning representatives are employee representatives with special responsibility for analysing the training needs of the organisation for which they work, providing information and advice on training matters, arranging training and promoting its value. See also **learn, shop steward, health and safety**.
The UK Employment Act of 2002 gives recognised trade unions the right to appoint learning representatives and allows these officials paid leave to train for and perform their duties.

lockout (n)
/'lɒkaʊt/

A lockout is when the management locks the doors of the workplace during an industrial dispute in order to stop the workers getting in, as a way of trying to force them to agree eventually to the management's demands.

mediate (v)
/'miːdieɪt/
mediator (n)
mediation (n)

Someone who mediates in an industrial dispute is a third party who talks to both sides and tries to find things they can both agree about. While a conciliator only facilitates discussion, a mediator can make recommendations for each side to consider carefully. See also **arbitrate, conciliate, party**.
One big advantage of mediation over litigation is cost savings since organisations avoid the expense of fighting cases in courts or tribunals.

merge (v)
/'mɜːdʒ/
merger (n)

When two or more unions merge, they join together to form a single organisation. See also **amalgamate**.

militant (n, adj)
/'mɪlɪtənt/
militancy (n)
militate (v)

A militant is usually an active trade union member who believes that the frequent use or threat of industrial action is an important way for workers to improve their pay and conditions. A militant union is one that often uses or threatens to use industrial action to achieve its objectives. See also **activist, industrial action**.

Employee relations and representation

7

Employee relations and representation

7

misconduct (n)
/mɪs'kɒndʌkt/

Your **conduct** is the way you behave. Employees who are guilty of misconduct are ones who break the rules on how employees should behave. An employer can take action against an employee who is guilty of misconduct.

persistent misconduct (n ph) An employee who is guilty of persistent misconduct is one who breaks the company's disciplinary rules and commits misdemeanours again and again. See also **discipline, misdemeanour, warning.**

➡ be guilty of (gross) misconduct

misdemeanour (n)
/mɪsdə'miːnə/

If you commit a misdemeanour, you break one of the organisation's rules for its employees. See also **discipline, misconduct, warning.**

➡ a minor / petty misdemeanour
➡ a serious misdemeanour
➡ be guilty of a misdemeanour
➡ commit a misdemeanour

The management claimed that he had committed a serious misdemeanour and he is now the subject of disciplinary proceedings.

motion (n)
/'məʊʃən/

A motion is a subject for formal discussion and / or policy decision at the conference of a trade union or political party, followed by a vote.

composite motion (n ph) A composite motion is a group of motions on the same subject which have been put together to save time at a conference.

➡ pass a motion
➡ put down / table a motion for debate
➡ reject a motion
➡ vote on a motion

national executive
(n ph, Br Eng)
/'næʃənəl ɪg'zɛkjətɪv/

The national executive (committee) is a common British name for the central governing body of a trade union.

negotiate (v)
/nɪ'gəʊʃɪeɪt/
negotiation (n)
negotiator (n)
negotiable (adj)

Management and employees' representatives negotiate when they have formal discussions in order to solve a problem or reach an agreement on, for example, pay or conditions. If one party refuses to negotiate on a certain issue, it says that this issue is **non-negotiable.** To negotiate is to bargain. Negotiations are also known as **talks.** See also **bargain, party.**

negotiating machinery
(n ph)

Negotiating machinery is the rules and procedures for negotiation between management and unions within an organisation.

➡ a breakdown in negotiations
➡ a pay negotiation
➡ a round of negotiations
➡ a skilled negotiator
➡ a strong / weak negotiating position
➡ a top level negotiation
➡ a tough negotiation, a tough negotiator
➡ abandon / break off / call off negotiations
➡ call for negotiations
➡ enter into negotiation with

➡ face-to-face negotiations
➡ joint negotiations
➡ negotiate an agreement
➡ refuse to negotiate
➡ return to the negotiating table
➡ sit down at the negotiating table
➡ take part in negotiations
➡ the chief negotiator

When negotiations break down, the two sides sometimes agree to return to the negotiating table after the intervention of a mediator.

organise (v)
/ˈɔːgənaɪz/
organiser (n)
organisation (n)

When workers organise, they join a union or form a union or union branch.

parity (n)
/ˈpærɪti/

When you achieve wage parity with another group of employees, you rise to the same wage level as that group.

➡ achieve parity
➡ gain parity
➡ income parity
➡ pay parity
➡ wage parity

In spite of laws on equal opportunities in Britain, working women are still a long way from achieving parity with men in many occupations.

partnership (n)
/ˈpɑːtnəʃɪp/
partner (n)

Partnership means management and employees working together in the best interests of both the organisation and the people who work for it. A partnership agreement is a general agreement between management and employee representatives to work together for the benefit of the organisation and of its employees. See also **business partnering**, **co-determination**, **confrontation**, **consultation**, **employee**, **supervisory board**, **worker director**.

social partners (pl n ph)

Social partners is Euro-speak for management and employee representatives.

picket (n, v)
/ˈpɪkɪt/
picketing (n)
flying picket (n ph)

A picket is a person or a group of people who stand outside a factory or office to protest against something, to encourage other workers to join a strike or to discourage people from entering the workplace.
A flying picket is someone who travels from one picket line to another, perhaps several times in the same day.

secondary picketing (n ph)

Secondary picketing happens when the people picketing outside a company's building are not employed at the site where the strike is taking place.

➡ cross a picket line
➡ respect a picket line
➡ engage in secondary picketing

Employee relations and representation

7

Employee relations and representation

poach (v)
/'pəʊtʃ/

A union poaches members when it takes members from another union.

political fund (n ph)
/pə'lɪtɪkəl 'fʌnd/

A union's political fund contains money which the union uses for political campaigns and to give to political parties.

ratify (v)
/'rætɪfaɪ/
ratification (n)

When union members ratify an agreement negotiated by union officers with management, they agree to accept and support the deal.

recognise (v)
/'rɛkəgnaɪz/
recognition (n)
derecognise (v)
derecognition (n)

A company recognises a union when its management agrees to accept the union as the official organisation representing some or all of the company's workforce. When a company **derecognises** a union, it tells the union that it will no longer accept it as the organisation representing the employees in negotiations on wages, health and safety and so on.

➡ a recognised union
➡ gain recognition
➡ seek recognition
➡ statutory recognition
➡ union recognition

reinstate (v)
/ri:ɪn'steɪt/
reinstatement (n)

You are reinstated if you are suspended or sacked and then get your old job back, perhaps as a result of a court ruling. Also known as **re-engage**. See also **sack**, **suspend**.
The tribunal ruled that the employee had been unfairly dismissed and that he should be reinstated.

renege (v)
/rə'neɪg/

If you renege on an agreement, you refuse to keep to an agreement you previously made.
German unions claimed that the employers had reneged on an agreement to bring the wages of workers in the eastern part up to the same level as their colleagues in the western part within a certain period of time.

repudiate (v)
/rɪ'pju:dɪeɪt/
repudiation (n)

When you repudiate something, you refuse to accept it or agree with it.
➡ repudiate an agreement
➡ repudiate industrial action
The members repudiated the deal negotiated by the union because they felt the terms were not generous enough.

reserved seat (n ph)
/rɪ'zɜ:vd 'si:t/

Reserved seats are places on a committee which can only be taken by a certain kind of member. Some unions have reserved seats on their national executive and other committees for women or members of minority groups in order to increase their presence and their influence in the organisation.

restrictive practice
(n ph)
/rɪs'strɪktɪv 'præktɪs/

A restrictive practice is a way of working of a group of employees which gives them an unfair advantage over other employees or which stops other employees or the business as a whole from working in an efficient and productive way. See also **demarcation**.

➡ engage in a restrictive practice

Although there are fewer restrictive practices in British industry than there were thirty years ago, there are still many restrictive practices in the professions.

shop steward (n ph)
/'ʃɒp 'stjuːəd/

A shop steward is a member of a trade union and an employee of a company who is elected by the other members of the union in the company to represent them in day-to-day discussions and negotiations with the management. See also **convenor**, **health and safety**, **learning representative**.

In a large organisation, a shop stewards' committee may exist to discuss all aspects of employee-management relations.

show of hands (n ph)
/'ʃəʊ əv 'hændz/

There is a show of hands, for example at a trade union meeting, when a group of people vote by raising their arms. See also **ballot**, **elect**.

It is no longer legal in the UK to call a strike following a vote based on a show of hands only.

social dialogue (n ph)
/'səʊʃəl 'daɪəlɒg/

Social dialogue is the name given by the European Union to meetings and discussions between business management and employee representatives, particularly at European level. See also **partnership**, **works council**.

solidarity (n)
/sɒlɪ'dærɪti/

When you show solidarity with, for example, a group of workers involved in an industrial dispute, you give them your active support. See also **activist**.

➡ demonstrate / express / show solidarity towards

staff association (n ph)
/'stɑːf əsəʊsi'eɪʃən/

A staff association exists to represent employees of a company and may discuss and negotiate with the company's management but, unlike a trade union, it may have been started by the company itself and may exist only within that company. It may also play an important welfare and social role. See also **staff**, **welfare**.

stoppage (n)
/'stɒpɪdʒ/

There is a stoppage when people stop working during a dispute. See also **deduction** (chapter 4), **down tools**, **industrial action**, **strike**, **walk-out**, **withdrawal of labour**.

strike (n, v)
/'straɪk/
striker (n)

The employees of a company go on strike when they stop working because they want better pay or conditions or because they want to protest to the management about something. A strike is a form of industrial action. A **striker** is someone who goes on strike. See also **down tools**, **industrial action**, **withdrawal of labour**.

advocate strike action
(v ph)

If you advocate strike action, you call for a strike or say that you think a strike should take place.

Employee relations and representation

7

Employee relations and representation

avert a strike (v ph) — When you avert a strike, you stop it from happening.

call off a strike (v ph) — When strike organisers call off a strike, they end it by telling the strikers to go back to work.

general strike (n ph) — A general strike is one involving the whole union movement in a country.

official strike (n ph) — An official strike is one which has the official support of the union.

selective strike (n ph) — In a selective strike, a union calls on its members in some but not all workplaces involved in the dispute to go on strike.

sympathy strike (n ph) — A group of workers strikes in sympathy when it takes strike action in support of another group which is protesting about something. A sympathy strike is a form of **sympathetic action**.

strike breaker (n ph) — Employees who work during a strike are called strike breakers by their striking colleagues. Union supporters may also describe someone who continues to work during a strike or who takes the job of someone on strike as a **blackleg**. An even more strongly negative informal term for a strike breaker is a **scab**.

token strike (n ph) — A token strike is a short strike, normally lasting just a few hours. The objective of a token strike is to show the strong feelings of the workers about an issue which may not directly concern the company.

unofficial strike (n ph) — An unofficial strike is one which does not have the official support of the union.

wildcat strike (n ph) — A wildcat strike is an unofficial strike which happens suddenly.

- a damaging strike
- a sit-down strike
- a strike ballot
- a strike fund
- a wave of strikes
- an all-out strike
- an industry-wide strike
- be on strike
- call a strike, a strike call
- call the workforce out on strike
- days lost through strikes
- go on strike / come out on strike (over pay, conditions, ...)
- strike for
- strike pay, get / receive
- take strike action
- the right to strike
- the strike weapon, use ~ as a last resort
- the threat of strike action, threaten strike action

subscription (n)
/sʌb'skrɪpʃən/
subscribe (v)

A subscription is the money that someone pays to be a member of a union. Also known as **dues**. See also **check off**.

supervisory board
(n ph)
/suːpə'vaɪzəri 'bɔːd/

A supervisory board is a joint management committee whose members come from management and from representatives of the employees. See also **co-determination**, **partnership**.

7

In Germany, the supervisory board appoints the executive board which is responsible for the overall running of the company; and the employee representatives on the supervisory board appoint the company's labour director.

suspend (v)
/səs'pɛnd/
suspension (n)

When an employer suspends an employee, the employee is not allowed to continue working although he or she has not been dismissed. See also **discipline**, **reinstate**.
- suspended from duty
- suspended on full pay
- suspended pending an investigation
- suspended without pay
- suspension pending disciplinary procedure

Suspension from duty is a temporary situation which may result in reinstatement or dismissal.

sweetheart deal
(n ph informal)
/'swi:thɑ:t 'di:l/

A sweetheart deal is a single-union agreement between a union and a company which includes a no-strike clause. See also **beauty contest**, **single union agreement**.

Supporters of sweetheart deals say that they help people for whom it might otherwise be difficult to get union representation. Those against say that they take away basic union rights.

'them and us'
mentality (n ph, informal)
/'θɛm ənd 'ʌs mɛn'tælɪti/

People who are criticised for having a 'them and us' mentality behave as if management and employees have different interests and that it is impossible for the two sides to cooperate. See also **confrontation**.

Partnership agreements are one way of trying to break down the traditional 'them and us' mentality which is still strong in many British companies.

trade union (n)
/'treɪd 'ju:njən/
trade unionist (n)

A trade union, trades union, union or **labor union** (Am Eng) is a democratic organisation of workers which exists to protect and promote the interests of its members and which represents them in discussions and negotiations with management. See also **union**.

trade union confederation
(n ph)

A trade union confederation is an organisation of independent unions, with its own full-time staff and budget, which works at national level, for example to communicate union policies and opinions to the government. See also **affiliate**.

trade union official (n ph)

A trade union official or **trade union officer** is any representative of the union, appointed or elected, paid by the company or by the employer, full-time or part-time.
- a trade union leader
- trade union opinion
- the trade union movement

tripartism (n)
/traɪ'pɑ:tɪzm/
tripartite (adj)

Tripartism is a process or a structure for discussion and possibly negotiation between employers, unions and government.
- hold tripartite talks

Employee relations and representation

7

union (n)
/'juːnjən/
unionise (v)

To unionise is to organise workers and encourage them to join a union. See also **organise**, **trade union**.

breakaway union (n ph)

A breakaway union is one formed by members who have split from another union.

craft union (n ph)

A craft union's members all do the same kind of skilled job. An electricians' union is an example of a craft union.

general union (n ph)

A general union has members who do a variety of jobs with different occupational groups organised into different sections.

industrial union (n ph)

An industrial union is one which recruits members from one industry or economic sector, for example unions for coal miners or rail workers.

super union (n ph)

In Britain, a super union is a very large union, often the result of two or more already large unions joining together. See also **merge**.

union buster
(n ph, informal)

A union buster is someone who wants to break the power of a union generally or in a particular company or workplace.

➠ a non-unionised company
➠ a company union
➠ non-unionised workers

victimise (v)
/'vɪktɪmaɪz/
victim (n)
victimisation (n)

If you are being victimised, you are being unfairly treated by your employer or by another employee or group of employees in your company. See also **bully**, **harass**, **intimidate**.

walk-out (n)
/'wɔːk aʊt/
walk out (v)

When workers walk out, they stop work, usually without warning, as a form of protest to management about something. Walk-outs are usually unofficial. See also **down tools**, **industrial action**, **stoppage**, **strike**, **withdrawal of labour**.

➠ stage a walk-out

warning (n)
/'wɔːnɪŋ/
warn (v)

A warning from an employer is a formal criticism: it tells an employee that the employer thinks that his or her work is unsatisfactory in some way. Official warnings are often issued as part of an organisation's official disciplinary procedure. Also known as a **reprimand**. See also **discipline**, **warning** (chapter 6).

➠ a final warning
➠ a formal warning
➠ a spoken warning
➠ a written warning
➠ an official warning
➠ issue a warning
➠ receive a warning

whistle blower (n)
/'wɪsəl bləʊə/
whistle blowing (n)

Whistle blowers are employees who draw attention to something which they think is wrong in the workplace. See also **disclose**.

➠ a whistle blowing claim
➠ a whistle blowing policy
➠ blow the whistle on (a company, a colleague)

One of the most famous whistle blowers in recent times was the American, Karen Silkwood, who believed her employer was hiding the truth about the safety of its nuclear power plant and who later died in mysterious circumstances.

withdrawal of labour
(n ph)
/wɪð'drɔːəl əv 'leɪbə/
withdraw labour (v ph)

A withdrawal of labour is any form of industrial action which involves employees stopping work or doing less work than usual. See also **down tools, industrial action, walk out, stoppage, strike.**
➡ a partial withdrawal of labour
When the management withdrew its pay offer, the union withdrew its members' labour.

work-to-rule (n)
/'wɜːk tə 'ruːl/
work to rule (v ph)

When employees work to rule, they do only the work they have to do according to their contracts of employment and no more. They therefore work more slowly and produce less. See also **go slow, industrial action.**
➡ follow a work-to-rule

worker director
(n ph)
/'wɜːkə dɪ'rɛktə/

A worker director is a representative of the employees who sits on the management board of the company.
Worker directors are common in Germany because of its co-determination laws.

works council (n)
/'wɜːks 'kaʊnsəl/

A works council is a committee of employees' representatives and management. Also known as a **works committee**. See also **co-determination, consultation, employee, partnership, social dialogue.**

European Works Council
(n ph)

Under European law, companies with 1,000 employees of whom 150 or more are in each of two or more states in the European Union and the European Economic Area (Iceland, Norway and Liechtenstein), must organise a meeting of a European works council (EWC) at least once a year to discuss transnational issues such as business plans, organisation and employment trends.
Although the powers and activities of works councils can vary a great deal, most of them are information-sharing and consultative bodies rather than ones with real negotiating powers.

Employee relations and representation

7

Exercises

Exercise 1

Choose the best term (A, B, C or D) to complete each sentence.

1 _____ represent a higher percentage of the national workforce in Scandinavian countries than in most other countries in the world.
A trade representatives   B trade unions   C staff associations D employee clubs

2 Companies in France have an obligation to set up _____ which provide a forum for information exchange between management and union representatives.
A enterprise councils   B supervisory boards   C works councils   D company councils

3 Large companies often employ _____ directors who specialise in working with the unions on issues such as pay negotiation, discipline, health and safety, and grievance handling.
A industrial relations   B public relations   C work relations   D craft

4 Because many organisations prefer to adopt a more human approach to workplace issues and because of the rise of services and the decline in manufacturing in some countries, the term preferred today by many companies to the above is _____.
A employee association   B employee relations   C investment in people
D service relations

5 In many works councils, _____ takes place with the unions on issues such as decisions to relocate, redundancy and reorganisation.
A counselling   B dispute   C consultancy   D consultation

6 In order to avoid disputes over plans to privatise some public services, the government decided to encourage _____ between employers and the main trade union confederation.
A social dialogue   B social talking   C social work   D transfer of opinion

7 Owners and directors of companies in a particular sector often create _____ to protect their interests.
A boss clubs   B patron associations   C employers' associations
D owners' committees

8 In some sectors such as banking, attempts have been made in the past to replace unions with _____, in the hope that they may play a less militant role in industrial relations.
A boards   B staff associations   C activity committees   D partnerships

Exercise 2

All the terms on the left (1 - 10) refer to the negotiation process. Match each one with a word in the right-hand column (a – j) which means the same.

1	bargain	a	break
2	conciliate	b	leave unclear
3	deal	c	mediate
4	binding	d	support
5	ratify	e	agreement
6	deadlock	f	negotiate
7	fudge	g	blockage
8	renege	h	compulsory

Exercise 3

All the terms 1 - 8 can be used with 'agreement'. Match each kind of agreement with its definition (a - h).

a when management agrees to treat blue and white collar workers in the same way

1 dilution
2 no-strike
3 no-union
4 partnership
5 single status
6 single union
7 threshold
8 collective

} agreement

b when a union signs an agreement with management not to go on strike

c when employees receive an automatic pay rise if inflation reaches a certain level

d when unions and management agree to work together for the good of the company and of the workforce

e when unions agree that unskilled labour may be used if skilled labour is unavailable

f when employees agree not to join a union

g when a union agrees to a management request to work with only one union

h when a deal is reached after bargaining between management and unions centrally

Exercise 4

Fill in the gaps (1-9) in the text which describes different forms of action which might be taken by employers or employees during industrial disputes.

strike	work-to-rule	picket	down tools	industrial action
walk out	stoppage	withdrawal of labour		unofficial action

When a union fails to reach agreement with management and the membership wishes to take (1)_____ , the union faces a number of options because (2) _____ can take a number of different forms. Sometimes, workers may feel so angry that they immediately (3) _____ and (4) _____ but this kind of (5) _____ is not usually a good idea and in some countries may indeed be illegal. One possible form of action, which does not involve an actual (6) _____ of work is a (7) _____, where employees strictly follow the terms of their contracts and slow down work. If there is real deadlock, the union may call a (8) _____ . The striking workers will then (9) _____ the workplace to show people that they are taking action and to communicate their strong views to management and to the general public.

Exercise 5

Use the terms in the box to create word clusters (groups of words belonging to the same family) on this and the next page.

suspend	convenor	general secretary	ballot	misconduct
branch	militant	warn	affiliate	merge	lay member
shop steward	closed shop	motion	national executive
discipline	worker director	show of hands	activist
subscription	misdemeanour	disaffiliate	check off

Disciplinary action {   suspend

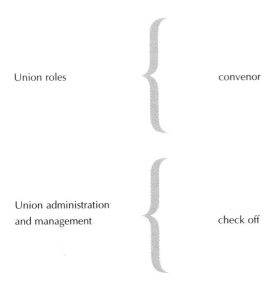

Union roles   convenor

Union administration
and management   check off

Exercise 6

Match each term in the box with one of the cryptic definitions (1–5).

beauty contest	sweetheart deal	black
blackleg	poach	'them and us' mentality

1   A darker member of the body which continues to work?
2   A loving agreement?
3   The brain sees two sides to the argument?
4   Hunt in someone else's workplace? A cooked egg?
5   Management prefers the prettiest one in the competition?
6   A night-time activity?

For discussion

1   What are unions for? Do they have a future? What are the biggest challenges facing the trade union movement today?
2   What are the advantages for management of having a unionised workforce? What arer the disadvantages? Do the advantages outweigh the disadvantages?
3   Do works councils play a useful role? In what ways would you like to see the activities of works councils scaled up or down?
4   What disciplinary procedures operate in your organisation? How are people who are guilty of persistent misconduct handled? Are there any changes you would like to see to these procedures?

Employee relations and representation

7

Case studies

Introducing a works council

A British group has recently bought a French company which owns subsidiaries in several European countries. The British parent company must therefore now create a European Works Council which will include representatives from the different countries in the EU. Up to now, the top management in Britain has only worked with the unions in places where they have been strong, and is rather worried about being forced to work with union and employee representatives from a number of different countries. At the same time, employee representatives from the different European subsidiaries are distrustful of a British management which only talks to unions when it has to.

The company has asked you to decide how best to set up its EWC. It is your job to make it work. You must therefore:

- recommend what the works council should do
- identify ways in everyone may benefit from the works council
- decide on a plan for setting up the council
- suggest ways to make sure that the EWC is successful.

How to market a trade union

The print workers union in one large European country has seen its membership decrease even more dramatically than the workforce in this sector as a whole – from 43% in the early 1980s to around 17% today. The main causes of this have been changes in the business including outsourcing abroad, changes in technology, and improvements in pay and working conditions. However, the results of a recent survey of management in the industry has revealed that companies consider union presence in the workplace to be desirable.

Working with consultants, the union executive has decided on a radical plan to attract membership. In addition to traditional representation of the craft and its employees, the union has decided to offer new members a range of services including the following:

- a partnership with a national bank offering low interest loans
- a legal and financial advice service
- a telephone help desk to assist members with welfare and work-related issues
- access to the union internet site and free subscription to a monthly newsletter

and to adopt the following approach:

- an industry-wide partnership agreement with management
- union representatives taking on the role of advisors and mediators between management and employees.

Consider:

- In what other ways can the union recover its membership?
- Do you think the union is right to adopt a services provider approach in addition to its traditional role?
- What are the pros and cons of a partnership approach with management?

Employee relations and representation

7

8

Employment law

Key terms to talk about
employment law and about
cases going before labour
courts.

8

Employment law

**These are the key terms in this chapter.
Which of them do you understand?
Which of them can you use?**

Accuse
adjudicate
allege
amendment
appeal
award
Breach
Capability
case
civil law
claim
clause
compensation
compliance
contract
costs
court
criminal
Damage
damages
data
derogation
directive
disclaimer
disclosure
dismiss
Employment tribunal
enforce
evidence
exempt

Fine
Hearing
Infraction
injunction
injury to feelings
Judgement
Legal
legislation
liable
litigation
Oath
offence
opt out
Panel
party
proceedings
proof
Rehearing
restrictive covenant
rights
ruling
Sequestrate
settle
statutory
submission
sue
Terms
transfer of undertakings
Witness

8

accuse (v)
/ə'kjuːz/
accusation (n)

You accuse someone when you say formally that they have committed a crime or have broken a rule. See also **allege**.
➡ accuse someone of (doing / having done) something
➡ make a serious accusation against
His employer accused him of stealing company property over a period of several months.

adjudicate (v)
/ə'dʒuːdɪkeɪt/
adjudication (n)
adjudicator (n)

When a judge or someone else adjudicates (in) a case, dispute or conflict, he or she studies the problem or hears the case and then makes a decision about it. See also **case**, **hearing**, **judgement**.
➡ adjudicate a conflict
➡ adjudicate a claim
➡ adjudicate in a dispute
➡ an adjudication officer
➡ adjudicate between the parties

allege (v)
/ə'lɛdʒ/
allegation (n)

If someone alleges that you have done something, they claim that you have done it. The allegation is usually that you have done something bad, for example committed a crime or a civil wrong. See also **accuse**.
➡ allege physical abuse
➡ make a serious allegation against (someone)
The employee alleged that the employer's behaviour amounted to sexual discrimination.

amendment (n)
/ə'mɛndmənt/
amend (v)

If you make an amendment to a law, you make a change to it. See also **legislation**.
➡ make an amendment
➡ propose an amendment

appeal (n, v)
/ə'piːl/
appellant (n)
appellate (adj)
internal appeals procedure
(n ph)

If you do not like the decision of a tribunal, you may decide to appeal to a higher court. An appeal is a request to a higher court to reconsider the judgement of a lower court. See also **discipline**, **employment tribunal**, **hearing**.
If you are not satisfied with the way that your organisation has handled your grievance, then you may decide to make a formal complaint. If there is an internal appeals procedure, your complaint will be handled by someone inside your organisation who will look at the decision about your grievance again and who may perhaps change the decision. See also **grievance**.

appeal proceedings (n ph pl) Appeal proceedings are all the actions and procedures in an appeal case.
➡ a court of appeal
➡ a disciplinary appeal
➡ a right of appeal
➡ a successful / an unsuccessful appeal
➡ an appeals procedure
➡ an employment appeal tribunal
➡ appeal against a decision
➡ bring / lodge / make an appeal

➡ hear an appeal
In the UK, you do not always have the right to appeal against the judgement of a tribunal, and if you do, you have to appeal within a certain period of time.

award (n, v)
/əˈwɔːd/

An award is the money paid by an employer to an employee after an employment tribunal rules for the employee in a dispute. See also **award** (chapter 4), **compensation**, **employment tribunal**.
➡ a compensatory award
➡ make an award
➡ receive an award

breach (n, v)
/ˈbriːtʃ/

There has been a breach of a rule or a law when someone breaks it. See also **contract**.
➡ a breach of contract, commit
➡ a breach of discipline
➡ a breach of duty
➡ a breach of policy
➡ a breach of procedure
➡ a breach of trust

repudiatory breach (n ph)

When a court judges that an employer has committed a repudiatory breach of the contract of employment, the court decides that the employer has broken the law because they have shown that they no longer plan to accept the terms of the contract, for example by reducing an employee's wages without consulting the employee. In this case, the employee can bring an action for constructive dismissal. See also **dismissal**, **repudiate**.

capability (n)
/keɪpəˈbɪləti/
capable (adj)

There is a problem of capability when an employee does not have the ability to do a job. It is important for the employer to see the difference between employees who do not work well because they cannot – for example because of lack of skills, training or good supervision – and others who do not work well for other reasons. See also **discipline**, **performance**.
➡ a capability case
➡ a capability meeting
Employers should make a clear distinction between a capability meeting and a disciplinary meeting. Questions of capability can arise from persistent short-term absence as well as from poor performance.

case (n)
/ˈkeɪs/

A case is a legal action. You take a case to a civil court when you feel that you should receive compensation for the loss or injury that you have suffered, for example from your employer. See also **case** (chapter 5)
➡ hear a case
➡ bring / take a case to / before a court / tribunal
➡ fight a case in court
➡ take on a case
In Britain, employees not eligible for legal aid may ask a lawyer to take on a case on a 'no win no fee' basis.

civil law (n ph)   Civil law is the branch of law which deals with disputes between
/ˈsɪvəl ˈlɔː/   individuals or companies. See also **dispute**.

claim (n, v)   If you make a claim against your employer, you go to court to ask for
/ˈkleɪm/   compensation, for example if you have an accident in a situation
claimant (n)   where the safety rules were not enforced. A **claimant** is someone who
    makes a claim. See also **claim** (chapter 7).
contest a claim (v ph)   When employers contest claims, they say (possibly in court) that they
    do not agree with the claim brought by the employee.
discrimination claim (n ph)   You make a discrimination claim (to a tribunal or court) if you feel that
    your employer has treated you less well because of your sex, sexual
    orientation, age, colour, religion, race, disability or trade union
    membership.
severance claim (n ph)   You make a severance claim when you ask your employer for extra
    money after you have lost your job without good legal reason, that is,
    if you lose your job through no fault of your own. See also **severance
    pay**.
    ➡ a claim culture
    ➡ a claim for damages / a damages claim
    ➡ a personal injury claim
    ➡ bring a claim against an employer
    ➡ make a claim for compensation / damages / payment
    *If you wish to take legal action of any kind, your lawyer should first
    tell you how much chance you have of winning the claim.*

clause (n)   A clause is a part of a contract. See also **contract**.
/ˈklɔːz/
confidentiality clause (n ph)   If there is a confidentiality clause in your contract of employment, you
    agree not to give secret information about the company or its
    employees to people outside the company. See also **disclose**.
flexibility clause (n ph)   Some employers include a flexibility clause in their contracts of
    employment so that they can ask their employees to do tasks or duties
    which are different from those in their job descriptions. For example,
    a flexibility clause might state that an employee should be ready to
    perform any of the duties normally carried out by other people of the
    same grade. Higher grade staff could be asked to perform duties
    normally performed by lower grade staff and, on a short-term basis,
    lower grade staff could be asked to cover for higher grade staff who
    are absent.
mobility clause (n ph)   A mobility clause in your contract of employment entitles your
    employer to ask you to work from different locations.
restraint clause (n ph)   If you sign a contract of employment with a restraint clause, you agree
    not to do something after you leave your current job. For example,
    you can agree not to work for a competitor for a certain period. See
    also **restrictive covenant**.
waiver clause (n ph)   If you sign a waiver clause, you agree to exclude certain employment
    rights from your contract. See also **rights**.
    ➡ a non-competition clause
    ➡ an arbitration clause
    ➡ an exemption clause

8

Employment law

Employment law

When I was hired by my current employer, I was required to sign a contract with a non-competition clause. Now I want to leave and work for a competitor in a different part of the country. Can my employer prevent me from doing that?

compensation (n)
/kɒmpən'seɪʃən/
compensate (v)
compensatory (adj)
compensation culture
(n ph)

When you claim compensation, you ask for money for injury, damage or loss that you have suffered. See also **compensation** (chapter 4), **claim**, **damage**.

An organisation or country with a compensation culture is one where members of that culture go to court a lot to claim damages if they have suffered any injury, loss or damage. The phrase is usually used in a negative way to suggest that too many people are trying to make money out of very small injuries, losses or damage.

➡ a compensatory payment
➡ appeal for compensation
➡ award compensation
➡ claim compensation
➡ compensation for damages
➡ compensation for loss of earnings
➡ grant compensation
➡ lump sum compensation
➡ pay compensation
➡ substantial compensation
➡ workers' compensation

An employment tribunal can award an employee substantial compensation if it decides, for example, that a company was responsible for an employee's injuries because of poor safety procedures.

compliance (n)
/kəm'plaɪəns/
comply (v)
compliant (adj)

You comply with a rule or a law when you do what it requires. Compliance with a rule is accepting and following the rule. The opposite of compliance is **non-compliance**. See also **code**, **directive**, **enforce**.

➡ comply with a directive
➡ comply with a code of practice
➡ compliance management
➡ compliance monitoring
➡ a compliance monitoring role

It can be difficult for employers to comply with all aspects of employment legislation when large numbers of new laws are passed every year.

contract (n v)
/'kɒntrækt/ (n)
/kɒn'trækt/ (v)
contractual (adj)
contract of employment
(n ph)

A contract is a legal agreement between two or more people or parties.

Your contract of employment should cover the conditions of your employment including working hours, holidays, sick pay and so on. See also **conditions of employment**.

8

breach of contract (n ph)	There is a breach of contract when either the employer or employee breaks a term of the contract of employment. See also **breach, discipline.**
draft a contract (v ph)	When you draft a contract, you prepare the agreement in writing. A draft contract can be changed and rewritten several times before it is finalised.
fixed term contract (n ph)	If you enter into a fixed term contract, then the agreement runs for a specific length of time. This length of time (the term) will be specified (fixed) in the contract.
no-hours contract (n ph)	If you sign a no-hours contract, you can decide yourself how many hours you will work. This kind of contract is used to employ, for example, software engineers in California who do not want any upper or lower limits on how many hours they work.
permanent contract (n ph)	If you enter into a permanent contract, then the agreement continues until one of the parties decides to end it (or there is a breach of contract).
temporary contract (n ph)	If you enter into a temporary contract, then the agreement ends at a specific time unless one of the parties decides to extend it.
vary a contract (v ph)	Varying a contract means changing the terms of the contract.
zero hours contract (n ph)	A zero hours contract is one where the employee agrees to be available to work but where there are no guaranteed hours and payment is only made for work done. It may be used, for example, for an employee who only works during very busy periods.

➡ a contractual entitlement
➡ a contractual issue
➡ a draft contract
➡ a fixed term contract
➡ a permanent contract
➡ a short-term contract
➡ a temporary contract
➡ an annual hours contract
➡ an open-ended contract
➡ be on / have a permanent (or other type of) contract
➡ offer a permanent (or other type of) contract
➡ the terms of a contract / contractual terms

costs (n pl) /'kɒsts/	If you take a case to court and the judge awards you costs, then the other party must pay you the money you spent on the action.

➡ award costs to

court (n) /'kɔːt/	The court is the place where legal actions are heard and usually decided by a judge or a panel of lawyers. See also **hearing, legal, settle, tribunal.**

➡ a civil court
➡ a court of appeal
➡ a criminal court
➡ a labour court
➡ appear as a court witness
➡ appear in / make an appearance in court

8

Employment law

⟶ court proceedings
⟶ give evidence in court
⟶ go to court
⟶ settle (a case) out of court
⟶ take a case to court

criminal (adj, n)
/'krɪmɪnəl/
crime (n)

A criminal is someone who breaks the law. If you do something criminal, you do something that is against the law. See also **civil law**, **offence**.

⟶ a criminal act
⟶ a criminal court
⟶ a criminal record
⟶ commit a (serious) crime
⟶ criminal justice, the criminal justice system
⟶ criminal law

criminal conviction (n ph)

You have a criminal conviction if you have been found guilty of an offence by a court of criminal law.

criminal offence (n ph)

If you commit a criminal offence, you do something which is against the law.

damage (n, v)
/'dæmɪdʒ/

You suffer damage if someone harms your property. If someone damages your property, you may have the right to claim damages. See also **damages**.

⟶ cause damage
⟶ criminal damage
⟶ damage to property
⟶ financial damage
⟶ suffer damage

Employers may take legal action against employees who cause damage to company property.

damages (n pl)
/'dæmɪdʒɪz/

If you win damages, you get compensation from a civil court for the injury, loss or damage that you have suffered. See also **compensation**, **civil law**, **damage**.

⟶ award damages
⟶ claim damages / make a claim for damages
⟶ compensation for damages, seek
⟶ sue for damages
⟶ win (substantial) damages

The tribunal awarded the claimant £35,000 in damages.

data (n)
/'deɪtə/

Data is information or facts about something. Personal data is information about individual people. A main function of computers is to store data. See also **exit**, **manual**.

data protection (n ph)

Data protection laws can protect your privacy in two ways: firstly, personal information about you can only be processed in fair and lawful ways; secondly the laws limit what can be done with information about you.

⟶ a data protection code

➡ a data protection policy
➡ data protection procedures
➡ data retrieval
➡ data security
➡ data storage

The UK Data Protection Act of 1998 allows employees to ask their employers to show them any personal data which they hold in computerised or manual files.

derogation (n)
/ˌdɛrəˈgeɪʃən/

A derogation is an exception to a rule or directive. For example, the derogation of senior managers and other groups from the EU directive on working hours means that they do not have to follow the same rules as most employees. See **directive**, **opt out**.
➡ apply a derogation to
➡ make a derogation for

directive (n)
/dɪˈrɛktɪv/

A directive recommends or requires a country, an organisation or a business to act in a particular way.
➡ a European (Union) directive
➡ carry out / implement a directive
➡ issue a directive

The EU has issued directives on a very wide range of HR subjects including health and safety, wage payment systems, training and the setting up of European Works Councils.

disclaimer (n)
/dɪsˈkleɪmə/

If you write a disclaimer, then you say that you are not responsible for something or give up your right to something. See also **clause**.
➡ a legal disclaimer
➡ add a disclaimer to

Corporate emails are often followed by detailed disclaimers to reduce the company's legal liability in relation to the content of the message.

disclose (v)
/dɪsˈkləʊz/
disclosure (n)

If you make a disclosure, then you give information which was previously secret or not generally known – for example, about a company's illegal activities – to someone, or you make that information known to a wider public. See also **clause**, **whistleblower**.

disclosure, protective (n ph)

If you give information that someone has done something wrong and you feel that you need legal protection against negative treatment because you have given this information, you can ask for protective (also called protected) disclosure.

disclosure, qualifying (n ph)

If you believe that your employer has committed a criminal offence, has failed to comply with a legal obligation, is responsible for a miscarriage of justice, a breach of health and safety regulations, or damage to the environment, you can make a qualifying disclosure which gives you legal protection against the possible harm you might suffer without it.
➡ disclose confidential information
➡ disclosure of documents / information
➡ make a disclosure
➡ public interest disclosure

Employment law

8

The Act makes it unlawful for an employee to suffer any damage or harm because he or she has made a protected disclosure.

dismiss (v)
/dɪsˈmɪs/
dismissal (n)

If an employer dismisses an employee, the employee no longer has a job and must leave the company. See also **discharge, fire, sack, termination.**

automatic unfair dismissal (n ph)

Under British law, there are certain situations where there cannot be a good reason for an employer to dismiss an employee. These include dismissal in relation to being pregnant, maternity leave, and making a request for flexible working. If an employer dismisses an employee in a situation like this, the employee can claim automatic unfair dismissal

constructive dismissal (n ph)

If you leave your job because you think that it is impossible for you to go on working – for example because the conditions are unsafe but your employer will not improve them – then you can make a claim of constructive dismissal to an employment tribunal. See also **claim.**

dismissal with notice (n ph)

Dismissal with notice may occur as the last stage in a disciplinary procedure where an employee has been persistently late or absent or performed to a low standard. In this case the employee works to the end of the period of notice or receives payment in lieu of notice.

fair dismissal (n ph)

In a case of fair dismissal, an employee is dismissed with good reason.

grounds for dismissal (n ph)

The grounds for dismissal are the reasons the employer gives for sacking someone.

summary dismissal (n ph)

Summary dismissal is instant dismissal or dismissal without notice.

unfair dismissal (n ph)

In a case of unfair dismissal, an employee is dismissed without good reason.

wrongful dismissal (n ph)

In a case of wrongful dismissal, an employee is dismissed in a way which is not legally correct.

➡ a claim of unfair / wrongful dismissal
➡ collective dismissal
➡ constitute grounds for dismissal
➡ dismissal without notice
➡ individual dismissal
➡ instant dismissal
➡ liable to dismissal
➡ summarily dismissed

Employees who think they have been unfairly or wrongfully dismissed, can take the case to an employment tribunal.

employment tribunal
(n ph)
/ɪmˈplɔɪmənt traɪˈbjuːnəl/

An employment tribunal is a special court which has the power to make decisions in disputes between employers and employees. Also known as a **labour court** and known in the past as an **industrial relations tribunal** or **industrial court**. See also **dispute, hearing, judgement.**

➡ a hearing of an employment tribunal
➡ a tribunal ruling in favour of / against
➡ an employment appeal tribunal
➡ appeal to an employment tribunal
➡ attend a tribunal
➡ take a case to an employment tribunal
➡ tribunal proceedings

In the UK, if you believe you are entitled to a redundancy payment, you should make a claim in writing to your employer or to an employment tribunal within six months of your redundancy, or your claim may be lost.

8

Employment law

enforce (v)
/ɪnˈfɔːs/
enforcer (n)
enforcement (n)
enforceable (adj)

When an organisation enforces a rule, it makes sure that everyone follows it. When a law is enforced, the police or some other agency tries to ensure that everyone obeys the law. See also **compliance**.
➡ enforce a law
➡ a law enforcement agency
Companies must ensure that all health and safety rules are enforced.

evidence (n)
/ˈɛvɪdəns/

When you give evidence in court, you tell the court what you know about the case being heard. See also **proof**, **submission**, **witness**.
➡ a piece of evidence
➡ documentary evidence
➡ give evidence against
➡ give evidence in court / before a tribunal
➡ give false evidence
➡ hear evidence from
➡ listen to evidence

exempt (v, adj)
/ɪgˈzɛmpt/
exemption (n)

If you are exempt from a rule or a procedure, you do not have to follow it. See also **derogation**, **opt out**.
➡ exemption from liability
➡ exemption from contributions

fine (n, v)
/ˈfaɪn/

A criminal court may ask you to pay money if they find you guilty of a minor criminal offence. The fine is the financial penalty. If a court finds you guilty of a more serious offence, then it will not fine you, it will imprison you. See also **infraction**, **offence**.
➡ a substantial fine
➡ an on-the-spot fine
➡ impose a fine
➡ pay a fine
The court has imposed a large fine on their company for non-compliance with stakeholder legislation.

hearing (n)
/ˈhɪərɪŋ/

A hearing is a session of a court or tribunal when the judge listens to what both sides have to say; or a formal part of a disciplinary procedure where the employer hears what the employee or employee representative has to say about a disciplinary problem. See also **accompany**, **court**, **discipline**, **employment tribunal**.
➡ a disciplinary hearing
➡ a grievance hearing
➡ a preliminary hearing
➡ conduct a hearing
➡ postpone a hearing

As from September 2000, British workers who have been asked to attend a disciplinary hearing or a tribunal, have had the right to be accompanied at the hearing by a 'companion', who can be a work colleague or an employee or union representative.

infraction (n)
/ɪnˈfrækʃən/

If you commit an infraction, you break a minor law. The penalty for an infraction is normally a fine. See also **fine, offence.**
➡ commit an infraction
➡ multiple infractions

injunction (n)
/ɪnˈdʒʌŋkʃən/

An injunction is an order from a court ordering someone not to do something or to stop doing something.
➡ a court injunction
➡ ask for / request an injunction
➡ grant an injunction
➡ take out an injunction against
Employers sometimes go to court to ask for an injunction against workers who are threatening to take industrial action.

injury to feelings
(n ph)
/ˈɪndʒʌri tə ˈfiːlɪŋz/

You may be able to claim damages for injury to feelings if you can prove to the court that you suffered from discrimination and that your feelings were hurt as a direct result. See also **damages, discrimination, injure.**
Employees who have been unfairly dismissed can sue for injury to feelings.

judgement (n)
/ˈdʒʌdʒmənt/
judge (n v)

A judgement is an official decision of a court or tribunal in a legal case. The **judge** is the lawyer whose job it is to make the decision after hearing all the evidence. See also **panel, ruling.**
➡ appeal against a judgement
➡ confirm a judgement
➡ deliver a judgement
➡ make a judgement
The judgement states that if an employee is suffering from stress, the employer must take steps to prevent the condition from worsening.

legal (adj)
/ˈliːgəl/
legalise (v)
legality (n)
legal aid (n ph)

Something which is legal is allowed by the law. Something which is not legal (against the law) is **illegal** or **unlawful.**

In some countries, people whose income is below a certain level can receive legal aid in the form of money which helps them to find a lawyer to present their case in court and to pay their legal fees.

take legal action against
(v ph)

If you have suffered injury, loss or damage at work you may decide to take legal action against your employer in a civil court. Your aim is usually to win damages (financial compensation). See also **case, damages, compensation, proceedings.**
➡ a legal adviser
➡ a legal argument

8

➠ a legal document
➠ a legally binding contract
➠ legal advice
➠ legal issues
➠ legal services
➠ start legal proceedings against
Our firm of lawyers offers legal help and advice on a wide range of employment issues.

legislation (n)
/ˈlɛdʒɪsˈleɪʃən/
legislate (v)
legislation (n)
legislature (n)

Legislation is law passed by the parliament or national assembly or other law-making body of a country. See also **amendment**.
➠ a (growing) body of legislation
➠ labour / employment legislation
➠ legislate against
➠ pass legislation

liable (adj)
/ˈlaɪəbəl/
liability (n)

Employers are liable when they are legally responsible for damage, loss or harm suffered by employees.
➠ accept liability for
➠ full liability
➠ limited liability
➠ refuse to acknowledge liability for
If a company does not accept liability for an employee's injuries, the employee may take the claim to an employment tribunal.

litigation (n)
/lɪtɪˈgeɪʃən/
litigate (v)
litigious (adj)
litigious society (n ph)

You engage in litigation when you go to a civil court to settle a dispute.

Litigious people go to court a lot to settle disputes. In a litigious society, many people prefer to take cases to court, often to win damages, rather than to settle their disputes in another way. See also **compensation**, **damages**, **dispute**, **sue**.
➠ commercial litigation
➠ cost-effective litigation
➠ employment litigation
➠ engage in litigation
➠ undertake litigation
The new law aims to help to build constructive employment relations and avoid the need for litigation through better communication in the workplace.

oath (n)
/ˈəʊθ/

When you swear an oath in court, you make a formal promise to tell the truth, the whole truth and nothing but the truth. See also **evidence**, **witness**.
➠ swear an oath
➠ take the oath
➠ administer an oath to a witness

Employment law

8

Religious people swear an oath while at the same time putting their hand on the holy book of their religion.

offence (n)
/ə'fɛns/
offend (n)
offender (n)

You commit an offence when you break the law. See also **criminal, fine, infraction.**
➡ a minor offence
➡ a serious offence
➡ commit an offence

opt out (v)
/'ɒpt 'aʊt/
opt-out (n)

If you opt out of a clause in a contract, the clause does not apply to you any more. See also **derogation, exempt.**
For some years, British employers had the right to invite their employees to opt out of the European working time directive, a right which was widely abused.

panel (n)
/'pænəl/

A panel is a group of judges or lawyers who sit in a court or tribunal to hear a case. See also **judgement, panel** (chapter 3).
➡ sit on a panel

party (n)
/'pɑːti/
third party (n ph)

Management and employee representatives are the two parties in organisations which are involved in negotiations or disputes. When two parties cannot agree, they may ask a third party to conciliate, mediate or to arbitrate. The third party is someone who is not a member of either side in the dispute. See also **arbitrate, conciliate, mediate.**
➡ a party to a dispute
➡ an independent third party
In some countries, a government arbitration service exists to mediate and to arbitrate between the different parties to a dispute. In Britain, this job is done by ACAS - the Arbitration, Conciliation and Advisory Service.

proceedings (n)
/prə'siːdɪŋz/
bring proceedings (v ph)

The proceedings of a court or tribunal cover all the actions and procedures in a case from the beginning to the end.
You bring proceedings against someone when you take legal action against them in a civil court. See also **legal.**
➡ court proceedings
➡ start proceedings against
➡ take proceedings against

proof (n)
/'pruːf/
prove (v)

The proof is the evidence presented to a criminal court which shows clearly that the person against whom legal action is being taken is really guilty of the crime of which he or she is accused. See **accuse, legal, evidence.**

burden of proof (n ph)

The burden of proof falls on the person who is responsible for showing that the person accused is really guilty.

re-hearing (n)
/'riː'hɪərɪŋ/

If there is a re-hearing of your case, then your case will be presented again before the same court in which it was originally heard. See also **appeal, hearing.**

The re-hearing overturned the decision of the tribunal and stated that the employee had been discriminated against.

restrictive covenant
(n ph)
/rɪs'trɪktɪv 'kʌvənənt/

If you enter into a restrictive covenant, you promise not to do something, for example to work for a competitor after the termination of a contract of employment for a specific period of time. See also **clause, contract**.

It is quite normal for employers to protect their business against the actions of ex-employees by means of a restrictive covenant in the contract of employment.

rights (n pl)
/'raɪts/

Your rights tell you what you can do according to the law.

acquired rights (n ph pl)

In many countries, employment law includes a concept called acquired rights. This means you cannot take away anything from an individual. So, for example, job content, responsibilities, pay and benefits must stay the same. See also **transfer of undertakings**.

human rights (n ph)

Human rights are a group of fundamental rights which belong to all people. They are found in many treaties and in the Universal Declaration of Human Rights, passed by the United Nations General Assembly in1948.

transsexual rights (n ph)

Transsexual rights refer to what a person who has undergone a sex change operation can do under the law, for example marry, change their birth certificates and be legally recognised under their new gender. See also **gender, sexual orientation**.

waive a right (v ph)

If you waive a right, you give it up. See also **clause**.

- a statutory right, to assert
- civil rights
- employment rights
- gay rights
- know your rights
- legal rights
- the exercising of rights in relation to
- the right to strike

A British transsexual has won her fight in the European Court of Human Rights to be recognised as a woman and to be allowed to marry .

ruling (n)
/'ruːlɪŋ/

The ruling of an employment tribunal is the decision the court makes in a particular case. See also **appeal, judgement**.

overturn a ruling (v ph)

If an appeal court overturns the ruling of a lower court, it says that the decision of the lower court was wrong.

- a court / tribunal ruling
- appeal against a ruling
- dispute a ruling
- respect a ruling
- the court's / tribunal's ruling

The tribunal overturned the ruling that the claimant was not entitled to redundancy pay on the grounds that he was over 65.

Employment law

Employment law

sequestrate (v)
/si'kwɛstreɪt/
sequestration (n)

When a court sequestrates the property or assets of an individual or an organisation, it takes control of property or assets as a punishment after ruling that the individual or organisation has broken the law.
In Britain, courts have the power to sequestrate the financial assets of trade unions which are ruled to have broken the law.

settle (v)
/'sɛtəl/
settlement (n)
settle out of court (v ph)

You settle a dispute when you bring it to an end. See also **agreement, dispute**.

If you settle your dispute out of court, it is not then necessary to bring an action in court. In this case, the parties will usually agree the compensation that is to be paid.
➡ make / reach an out-of-court settlement
➡ settle a dispute
➡ settle a matter
➡ settle the case
Among the many good arguments for encouraging more out-of-court settlements are cost savings, reducing the workload of the courts, and encouraging parties to disputes to find alternatives to litigation which may also help improve communication between them.

statutory (adj)
/'stætjətəri/
statute (n)

If something – like a right – is statutory, then it is recognised by the law. For example, if you have a statutory right to benefit, then this right is protected by law.
➡ a statutory disciplinary procedure
➡ a statutory instrument
➡ a statutory procedure
➡ a statutory right
➡ statutory adoption / maternity / paternity / sick pay
➡ statutory dispute resolution
➡ statutory legal protection

submission (n)
/səb'mɪʃən/
submit (v)

If someone makes a submission to a court, they present information as part of the case that they are arguing. See also **evidence**.
➡ make a submission

sue (v)
/'suː/
suit (n)

If you sue someone, then you bring an action or **lawsuit** against them in a civil court for the injury, loss or damage that you have suffered. See also **damages**.
➡ sue for damages
➡ the right to sue
The lawyer agreed to represent the employee who had been injured at work and who wanted to sue his employer for compensation.

terms (n pl)
/'tɜːmz/

express terms (n ph)

The terms of an agreement or contract are the conditions which an employer and an employee agree to. See also **agreement, contract, conditions of employment**.
You can read the express terms in the agreement, because they are in writing.

8

implied terms (n ph)

You cannot find the implied terms in the agreement, because they are not in writing. But they are considered part of the agreement and bind the parties. For example it is an implied term of a contract of employment that the employer will provide a secure, safe and healthy environment for employees.
- a statement of terms of employment
- accept the terms of an agreement
- agree on terms
- agree to the terms of
- terms of employment / employment terms
- under the terms of the contract

Under the terms of the new agreement, staff will work an extra half hour two afternoons per week in exchange for a half day off every fourth Friday in the month.

transfer of undertakings (n ph)
/ˈtrænzfɜː əv ʌndəˈteɪkɪŋz/

When one organisation passes responsibility for an activity to another, there is a transfer of undertakings. Also known as a **business transfer**.

Transfer of Undertakings (Protection of Employment) (n ph)

The British Transfer of Undertakings (Protection of Employment) Regulations, known as TUPE (pronounced /ˈtjuːpiː/) is a 1981 law making new employers accept the employment rights of the employees of a business which they have bought.

TUPE also covers areas such as protection against dismissal and the right of employees to consultation.

witness (n, v)
/ˈwɪtnəs/

A witness is someone who has seen an event, for example a crime, and reported on it, for example to the police. Witnesses can appear in a court of law to say what they know about the case being heard and to answer questions from the judge and the lawyers working on the case. See also **evidence, oath**.

brief a witness (v ph)

Before the court case, a lawyer briefs witnesses by preparing them for what will happen in the court, telling them how they should behave and suggesting how to present the information they want to give to the court.

witness statement (n ph)

If you are asked to make a witness statement, then what you say will be written down and presented to the court.
- an expert witness
- call a witness
- come forward as a witness
- cross-examine a witness
- prepare a witness statement

If you are bullied at work, keep a diary of all incidents - records of dates, times, any witnesses, your feelings, etc.

Employment law

Exercises

Exercise 1

Match each of the terms (1 – 5) with a definition (a – e).

1	appeal	a	to request or demand something you think is due to you
2	sue	b	to bring action against someone in a civil court
3	award	c	when there is no solution to a dispute, the case goes to court
4	claim	d	a request to a higher court to reconsider a judgement
5	litigation	e	money paid after a tribunal rules for the employee in a dispute

Exercise 2

Write in the missing verbs and nouns.

	Verb	Noun
1	adjudicate	_____
2	allege	_____
3	_____	compensation
4	legislate	_____
5	_____	compliance
6	_____	disclosure
7	fine	_____
8	_____	ruling
9	settle	_____
10	witness	_____

Exercise 3

Fill in the gaps (1 – 8) with the best term from the box.

statutory	panel	Data	directive
rights	amendment	submission	opt-out

1   The European Union issued a _____ requiring companies over a certain size which operated in two or more European countries to set up a European works council.

2   The employees stated their case in court before a _____ composed of a full-time judge, a labour representative and an employer's representative.

3   The standard contract applies the same conditions to all employees although there is an _____ clause to allow senior managers to work more hours if they choose to.

4   The new _____ to the law on working time, effectively makes several changes to the way overtime can be calculated.

5   When the organisation issued a statement to employees requesting them to limit rest

periods during working time, employees went to court, claiming that breaks were part of the acquired _____ of the trade.

6   After several cases of abuse, employees went to court claiming damages under the _____ Protection Act which states that personal information must not be shared with any external body unless authorised by the employees themselves.

7   Since employees' rights to participate in training during working hours became _____ under law, employees have been able to take legal action against any abuse of this right.

8   As part of her case before the employment tribunal for unfair dismissal, she was asked to make a _____ about her level of attendance.

Exercise 4
Fill each gap in the text with a key employment contract term from the box.

| clause | disclaimer | opt-out |
| restrictive covenant | breach | comply with |

Many employment contracts contain a confidentiality (1) _____ which require the employee not to give confidential information about the company to its competitors. In addition, a (2) _____ can oblige the employee not to work for a competitor for a given amount of time after termination of the contract of employment. An employer can take the (ex-) employee to court if there is a (3) _____ of these terms. Contracts can also contain (4) _____ clauses which make it possible for certain standard conditions of employment, for example on working hours, not to apply to a particular employee. Finally, some contracts contain a (5) _____ in which the employers state that they are not responsible for something or invite employees to give up their rights on a given point. By signing the contract, the employer and employee agree to (6) _____ the terms which constitute the basis for their working relationship.

Exercise 5
Which verbs (1 – 10) are used with the following key terms (a – j)?

1	agree to	a	court
2	enforce	b	damage
3	appeal against	c	a witness
4	suffer	d	a case
5	award	e	an oath
6	swear	f	a ruling
7	commit	g	the terms
8	take (someone) to	h	an infraction
9	call	i	a law
10	hear	j	compensation

For discussion

1 Describe the basics of the system of employment law in your country? Does it work?
2 How far does employment law have an impact on your everyday work? Would you like this to be more or less than it is now?
3 If you could draft one new piece of employment legislation, what would it be?
4 There is too much employment law and the ever-increasing body of law is killing human resources management and good employee relations. Do you agree?

Case studies

A case of unfair dismissal?

An executive working in a computer services company showed an inability to work with colleagues and customers. According to his immediate superior, and supported by comments made to this manager by other staff and several customers, the employee lacked the skills and personality to offer internal and external customers an appropriate attitude and behaviour in terms of cooperation and assistance. After a year, the manager dismissed the employee and the employee took his case to the employment tribunal. The tribunal initially rejected the manager's right to dismiss the employee, though on appeal, the judgement was overturned.

Consider:
• Why do you think the tribunal was initially in favour of the employee?
• Why do you think the tribunal then passed judgement in favour of the manager?
• How could the situation have been avoided?

Forced or voluntary resignation?

An airline employee, on duty after a long and difficult flight, accidentally overturned the drinks trolley in the plane. Her initial reaction was one of anger and frustration. Other members of the crew helped the employee and calmed her nerves. After the plane landed, the crew then spent a period of rest together. A manager entered the room and severely reprimanded the employee in front of her colleagues. The employee's reaction was to resign. However, two days later, she claimed that she had had no other option but to resign on the grounds that she had been humiliated and ridiculed by the manager. The tribunal accepted the employee's claim and ordered the airline to reinstate her due to their opinion that the manager's behaviour represented a breach of "trust and confidence" stated in the contract of employment.

Consider:
• Would the employee's initial behaviour be grounds for dismissal?
• Should the manager have adopted a more tolerant attitude?
• How was the employee right in claiming that she had been "forced" to resign?
• How would you define such a term ("mutual trust and confidence") in a contract of employment?

9

Communication and culture

Key terms to talk about communication
within organisations, organisational
culture and intercultural communication.

These are the key terms in this chapter.
Which of them do you understand?
Which of them can you use?

Communication and culture

9

Achievement
active listening
adapt
ambiguity
appreciative enquiry
appropriate
artefact
ascription
assimilate
Bell curve
blame
body language
brainstorm
Champion
collectivism
command and control
communication
confrontation
corporate social responsibility
critical incident
culture
Directness
dress
Emotional intelligence
empathy
ethnocentric
eye contact
Face
femininity
fog index
functional silo
Gender
Hall
hierarchy
high context
Hofstede

house magazine
Indirectness
individualism
integrate
Johari window
Kluckholn and Strodtbeck value orientations
Leadership
low context
Masculinity
monochronic
morale
Native speaker
norm
notify
Open door policy
organic
organisation
Particularism
peach and coconut
polychronic
power distance
prejudice
punctual
Small talk
sojourner
statement
stereotype
suggestion scheme
systematic
Theory X and theory Y
Trompenaars
turn taking
Uncertainty avoidance
universalism
Vision

achievement (n)
/ə'tʃiːvmənt/

Trompenaars uses this term, in contrast to ascription, to describe how people in some cultures get status because of what they do, what they have achieved, what they know or how effective they are seen to be in their jobs. See also **ascription, Trompenaars**.
➡ an achievement-oriented culture

active listening (n ph)
/'æktɪv 'lɪsnɪŋ/

When you listen actively, you not only listen to someone's words but you also read their body language and other non-verbal signs, and you signal your positive response to what you hear through eye contact, facial expression, body language and so on. See also **body language, eye contact**.
➡ engage in active listening

adapt (v)
/ə'dæpt/
adaptable (adj)
adaptation (n)
adaptability (n)

An adaptable person can quickly get used to unfamiliar situations. Adaptability is important for intercultural competence.
➡ a short / long period of adaptation to
➡ highly adaptable, have a high degree of adaptability
➡ prove / turn out (to be) very adaptable

ambiguity (n ph)
/æmbɪ'gjuːɪti/
ambiguous (adj)

Something which is ambiguous has different possible meanings. You are in an ambiguous situation when you do not understand what is happening and what other people are thinking and feeling as well as you would like to. Interculturally competent people can tolerate and enjoy ambiguity in unfamiliar situations more than others.

tolerance of ambiguity
(n ph)

If you are tolerant of ambiguity, you accept a situation which you do not necessarily understand and do not feel too uncomfortable or worried by its strangeness.
➡ a strong dislike of ambiguity
➡ a love of ambiguity
➡ low tolerance of ambiguity

appreciative enquiry
(n ph)
/ə'priːʃətɪv ɪŋ'kwaɪri/

Organisations which encourage appreciative enquiry encourage people from different parts and different levels of the organisation to talk to each other to find out what they like about their jobs and what they would like to change.
➡ a process of appreciative enquiry, engage in

appropriate (adj)
/ə'prəʊprɪət/
appropriacy (n)

Doing the appropriate thing means doing the right thing for that situation. Interculturally competent people understand that what is appropriate behaviour in a familiar situation may be inappropriate in an unfamiliar situation, so they watch and try to understand in order to be able to adapt quickly.
➡ entirely / highly appropriate

artefact (n)
/'ɑːtɪfækt/

An artefact is an object made by a human being. Cultural artefacts – buildings, paintings, clothes, jewellery and so on – give us information about the societies which produced them.

9

Communication and culture

Communication and culture

9

ascription (n)
/ə'skrɪpʃən/

Trompenaars uses this term, in contrast to achievement, to describe how people in some cultures get status because of who and what they are more than what they do. For example, an ascription-oriented culture could give status to people because of their age, their gender or their social class. See also **achievement, seniority, Trompenaars.**
➡ an ascription-oriented culture

assimilate (v)
/ə'sɪmɪleɪt/
assimilation (n)

Assimilation is the process of becoming part of another group, community or society while at the same time losing or giving up an important part of your original identity. See also **integrate.**
➡ a good / a poor degree / level of assimilation

bell curve (n ph)
/'bɛl dʒɑː/

Bell curves are a visual reminder to us of the dangers of over-generalising when we talk about people from different cultures. For example, we can claim that business people from group X tend to be more punctual for meetings than people from group Y but we cannot say that (all) members of group X are more punctual than (all) members of group Y. See also **stereotype.**

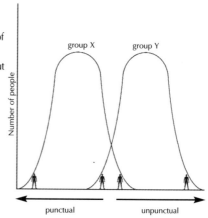

blame (n, v)
/'bleɪm/
blameless (adj)
blame culture (n ph)

If someone blames you for something, they say you are responsible for something bad which happened.

An organisation with a blame culture is one where the employees spend more time avoiding responsibility and finding fault with others than looking after the business. See also **culture.**
➡ attach the blame to
➡ be partly to blame for
➡ get the blame for
➡ lay (the) blame on
➡ share the blame with

body language (n ph)
/'bɒdi 'læŋgwɪdʒ/

Body language is a general term for the physical signals we send to other people. We are aware of some of these but not all, and the non-verbal messages that we send may be understood quite differently by people with different backgrounds from ours. Physical contact (for example, shaking hands), physical distance, facial expressions and gestures (signals we make with our hands) can all vary a great deal from one culture to another. See also **active listening**, **eye contact**.

brainstorm (v, n)
/'breɪnstɔːm/
brainstorming (n)

When a group of people brainstorms ideas, for example to solve a problem, everyone in the group suggests ideas which one person writes on a board without comment. The group can then begin to consider some of the ideas more carefully. Brainstorming is a technique which encourages creative thinking.
➡ a brainstorming session

champion (n, v)
/'tʃæmpɪən/

The job of a champion in an organisation is to bring about change in a particular area, for example diversity, by taking the main responsibility for educating and informing people, communicating the issue to them, and publicising and promoting its importance.
➡ a diversity champion
Champions have more chance of success if they are appointed by senior management and are seen to have the support of and full authority from senior management to work on a particular brief.

collectivism (n)
/kə'lɛktɪvɪzəm/
collectivist (adj)

Hofstede uses this term, in contrast to individualism, to describe how people in some cultures see an important part of their own identity as coming from the group they belong to. The group could be a family, a company, a nation, and so on. People from collectivist cultures may use 'we' more than 'I'. See also **collective**, **individualism**, **Hofstede**, **Trompenaars**.

command and control (n ph, v ph)
/kə'mɑːnd ən kən'trəʊl/

Command and control is a top-down management style which is based on giving instructions to employees lower in the hierarchy and then checking that the instructions have been carried out. See also **hierarchy**.

communication (n ph)
/kəmjuːnɪ'keɪʃən/
communication policy (n ph)

Communication is the exchange of messages with others, normally through speaking or writing. See also **culture**.
A communication policy is a set of guidelines to help people to communicate successfully. In particular, some international companies have rules about which languages can be used for international communication and guidelines for both native and non-native speakers of those languages about how to speak clearly and make themselves understood. See also **statement**, **turn taking**.

intercultural communication (n ph)

Intercultural communication is communication between people from significantly different cultural groups.

paralinguistic communication (n ph)

A study of the paralinguistic features of communication can tell us what people communicate to others, both consciously and unconsciously, through their tone of voice, the speed at which they talk, the pitch of their voice (that is, how high or low the voice is), and so on.
➡ a (complete / total) breakdown in communication, experience
➡ internal / external communication
➡ non-verbal communication

9

Communication and culture

Communication and culture

9

confrontation (n)
/kɒnfrən'teɪʃən/
confrontational (adj)
confront (v)

Confrontations happen when two people or groups of people deliberately argue and become aggressive. A confrontational culture is one where there is a lot of strong argument and disagreement about how best to do things. See also **'them and us' mentality**.
➡ a culture of confrontation / a confrontational culture
Many people prefer a cooperative approach to problem-solving but some believe that confrontation can be creative and productive.

corporate social responsibility (n ph)
/'kɔːpərət 'səʊʃəl rɪspɒnsɪ'bɪliti/

Companies with a sense of corporate social responsibility (CSR) actively recognise their responsibility not only to their shareholders but also to the local community which hosts the organisation and to the wider society within which it operates. Organisations can show this sense in a number of ways including helping local community projects, supporting charities, sponsoring local organisations and individuals, and seconding employees to work on any of these. See also **second, stakeholder**.
➡ exercise corporate social responsibility
➡ implement corporate social responsibility

critical incident (n ph)
/'krɪtɪkəl 'ɪnsɪdənt/

In intercultural communication studies, a critical incident is an event or a situation which can be used as a case study to help people learn and develop their intercultural competence. You can read about critical incidents, watch videos of them, etc.

culture (n)
/'kʌltʃə/
cultural (adj)
corporate culture (n ph)
cultural briefing (n ph)
cultural conditioning (n ph)

A culture is a set of beliefs, values, attitudes and behaviours shared by the members of a group. See also **blame, communication, compensation** (chapter 8).
Corporate culture is the culture of a company.
Cultural briefing teaches you about one particular culture.
Your cultural conditioning shapes your behaviour so that you act in similar ways to other people from the same group.

cultural due diligence (n ph)

Due diligence is a process which is launched when there is a plan for two companies to merge. The aim of cultural due diligence is to see how far the cultures of the two companies can be successfully integrated. In particular, cultural due diligence can involve doing an audit of the human resources management and employee relations policies of the two businesses as a first step towards ensuring the successful cultural fusion of the two.

cultural sensitisation (n ph)

Cultural sensitisation is a form of training which aims to help people to develop their general intercultural competence so that they can manage successfully in a variety of unfamiliar and unpredictable situations.

culture clash (n ph)

There is a culture clash or a clash of cultures when there is a problem because two people with different cultural backgrounds have misunderstood each other.

culture mapping (n ph)

Culture mapping is a process which shows the difference between the values expressed in a company's mission statement and employees' and perhaps other stakeholders' views of the real culture of the organisation. See also **statement, vision**.

culture onion (n ph) The culture onion is a way of visually representing layers of culture. The individual is at the centre and the layers can represent the different cultural influences on the individual – country, region, organisation, profession, and so on.

culture shock (n ph) Culture shock is a negative reaction, which can be physical as well as psychological, to a new culture where the unfamiliarity of the situation makes you feel anxious and insecure.

professional culture (n ph) A professional culture is the set of cultural characteristics shared by a particular profession – for example accountants or architects – or other job group.

➥ a blame culture
➥ a claims culture
➥ a compensation culture
➥ a long hours culture
➥ an organisational culture
➥ experience culture shock

Trompenaars' short definition of culture is: 'the way we do things round here.'

directness (n)
/dɪ'rɛktnəs/
direct (adj)
Directness is the open communication of meaning. In low context cultures, directness is used and valued as a strategy for showing honesty and openness. People who value direct communication may see indirect communicators as unreliable and even dishonest. See also **indirectness**, **low context**.

dress (n, v)
/'drɛs/
Your dress is the clothes you wear. You may dress formally or informally at work and your dress may vary from day to day, depending on who you are going to meet.

dress code (n ph) The organisation's dress code is the set of written or unwritten rules about the clothes its employees should wear at work. See also **code**.

dress down Friday (n ph) When a company has a dress down Friday, its employees wear less formal clothes at work on Fridays.

Mathew Thompson argued in an employment tribunal that the dress code at the Jobcentre in the UK where he was an employee discriminated against men because they were made to wear collars and ties while women had to dress "appropriately and to a similar standard". He won his case.

emotional intelligence (n ph)
/ɪ'məʊʃənəl ɪn'telɪdʒəns/
Your emotional intelligence (or **EQ**, your emotional intelligence quotient) is your ability to understand and control your emotions and to recognise and respond to the emotions and feelings of others. See also **empathy**, **multiple intelligences**, **skills**, **test**.

➥ score high / well on emotional intelligence

Emotional intelligence involves intrapersonal skills (understanding yourself) as well as interpersonal skills (understanding others).

empathy (n)
/'ɛmpəθi/
empathise (v)
empathetic or empathic (adj)
People who feel empathy understand and are sensitive to how other people feel. See also **emotional intelligence**, **skills**.

Communication and culture

ethnocentric (adj)
/ˌɛθnəʊˈsɛntrɪk/
ethnocentricity (n)

Ethnocentric people believe that the cultural groups they belong to are better than other people's. Ethnocentric people tend to misunderstand members of these other groups quite seriously.

eye contact (n ph)
/ˈaɪ kɒntækt/

You make eye contact when you look directly into the eyes of someone else and they look into yours. In some cultures, making eye contact is important for successful communication while in others, it may, for example, show a lack of respect.

face (n)
/ˈfeɪs/

Face is the exterior dignity of a person. When we **save face**, we do and say things in order to keep our external dignity. To **lose face** means to fail to maintain our external dignity. See also **indirectness**.
➡ a face-saving device / strategy

femininity (n)
/fɛmɪˈnɪnɪti/
feminisation (n)

Femininity is a term used by Hofstede to describe cultures where relationships, empathy, life outside work and compromise rather than conflict are valued. The term has been criticised for stereotyping gender. **Feminisation** takes place when the presence and power of women grow within, for example, a profession or an organisation. See also **gender**, **Hofstede**, **masculinity**.
In Britain, a number of professions and sectors are becoming increasingly feminised, including law, the media and human resources.

fog index (n ph)
/ˈfɒg ɪndɛks/

The fog index is a way of measuring how difficult your writing is to understand. For example, the longer the sentences you write, and the longer the words you use, the higher your fog index is. All writers should aim to keep their fog index low.

functional silo
(n ph informal)
/ˈfʌŋkʃənəl ˈsaɪləʊ/

A silo is a large metal cylinder used to store animal feed. A functional silo in an organisation is a department which does not communicate enough with others. See also **function**.

gender (n)
/ˈdʒɛndə/

You have either male or female gender. Your gender has a major influence on your identity. Attitudes to gender vary considerably from one culture to another. See also **mainstreaming**, **sexual orientation**.

gender reassignment (n ph)

Gender reassignment is a medical process which allows transsexual people to alter their bodies to match their gender identity.
The Sex Discrimination Act 1975 (SDA) makes discrimination unlawful on the grounds of sex, and marital status, and gender reassignment in a limited manner.

Hall
/ˈhɔːl/

Edward T. Hall is one of the founders of intercultural communication. His books, notably *The Silent Language* (1997), *Beyond Culture* (1997) and (with Mildred Reed Hall) *Understanding Cultural Differences* (1989) show the importance to culture of space, time and context. See also **high context**, **low context**, **monochronic**, **polychronic**.

hierarchy (n)
/ˈhaɪərɑːki/
hierarchical (adj)

A hierarchical organisation has levels. Employees at higher levels in the organisation give orders and instructions to employees at lower levels. Hierarchical societies have high power distance. See also **command and control**, **organisation**, **power distance**.

high context (n ph)
/ˈhaɪ ˈkɒntɛkst/

In high context cultures, according to Hall, a great deal of information is shared by the members of the group so that this does not need to be communicated explicitly. Outsiders, who do not share the same information, can therefore find it difficult to understand what members of the group are saying. People in high context cultures tend to believe that harmony and the avoidance of conflict are important in social relationships and will therefore avoid communicating too directly, for example, by saying "no". Importance is also given in high context business cultures to building and relying on personal relationships rather than on written contracts. Trompenaars uses the term **diffuse** to describe high context cultures. See also **indirectness**.

Hofstede
/ˈhɒfstɛdə/

Geert Hofstede is a major figure in the field of intercultural communication. In his 1980 book, *Culture's Consequences*, he presented the results of research done for IBM which involved 116,000 individuals from 40 countries. His model for national cultures has four dimensions: power distance, individualism / collectivism, uncertainty avoidance, and masculinity / femininity. His other best-known book is (with G. J. Hofstede) *Cultures and Organizations* (1991). See also **collectivism**, **femininity**, **individualism**, **masculinity**, **power distance**, **uncertainty avoidance**.

house magazine (n ph)
/ˈhaʊs mæɡəˈziːn/

A house magazine is a magazine written for the employees of a company. Also known as **house journal**, **in-house magazine** and **in-house journal**.

indirectness (n)
/ɪndɪˈrɛktnəs/
indirect (adj)

Indirectness is the implicit communication of meaning. In high context cultures, indirectness is used and valued as a strategy for not losing face. People who value indirect communication may see direct communicators as blunt and rude. See also **directness**, **face**, **high context**.

individualism (n)
/ɪndɪˈvɪdjʊəlɪzəm/

Hofstede and Trompenaars use this term, in contrast to collectivism, to describe how people in some cultures see the important part of their own identity as coming from themselves and their immediate family rather than from larger groups. People from individualist cultures may use 'I' more than 'we'. See also **collectivism**, **Hofstede**, **Trompenaars**.

integrate (v)
/ˈɪntəɡreɪt/
integration (n)
integrationist (n)

Integration is the process of becoming part of another group, community or society while keeping an important part of your original identity. See also **assimilation**.

Johari window (n ph)
/dʒəˈhɑːri ˈwɪndəʊ/

The Johari window (the name comes from a combination of the names of its creators, Joseph Luft and Harrington Ingram) offers a visual model for developing self understanding as a basis for cultural learning. In a box divided into four squares or windows, one window is for what I know about myself and what other people know about me; the second is for what other people know about me but which I don't know about myself; the third is for what I know about myself but

9

Communication and culture

Communication and culture

which other people don't know about me; the fourth is for what neither I nor other people know about me. The model reminds us that we can develop better understanding of the beliefs, attitudes and behaviours of others through developing better understanding of ourselves.

Kluckholn and Strodtbeck value orientations (n ph)
/'klʌkhəʊn ən strəʊtbɛk 'vælju: 'ɔːrɪən'teɪʃənz/

The two anthropologists, Florence Kluckhohn and Fred Strodtbeck, have named five key areas or orientations for identifying differences between people and cultures relating to: 1 human nature (seeing people as basically good, a mixture of good and bad, or basically evil); 2 our relationship with nature (submitting to nature, living in harmony with nature, dominating nature); 3 our time orientation (past, present or future); 4 our activity orientation (from being to doing); 5 relational, from the hierarchical to the egalitarian. See also **hierarchy**.

leadership (n)
/'li:dəʃɪp/
lead (v)
leader (n)

Leadership is getting people to perform above their own expectations. One view of leadership (sometimes called **transformational leadership**) emphasises vision and performance while management (sometimes called **transactional leadership**) is about systems and processes. Both are important for the success of an organisation.
➡ leadership behaviour
➡ leadership development
➡ leadership potential, show / display
"When the best leader's work is done, the people say 'We did it ourselves.'" (Lao Tzu)

low context (n ph)
/'ləʊ 'kɒntɛkst/

In low context cultures, according to Hall, a great deal of information is communicated explicitly. People in low context cultures tend to say what they mean, to confront difficulties and problems openly and to expect them to be solved by discussion. Written text plays an important role in low context cultures as do laws, rules and regulations. Low context communicators depend on words rather than on non-verbal signals to communicate meaning, and place emphasis on detail. Trompenaars uses the term **specific** to describe low context cultures. See also **directness**.

masculinity (n)
/mæskjə'lɪnɪti/

Masculinity is a term used by Hofstede to describe cultures where things rather than people, and success, work and conflict rather than consensus are valued. The term has been criticised for stereotyping gender. See also **gender, femininity, Hofstede**.

monochronic (adj)
/mɒnəʊ'krɒnɪk/

People in monochronic cultures tend to do one thing at a time and to respect deadlines. See also **polychronic**.

morale (n)
/mə'rɑːl/

The morale of an organisation is the general level of satisfaction of its workforce.
➡ a high / low level of morale
➡ be bad / good for morale
➡ boost morale

➡ damage morale
➡ rock bottom morale

native speaker
(adj ph, n ph)
/'neɪtɪv 'spiːkə/

Your native language is the first language you learn. A native speaker of, for example, English, is someone whose first language is English. A **non-native speaker** is someone for whom that language is not the first language.

norm (n)
/'nɔːm/
normative (adj)

Norms are the values, attitudes and behaviours which are considered to be most normal by members of a particular cultural group.

notify (v)
/'nəʊtɪfaɪ/
notification (n)

When you notify someone of something, you tell them about something officially.
➡ give (prior) notification of

open door policy (n ph)
/'əʊpən 'dɔː 'pɒlɪsi/

If you have an open door policy towards the people who work for you, you encourage them to discuss with you any problem they may have at any time.

organic (adj)
/ɔː'gænɪk/

An organic organisation, according to John Mole, is one where personal relationships and social hierarchy count for more than functional systems. See also **systematic**.

organisation (n)
/ɔːgənaɪ'zeɪʃən/
organise (v)
organiser (n)
organisational (adj)

An organisation is a group of people – formed into a company, a business, etc. – who work together to achieve a common objective.

boundaryless organisation (n ph)

A boundaryless organisation is one which can adapt very quickly to a changing business environment because it is not held back by rigid hierarchies, geography or cultural inflexibility and other typical brakes on performance.

change organisation (n ph)

A change organisation is one with structures which, and people who are flexible enough to be able to, adapt quickly and frequently to a constantly changing business environment.

flat organisation (n ph)

A flat organisation has few layers or levels. It is the opposite of a hierarchical organisation. See also **hierarchy**.

knowledge organisation (n ph)

Knowledge management is the process of using the knowledge and expertise within an organisation to create value and achieve business goals. Organisations, especially large ones, need knowledge management to create and share knowledge and so use their intellectual capital to add to the growth of the business. Knowledge managers have to identify experts and tell everyone who they are; and encourage all employees to share rather than hide the information they have.

lean organisation (n ph)

A lean organisation employs as few employees as possible.

virtual organisation (n ph)

A virtual organisation is one which does not have a physical identity but exists because its members can communicate using computers, the telephone and so on.

9

Communication and culture

Communication and culture

9

➠ organisational development

➠ organisational change

particularism (n)
/pə'tɪkjələrɪzəm/

In a particularist culture, according to Trompenaars, the particular situation may have a more important influence on people's behaviour and on their relationships than the rules which govern that situation. See also **universalist**.

peach and coconut
(n, n)
/'piːtʃ ən 'kəʊkənʌt/

The peach and coconut model gives us a visual picture of two kinds of culture. In one (the peach, with a thicker soft exterior and a smaller hard interior), the outer public sphere is bigger than the inner private sphere. It can seem easy to make initial contact with peaches but difficult to get to know them really well. In the other (the coconut, with a thinner hard exterior and a bigger soft interior), the outer public sphere is smaller than the inner private sphere. It can seem difficult to make initial contact with a coconut, but – when finally you have been accepted – you may be allowed to enter the private sphere. Peaches and coconuts have different views of social relationships and friendship and it can be difficult for them to understand each other.

polychronic (adj)
/pɒli'krɒnɪk/

People in polychronic cultures are happy to do several things at the same time, tend to be flexible about deadlines, and tend to make a less clear distinction between their working lives and their lives outside work. See also **monochronic**.

power distance (n, n)
/'paʊə 'dɪstəns/

Power distance is a concept developed by Hofstede to explain the differences between national cultures. It refers to the degree to which people in a group accept an unequal distribution of power. In organisations with high power distance, people accept that senior managers have a lot of power. In low power distance cultures, there is a greater distribution of power across the organisation. See also **Hofstede**.

prejudice (n)
/'prɛdʒədɪs/
prejudiced (adj)
prejudicial (adj)

Someone is prejudiced if he or she does not like a group of people with another race, religion, sexual orientation, etc., simply because they are different. See also **ethnocentric**.

➠ racial prejudice

punctual (adj)
/'pʌŋktjʊəl/
punctually (adv)
punctuality (n)

If you are punctual, you arrive on time for meetings and appointments. If you often arrive late for meetings, you are **unpunctual**. Attitudes towards punctuality vary a great deal from one culture to another.

small talk (n ph)
/'smɔːl tɔːk/

Small talk is light conversation. Being good at small talk can be an important communication and intercultural skill, especially when dealing with people from high context cultures who place value on building relationships with the people they do business with. See also **high context**.

sojourner (n)
/'sɒdʒɜːnə/
sojourn (v)

A sojourner is the term used by intercultural specialists for someone who goes to live in another country temporarily. See also **expatriate**.

statement (n)
/'steɪtmənt/

Organisations produce written statements of various kinds to communicate important messages about themselves internally (to employees) and externally (to promote a certain image). These various kinds of statement may sometimes be supported more enthusiastically by the people who wrote them than by other employees. See also **culture, diversity, vision**.

mission statement (n ph)

A mission statement is a written text which tells you where an organisation wants to go or where it wants you to think it is going.

value statement (n)

Your values tell you what is right and wrong and what is important in life. Value statements (or statements of values) claim to tell us what the organisation stands for and what the people in the organisation believe in. In fact they are often better at telling us what some senior managers would like them to believe.

➡ draft a mission / value / vision statement
➡ draw up a mission / value / vision statement
➡ publish a mission statement

stereotype (n, v)
/'stɛrɪəʊtaɪp/
stereotypical (adj)
stereotyping (n)

A stereotype is an over-simplified, untrue or inaccurate view held by one person or group of people about what another different person or group of people is like.

➡ engage in stereotyping
➡ be guilty of stereotyping

suggestion scheme (n)
/sə'dʒɛstʃən 'skiːm/
suggest (v)

When you make a suggestion, you propose to the organisation a way of doing something better. A suggestion scheme is a way of getting employees to suggest improvements in the way things are done.

➡ run a suggestion scheme

The success of suggestion schemes depends on commitment from top managers, decentralised decision-making, good marketing and the use of pilot schemes.

systematic (adj)
/sɪstə'mætɪk/

A systematic organisation, according to John Mole, is one where functional systems count for more than personal relationships and social hierarchy. See also **organic**.

theory X and theory Y (n ph)
/'θɪəri ɛks ən 'θɪəri waɪ/

According to Douglas McGregor, an American management writer, theory X people do not like work and do everything possible to avoid it. People who believe in theory Y think that everyone can find satisfaction in their work if the conditions are right.

Trompenaars
/'trɒmpɛnɑːz/

Fons Trompenaars is the son of a French mother and a Dutch father who has made a life-long study of cultural differences in organisational structure. His work has focused on the interface of corporate and national cultures, particularly on how the successful management of

9

Communication and culture

Communication and culture

cultural difference within organisations can lead to competitive advantage. His dimensions for cultural difference include universalism / particularism, specific / diffuse, neutrality / affectivity, and achievement / ascription. His best-known book (with Charles Hampden-Turner and Alfons Trompenaars) is *Riding the Waves of Culture: Understanding Cultural Diversity in Business*. See also **achievement, ascription, high context, low context, particularism, universalism.**

turn taking (n ph)
/'tɜːn teɪkiŋ/

The way people take turns when talking varies from culture to culture. In some cultures, one person waits until the other person has finished before beginning to talk. In others, there may be a period of silence before another person begins to talk. In others, there may be a lot of interrupting and people talking at the same time. The way people take turns can have an important influence on the way they see each other and also, in intercultural contexts, on how far people can understand what other people are saying.

uncertainty avoidance (n ph)
/ʌn'sɜːtənti ə'vɔɪdəns/

Uncertainty avoidance, according to Hofstede, is the degree to which people feel worried or threatened by the unknown. People in a low uncertainty avoidance culture can live with a lot of uncertainty. People in a high uncertainty avoidance culture try to avoid uncertainty and so like to make plans and like a structured decision-making process in order to identify possible problems before facing them.

universalism (n)
/juːnɪ'vɜːsəlɪzəm/
universalist (adj)

In a universalist culture, according to Trompenaars, rules have a more important influence on people's behaviour and on their relationships than in a particularist culture. See also **particularist**.

vision (n)
/'vɪʒən/
visionary (adj, n)

An organisation's vision is a set of ideas about why it exists, what its people believe in and where it wants to go. Since groups with a strong common purpose are often more successful than groups without, managers in many organisations try to write down what they think the organisation is for in a vision statement. See also **culture, statement.**

Exercises

Exercise 1

Choose a term from the box to complete each sentence (1 – 8).

stereotypes	eye contact	native speakers	body language
mission statement	house magazine	change	dress down Fridays

1   As part of group communication policy, all employees receive a copy of the quarterly _____ which includes news and articles about the company.

2   Communication can be verbal (through language) or non-verbal (including factors such as eye movement and _____).

3   When organisations acquire both national and foreign subsidiaries, training in _____ management helps employees with the process of accepting a new culture.

4   One of the initial difficulties in working with employees of different nationalities and cultures are national _____ which generalise behaviour, appearance and ways of thinking.

5   In some cultures, it is considered polite to keep _____ in a conversation, whereas in others it can be taken as a sign of aggression.

6   Many organisations have adopted _____, meaning that employees may come to work in casual clothes before finishing for the weekend.

7   The working group was composed of several nationalities, some of whom spoke English as a foreign language and some of whom were _____.

8   The company has asked all employees to attend a series of meetings to discuss what the organisation stands for and where it is going so that a special team can then write a corporate _____ .

9

Communication and culture

Communication and culture

9

Exercise 2

Match the terms (1 – 5 and 6 – 10) with their definitions (a – e and f – j).

1	culture shock	a	an audit to establish if an organisation is culturally matched to your own
2	cultural briefing	b	measure the gap between what the mission statement says and what employees really think
3	cultural due diligence	c	when an expatriate employee first arrives in a different cultural environment
4	cultural mapping	d	developing trainees' general competence to interact successfully with people from a variety of different cultures
5	cultural sensitisation	e	studying a particular culture before being sent to work abroad
6	lean organisation	f	a network of employees linked and working via internet and email
7	flat organisation	g	an organisation where cultural, geographical and organisational barriers are made flexible and permeable by easy access to information sharing
8	knowledge organisation	h	an organisation with fewer layers of management
9	virtual organisation	i	an organisation which carries no fat.
10	boundaryless organisation	j	an organisation whose left hand knows what its right hand is doing.

Exercise 3

Match the terms in the box with the headers (1 – 5) in the diagram.

monochronic / polychronic   power distance   individualism / collectivism
transformational / transactional leadership   uncertainty avoidance

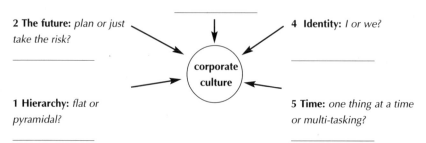

3 Management style:
motivator or bureaucrat?

2 The future: *plan or just take the risk?*

4 Identity: *I or we?*

corporate culture

1 Hierarchy: *flat or pyramidal?*

5 Time: *one thing at a time or multi-tasking?*

Exercise 4

Choose the correct definition (a or b) for each term (1 – 5).

1 Critical incident

a health and safety accident particular to a given culture

b something in training which demonstrates a specific point

2 Turn-taking

a what a person says and when and their respect for others' speech

b the study of how people interact for a given work task

3 Ethnocentric

a a culturally diverse organisation

b a monocultural organisation

4 High context

a a culture which values face and harmony

b a culture which values directness and plain speaking

Exercise 5

Match the terms in the box with the cryptic clues (1 – 4) and then match the terms with their definitions.

fog index	active listening	functional silo	open door policy

1 Large containers for stocking job families? : _____

2 Not shut to enquiries at any time? : _____

3 Difficult list to see on account of thick mist?: _____

4 Did you hear it with a big effort?: _____

a a measure to enable employees communication and access, at all times, to higher management

b a way of analysing written material to see how easy or difficult it is to understand

c when different parts of the organisation don't talk to each other

d intentionally focusing on who you are listening to in order to better understand and return communication

9

Communication and culture

For discussion

1 Should English be the language of international business communication?

2 Do you agree with the claim that the key to success in business is cultural diversity?

3 How do you define culture? What do you think are the cultural factors which have most impact on behaviour?

4 How do people develop intercultural competence? How can they be trained to develop this? How interculturally competent are you?

5 Give your own examples of successful and unsuccessful intercultural communication. What did you learn from these experiences?

Case study

When culture comes under attack

A British managing director was seconded to take charge of a continental European subsidiary recently acquired by his group. His first action was to call a meeting with the directors and to outline the parent company's approach to working together. His main message from the parent company was that things had to change, notably:

- working methods (judged too slow and methodical)
- company logo and colours (judged too old-fashioned)
- introducing the notion of empowerment (present system judged too hierarchical)
- working hours (executives staying too long on the premises are not efficient)
- relations with employee representatives (judged too conflictual)

His speech and subsequent outlining of the changes was met with little reaction (although he had hoped it would give rise to creative debate). A week later, during another board meeting, he repeated, more energetically, the key message that in order to progress, the subsidiary had to change its ways and adapt to a more modern approach. While the directors present did not disagree, they showed no over-enthusiasm for change.

A month later, he felt that the atmosphere in the subsidiary had become morose, not only among directors but among employees at all levels. His weekly tour of the premises was met with polite coldness and he became frustrated when his enthusiasm to get started with making the changes and improvements was met with passive resistance and what he considered to be a total disregard for keeping to schedule. He was also surprised that nobody in the plant had responded to his efforts to socialize. (In his last job, as head of a US subsidiary, he had been invited to employees' homes for dinner and had participated in numerous social events). A further point was that, despite his efforts at explaining and encouraging empowerment and delegation of decision-making, directors and managers still came to his office asking for advice in a way which he understood to be asking for direct orders. For him, they hadn't understood that he was offering them his trust in their skills and a chance to show him they were up to the job. After two months, there was still no change and his superiors from the parent company began to demand explanations. The message from headquarters was: be tougher and get results. When he tried to implement a new process in working methods, moving several teams to a different location, employees called for a strike. Relations became extremely tense and after another month abroad, the managing director was eventually repatriated.

You are his replacement. Consider:

- What can you learn from your predecessor's experience?
- How will you approach the subsidiary's directors? the employees?
- How and what can you learn about the subsidiary's set of beliefs and values?
- What are your views on headquarters' wishes to replace the subsidiary's beliefs and values with their own?
- How is 'changing somebody's culture' different from 'changing somebody's vision'?
- What can you do to ensure that you and your hosts understand each other better?
- How can the headquarters' list of changes be communicated in a more positive manner?

Appendices

Appendix 1

Abbreviations in human resources: general

AFL-CIO	American Federation of Labor – Congress of Industrial Organisations
AIDS	Acquired Immune Deficiency Syndrome
BO	body odour (see chapter 6)
BPR	business process re-engineering (see chapter 2)
C & B	compensation and benefits (see chapter 4)
CBT	competency-based pay (see chapter 4)
CCTV	closed circuit television
CPD	continuing professional development
CPIS	computerised personnel information system
CSOP	company share option plan (see share option, chapter 4)
CSR	corporate social responsibility (see chapter 9)
CV	curriculum vitae (see chapter 3)
DDP	discipline and dismissal procedure (see discipline, chapter 7 and dismiss, chapter 2)
DSE	display screen equipment (see VDU, chapter 6)
EAP	employee assistance programme (see chapter 6)
EI	emotional intelligence (see chapter 9)
EQ	emotional (intelligence) quotient (see chapter 9)
ESOP	employee share ownership plan (see share plan, chapter 4)
ETUC	European Trade Union Confederation (see trade union, chapter 7)
EU	European Union
EWC	European Works Council (see works council, chapter 7)
HCM	human capital management (see human capital, chapter 2)
HR	human resources (see chapter 2)
HRD	human resources development (see human resources, chapter 2)
	human resources director
HRM	human resources management
ICD	(European Union) Information And Consultation Directive (see directive, chapter 8)
ICFTU	International Confederation of Free Trade Unions (see trade union, chapter 7)
ILA	individual learning account (see learning, chapter 5)
ILO	International Labour Organisation
IR	industrial relations (see chapter 7)
LIFO	last in, first out (see chapter 7)
MBWA	management by walking around
MD	management development (see development, chapter 6)
NLP	neurolinguistic programming (see chapter 5)
NMW	national minimum wage (see wage, chapter 4)
OHP	occupational health practitioner (see occupational, chapter 6)
OHU	occupational health unit (see occupational, chapter 6)
PAQ	position analysis questionnaire (see chapter 2)
PBR	payment by results (see pay, chapter 4)
PRP	performance-related pay / profit-related pay (see chapter 4)
PTSD	post-traumatic stress disorder (see stress, chapter 6)

Appendices

R&R	ranking and rating (see chapter 5)
RSI	repetitive strain injury (see chapter 6)
SMART	specific, measurable, agreed, realistic, time-bound (see chapter 5)
SME	small or medium-sized enterprise
SMP	statutory maternity pay (see maternity, chapter 2)
TBT	technology-based training (see training, chapter 5)
TCN	third country national (see chapter 2)
VAK	visual, auditory and kinesthetic (see chapter 5)
VDU	visual display unit (see chapter 6)

Abbreviations in human resources: British

ACAS	Advisory, Conciliation and Arbitration Service
CBI	Confederation of British Industry (the main employers' organisation)
CIPD	Chartered Institute of Personnel and Development
CCT	compulsory competitive tendering
COSHH	control of substances hazardous to health
CRE	Commission for Racial Equality
EAP	Employment Appeal Tribunal
EOC	Equal Opportunities Commission
EMI	enterprise management incentive
ERA	Employment Rights Act
HSE	Health and Safety Executive
NICs	National Insurance contributions
NVQ	National Vocational Qualification
PAYE	Pay As You Earn
SAYE	Save As You Earn
SDA	Sex Discrimination Act
SIP	share incentive plan
TGIF	Thank God it's Friday
TUC	Trades Union Congress
TUPE	Transfer of Undertakings (Protection of Employment)

Appendices

Appendix 2

Job titles in human resources

This list aims to show the range of activities which HR professionals follow, and to help HR professionals from non-English-speaking countries to find an English translation of their own job title with which they feel comfortable. The list is drawn from the British specialist press over a short period and is a reflection of British practice only. No attempt has been made to be selective.

HR job titles in the UK can vary between the clear and informative on the one hand, and the obscure and even bizarre on the other. If you are looking for a translation into English for what you do, please choose something simple.

Note that 'adviser' can also be spelt 'advisor'.

Appendices

Area Human Resources Manager
Assistant Director of Human Resource
   Management
Assistant Director of Human Resources
Assistant Director of Human Resources
   Operations
Assistant Director of Resources
Assistant Human Resources Officer
Assistant Personnel Officer
Attendance Improvement Coordinator
Attendance Personnel Officer

Business Training Manager

Change and Development Manager
Chief Medical Officer
Chief Personnel Officer
Company Doctor
Compensation Advisor
Compensation Analyst
Compensation and Benefits Administrator
Compensation and Benefits Adviser
Compensation and Benefits Analyst
Compensation and Benefits Manager
Compensation and Benefits Officer
Compensation and Benefits Specialist
Compensation, Benefits and Payroll Manager
Compensation Manager

Deputy Director of Human Resources
Deputy Director of Personnel
Deputy Director, Policy and Performance
Deputy Personnel Manager
Development and Training Advisor

Development and Training Manager
Director of Company Career Development
Director of Company Pensions
Director of Human Resources
Director of Human Resources and
   Communications
Director of Human Resources and
   Organisational Development
Director of Personnel
Director of Training and Development
Diversity Adviser in Human Resources
Diversity Coordinator
Diversity and Recruitment Advisor
Divisional Human Resources Manager

Employee Development Manager
Employee Relations Consultant
Employee Relations Manager
Employee Resourcing Manager
Employee Reward Adviser
Employment Development Advisor
Employment Law Consultant
Employment Relations Adviser
Employment Relations Executive
Employment Relations Officer
Equalities Manager
Equal Opportunities Officer
Equal Opportunities Manager
Executive Director of Human Resources and
   Corporate Development
Expatriation Co-ordinator

Graduate Recruitment Assistant
Graduate Recruitment Officer

Group Head of Training and Development
Group Human Resources Manager
Group Human Resources Officer
Group Organisation and Development Manager

Head of Change Management and Work
  Structures
Head of Colleague Relations
Head of Employee Relations
Head of Employment Strategy
Head of Human Resource Operations
Head of Human Resources
Head of Human Resources Operations
Head of Human Resources and Organisational
  Development
Head of Human Resources Service Centre
Head of Learning and Development
Head of Organisational Development and
  Improvement
Head of People Services
Head of Personnel Administration
Head of Personnel and Organisational
  Development
Head of Personnel and Training
Head of Personnel Services
Head of Resource Planning and Services
Head of Resourcing
Head of Resourcing and Diversity
Head of Recruitment and Resourcing
Head of Reward and Information
Head of Staffing
Head of Training and Development
Head of Workforce Planning and Development
Health and Safety Inspector
Human Resource Advisor
Human Resource Officer
Human Resources Administration Officer
Human Resources Administrator
Human Resources Advisor
Human Resources Advisor (Training)
Human Resources and Change Director
Human Resources and Development Manager
Human Resources Assistant
Human Resources Business Partner
Human Resources Client Manager
Human Resources Consultant
Human Resources Director
Human Resources Executive
Human Resources Expert

Human Resources Generalist
Human Resources Manager
Human Resources Manager – Culture Change
  and Diversity
Human Resources Manager - International
  Deployment
Human Resources Manager – Operational
Human Resources Manager – Reward and
  Policy
Human Resources Modernisation Manager
Human Resources Operations Manager
Human Resources Operations Officer
Human Resources Officer
Human Resources Officer (Training)
Human Resources Outsource Relationship
  Leader
Human Resources Policy Adviser
Human Resources Policy Development Manager
Human Resources Policy and Equalities
  Manager
Human Resources Policy and Projects Advisor
Human Resources Projects Manager
Human Resources Project Officer
Human Resources Services Manager
Human Resources Strategy Director
Human Resources Strategy and Projects
  Manager
Human Resources Strategy Researcher
Human Resources Support Officer

Interim Human Resources Advisor
Interim Human Resources Consultant
Interim Human Resources Manager
Interim Human Resources Specialist
International Human Resources Manager

Job Analyst
Job Evaluation Manager

Learning and Development Advisor
Learning and Development Manager
Learning and development Director
Learning and Development Specialist
Learning Team Leader

Management Development and Training
  Manager
Management Development Officer
Management Trainer

Appendices

Management Training Officer
Management Training Scheme Co-ordinator
Manpower and Remuneration Officer
Manpower Profiling Officer
Monitoring Manager

National Training Manager

Occupational Psychologist
Operational Training Manager
Organisation Development Manager
Organisational Development Manager
Organisational Development and Learning
    Consultant
Organisational Development and Learning
    Manager

Pay and Benefits Manager
Pay Strategy Manager
Payroll Administrator
Payroll Manager
People Manager
People and Facilities Director
Pensions Manager
Personnel Administration Officer
Personnel Advisor
Personnel and Recruitment Officer
Personnel and Training Manager
Personnel and Training Officer
Personnel Assistant
Personnel Controller
Personnel Director
Personnel Manager
Personnel Officer
Personnel Officer - Recruitment
Personnel Projects Officer
Policy and Equality Personnel Officer
Principal HR Adviser
Principal Personnel Officer
Professional Development Manager

Recruitment and Selection Manager
Recruitment and Training Officer
Recruitment Consultant
Recruitment Services Consultant
Recruitment Manager
Recruitment Officer
Recruitment Specialist
Regional Human Resources Manager

Relocation Adviser
Remuneration and Benefits Analyst
Resource Manager
Resourcing Officer
Resourcing Manager
Reward Manager

Safety Officer
Senior Assistant Personnel Officer
Senior Nurse
Senior Human Resources Advisor, Recruitment
    and Selection
Senior Human Resources Consultant
Senior Personnel Advisor
Senior Personnel Advisor – Equality and
    Diversity
Senior Personnel Officer
Senior Rewards and Benefits Consultant
Senior Training Officer
Staff and Organisation Development Manager
Staff Development Manager
Staff Trainer
Strategic Personnel Manager

Talent Specialist
Trainer
Training Administrator
Training and Development Co-ordinator
Training and Development Consultant
Training and Development Design Manager
Training and Development Advisor
Training and Development Manager
Training and Development Officer
Training Co-ordinator
Training Commissioner
Training Consultant
Training Evaluation and Quality Assurance
    Officer
Training Executive
Training Manager
Training Manager (Management Development)
Training Officer

Vocational Training Officer

Welfare Officer
Workforce and Human Resources Systems
    Planner

Appendix 3

Questions for recruitment interviews

These questions have all been suggested by HR practitioners following courses with York Associates and are given as reference for interviewers. They embrace a range of interview styles and philosophies.

Starting up
Did you have any problems finding us?
Did you get my letter?
Have you brought all your papers with you?

Background and general
Could you tell me / start by telling me something about yourself? / Tell me something about yourself. / Tell me something about your career so far.
What sort of person are you? What sort of person are you socially?
How do other people see you?

Professional experience
What made you become a . . . ? / Why did you become a . . . ?
Why did you choose the . . . business? / How did you get into . . . ?
What was your most important contribution to . . . ?
What was your biggest success while you were at . . . ? / Tell me about your best / worst professional experience so far.
What was your most important contribution to . . . ?
Why did you leave your last job? / Why do you want to leave your current job?
Do you have any overseas experience? / Do you have any experience of living or working abroad?
How did your first / last job influence your career?
What do you think is your most important achievement?
What did you learn while you were working for company X?
What training have you had for this job?
Which of your jobs has given you the greatest satisfaction?
Why are you considering a move from your present company?
Why are you dissatisfied with your present job?
Why are you leaving your current job?
Why were you made redundant?
Why were you out of work for so long?

Capacities
What can you contribute to this company? / What contribution do you think you could make to . . .?
Why do you think we should give you this job?
How would you add value to our company?
What are you good at? / What are you not so good at?
What do you think your best / strongest qualities are? What are your main strengths?
What are your main weaknesses? / weak points?
Give me three adjectives which describe you particularly well.
Tell me three positive things / three negative things about yourself.
What decisions do you find difficult / easy to take?
Are you flexible? / Would you describe yourself as a flexible person?

Would you describe yourself as . . . ?
How many foreign languages do you speak?
How good is your German / Japanese / . . . ?
How would your boss describe your work?
If we asked for a reference, what would it say about you?
What makes you think you can be successful with us?

Critical incidents

Tell me about something you think you did particularly well last year? / What has been your greatest professional or personal success during the past year?
Give me an example of a situation where one of your weaknesses created problems for your organisation.
Describe a difficult situation you've experienced and what you did about it.
Describe a time when you felt things were not going too well.
Describe a time when you felt you were doing well.
Tell me about a high-risk decision you have had to take.
Give me an example of serious conflict which you have experienced.
Tell me about a success / failure you have experienced.
When were you most happy at work?

Motives and motivation

What do you know about our company?
Why have you applied for this job? / What made you apply for this job?
Why do you want to work for this company / for us?
Why should we offer you this job?
What motivates you? / What makes you tick?
What sets you alight? / What really excites you in your professional life?

Money

How much do you expect to earn in your next job? / What benefits do you expect from your next job?
Given the achievements described in your application, why is your salary so low?

Personal preferences and working style

How would you approach this job?
What's your ideal job?
What do you enjoy most about your present job?
Do you prefer to work in a team or on your own?
Do you prefer to work in an open plan office or to have an office of your own?
Are you free to travel?
Are you prepared to work abroad?
What kind of role do you usually play in teams?
What characteristics in other people disturb you most?
How do you get things done?
How do you manage your day?
How do your respond to stress?
What kind of working environment suits you best?

Ambitions and the future

How do you see this job developing?

How does this job fit in with your career plan?
How long do you plan to stay with us?
Where do you hope to be . . . . / What do you hope to be doing in five years' time?
What is your view / vision of the future of the . . . business?
Where are you heading?

Management style and philosophy
What skills do you need to be a . . . ?
What is your definition of a challenge? / What do you see as a real challenge?
What, in your opinion, are the most important shared values for a successful business organisation?
How do you get the best out of people? / How do you manage your staff?
How could your boss improve his / her management of you?
How do you typically approach a new project?
If you could change your current job / company in any way, what would you do?
In your view, what are the major challenges / opportunities facing this company?
What do you look for in a manager? / in a subordinate?
What's your definition of a challenge?

Personal
What do other people think of you?
Is your family happy with the (career) choices you have made so far?
What do you do in your spare time? / How do you spend your free time?
Do you think you have a good balance between your personal and your professional life?
How have you changed over the last five years?
If you did not have to work, what would you do?
What are you reading at the moment?
When do you plan to retire? What will you do?
How important is your work to you?
What do you miss most about your work when you're on holiday?

General applications
I have another question.
You talked about . . . / You mentioned . . .
Could you tell us a bit more about . . . . ? / Could you elaborate on . . . ?
Have you ever . . . ?
What in your opinion is . . . ?
How often do you . . . ?
How much time do you spend on . . . ?
What skills do you need to be a . . . ?
How did you deal with . . . ?
What do you understand by . . . ?
Do you have any questions?
How does the job sound to you?
Is there anything more you'd like to ask us?

Practical details / Finishing off
How much notice do you have to give in your present job?
You should hear from us in the next few days / week / . . .
Thank you for coming.
When could you start?

Appendices

Appendix 4

Describing people

More and more people managers have to recruit and appraise people internationally and this usually involves describing them to colleagues. These adjectives can all be used to describe people.

Appendices

able	confrontational	enquiring
adaptable	conscientious	entrepreneurial
aggressive	consensual	even-tempered
ambitious	conservative	exceptional
analytical	considerate	excitable
approachable	consistent	experienced
argumentative	conventional	extrovert
arrogant	convincing	
artistic	courageous	fit
assertive	courteous	flexible
at ease	creative	focussed
autonomous	critical	formal
awkward	cultured	forward-looking
	curious	friendly
backward-looking		funny
bad-tempered	decisive	
blunt	demanding	gentle
boring	dependable	gifted
bossy	detached	good-humoured
brave	determined	good-tempered
bright	difficult	gregarious
bureaucratic	diplomatic	
business-minded	direct	hard
	discourteous	hard-working
calm	dishonest	healthy
capable	distant	helpful
careful	down-to-earth	highly qualified
casual	driven	honest
casually dressed	dull	humorous
cautious	dynamic	humourless
chaotic		
charismatic	easy-going	ill-at-ease
cheerful	eccentric	illogical
clever	effective	imaginative
cold	efficient	immature
colourful	egotistical	impatient
committed	emotional	incompetent
competent	emotionally neutral	independent
competitive	empathetic	inefficient
confident	energetic	inexperienced

inflexible
influential
informal
innovative
inquisitive
insecure
insensitive
insincere
inspirational
intellectual
intelligent
intense
interesting
intolerant
introvert
involved
irresponsible
irritable

kind

lacking in ambition /
    determination / …
laid back
lazy
liberal
logical
loyal

methodical
moderate
modest
motivated

narrow-minded
neat
negative
nervous
nice

obstinate
open, open-minded
optimistic (about …)
organised
original
orthodox
outgoing
outstanding

over-ambitious
over-sensitive
overworked

passionate (about …)
patient
people-focused / people-
    oriented
persevering
persuasive
pessimistic (about …)
pig-headed
plain-speaking
pleasant
polite
pompous
popular
positive
predictable
prejudiced (against …)
proactive
punctual
pushy

quiet

reactionary
reasonable
reckless
relaxed
reliable
reserved
resilient
responsible
results-focused / results-
    oriented
rigid
rude

sad
self-assured
self-confident
self-conscious
self-important
sensible
sensitive
serious
shabby, shabbily-dressed

sharp
shrewd
shy
sincere
skilled (in …)
smart
smartly dressed
sociable
soft
softly spoken
straight
strange
stressed
strong
stubborn
stupid
successful
supportive
sympathetic
systematic

tactful
talented
talkative
tenacious
tense
thick-skinned
thin-skinned
thorough
tidy
timid
tolerant
touchy
touchy-feely
tough
tough-minded
traditional
trusting
trustworthy

unconventional
unconvincing
uncritical
undemanding
understanding
undiplomatic
unfriendly
unhelpful

Appendices

unorthodox
unpredictable
unreliable
unsociable
untidy
untrustworthy

vulnerable

warm
weak
weak-willed
well-balanced
well-dressed

well-mannered
well-qualified
well-rounded
wise
witty

Appendix 5

Business English verb + noun collocations

This is a list of verbs which are useful in general professional communication, plus some of the nouns which often go with them. These can form bridges between the specific words and phrases in this book and the complete sentences people managers use in business communication.

Accept: ~ criticism of, ~ a decision, ~ an offer, ~ the possibility that
Acknowledge: ~ receipt of
Achieve: ~ an aim, ~ a breakthrough, ~ growth, ~ an objective, ~ progress, ~ a result, ~ a target, ~ little
Acquire: ~ expertise, ~ a reputation for
Add: ~ value to
Address: ~ an issue, ~ a problem, ~ a meeting, ~ a group on
Adjust: ~ a target
Adopt: ~ an approach, ~ a formula, ~ a plan, ~ a policy, ~ a programme, ~ a proposal, ~ a practice, ~ a regulation, ~ a resolution, ~ a scheme, ~ a suggestion, ~ tactics
Agree on: ~ a plan, ~ a way to proceed
Agree to: ~ a demand, ~ a plan, ~ a proposal
Allocate: ~ resources to
Allow for: ~ a delay
Alter: ~ a decision
Analyse: ~ the causes of, ~ data, ~ information, ~ a problem, ~ a situation. ~ a trend
Announce: ~ a decision, ~ a result, ~ a new strategy
Apologise for: ~ a delay, ~ an inconvenience
Apply: ~ pressure to, ~ a regulation, ~ a rule
Appreciate: ~ someone's efforts, ~ someone's work
Approve: ~ a decision, ~ a plan, ~ a recommendation, ~ a scheme
Argue: ~ a case for, ~ in favour of
Arrange: ~ a meeting
Arrive at: ~ an agreement, ~ a compromise, ~ a deal, ~ a decision
Ask for: ~ an estimate, ~ further information about, ~ more details of, ~ permission to
Assess: ~ a situation, ~ an applicant
Assemble: ~ a team
Attend: ~ a meeting
Attract: ~ attention, ~ talent
Authorise: ~ expenditure, ~ payment
Avoid: ~ responsibility

Back: ~ a plan, ~ a policy, ~ a proposal, ~ a project
Base: ~ an argument on, ~ an opinion on
Beat: ~ the competition
Block: ~ change, ~ a deal, ~ a plan, ~ progress, ~ a proposal
Boost: ~ confidence, ~ morale, ~ production, ~ productivity, ~ revenues, ~ sales
Break down: ~ figures (into)
Break up: ~ a business
Bring about: ~ change, ~ a confrontation, ~ an improvement, ~ an increase

Bring down: ~ a price
Bring in: ~ (new) business, ~ outside expertise
Bring up: ~ a problem, ~ a subject
Build (up): ~ a business, ~ confidence, ~ a partnership, ~ a team
Buy in: ~ outside expertise / help

Call for: ~ a change
Cancel: ~ a meeting, ~ a project
Carry out: ~ an agreement, ~ an analysis of, ~ an assignment, ~ an audit, ~ a decision, ~ duties, ~ a
  function, ~ an inspection, ~ an instruction, ~ a plan, ~ a programme, ~ a project, ~ a
  recommendation, ~ a review, ~ a (market) survey, ~ a task, ~ research
Centralise: ~ authority, ~ the decision-making process
Chair: ~ a meeting
Change: ~ the culture, ~ direction, ~ an image, ~ a procedure, initiate ~, make a ~
Charge: ~ extra for, ~ expenses to
Chase: ~ a late payment, ~ an outstanding invoice, ~ a slow payer
Check: ~ quality
Choose: ~ the best option
Clarify: ~ a point, ~ a detail
Clear: ~ a debt
Close: ~ a deal, ~ a meeting, ~ a sale
Collaborate on: ~ a project
Collect: ~ data, ~ information
Combine: ~ business with pleasure
Come up with: ~ an idea, ~ a proposal, ~ a solution
Commission: ~ a report, ~ a survey
Commit oneself to: ~ a course of action, ~ a decision, ~ a policy
Complete: ~ a deal, ~ a form, ~ a phase, ~ a project, ~ a questionnaire, ~ a stage, ~ a task, ~ work
  on
Concentrate on: ~ the details, ~ the essentials, ~ the main issue(s)
Conduct: ~ business, ~ a correspondence with, ~ an interview, ~ a meeting, ~ talks with
Confirm: ~ an appointment
Consider: ~ a proposal
Consult: ~ a colleague
Consume: ~ energy
Construct: ~ a framework, ~ a questionnaire
Continue: ~ a process
Contribute: ~ to a discussion
Control: ~ costs, ~ expenditure, ~ quality, ~ spending
Cost: ~ a project
Cover: ~ the cost of
Cut: ~ costs, ~ jobs, ~ a price, ~ the workforce

Damage: ~ relations with, ~ sales, ~ a reputation
Deal with: ~ a complaint, ~ the consequences of, ~ a customer, ~ a (difficult) question, ~ an
  emergency, ~ a problem, ~ a situation
Decide on: ~ an approach, ~ a course / plan of action, ~ a policy, ~ a strategy
Decline: ~ an invitation, ~ an offer

Defeat: ~ a proposal
Defend: ~ an opinion, a position, ~ a policy, ~ a proposal, ~ a colleague
Define: ~ a course of action, ~ a policy, ~ a problem, ~ a procedure, ~ a role
Delay: ~ (the) implementation of, ~ the introduction of, ~ payment
Delegate: ~ responsibility for, ~ authority
Deliver: ~ a product, ~ an order, ~ a programme, ~ results, ~ goods
Demand: ~ payment
Depart: ~ from the agenda
Destroy: ~ confidence in
Develop: ~ an ability, ~ a capacity, ~ a competence, ~ a concept, ~ a partnership with, ~ a process, ~ a (new) product, ~ a project, ~ relations with, ~ resources, ~ a skill, ~ staff, ~ a structure, ~ a team
Devise: ~ a scheme
Direct: ~ operations
Discover: ~ an error / a mistake
Display: ~ enthusiasm for
Diversify: ~ into new areas
Divide: ~ a presentation into, ~ a task into
Do: ~ business with, ~ a deal, ~ a job, ~ a course, ~ research into
Downgrade: ~ the status of
Draft: ~ a contract, ~ a letter, ~ a reply, ~ a report, a proposal
Draw: ~ a conclusion from
Draw up: ~ an agenda, ~ a contract, ~ guidelines, ~ a plan, ~ a proposal / a set of proposals, ~ regulations, ~ a scheme
Drop: ~ a proposal, ~ a plan, ~ an idea
Duplicate: ~ effort

Earn: ~ a holiday, ~ money
Eliminate: ~ an option, ~ waste
Enclose: ~ details of, ~ information about
Endorse: ~ a recommendation
Enforce: ~ a rule, ~ a regulation, ~ a law
Enjoy: ~ an opportunity to, ~ (good) relations with, ~ a (good) reputation, ~ success, ~ support
Enter: ~ a (new) market
Enter into: ~ an agreement with, ~ discussions with, ~ a partnership with, ~ talks with
Entertain: ~ a client, ~ a visitor, ~ the possibility that
Equip: ~ someone with the skills to
Establish: ~ communication with, ~ contact with, ~ an identity, ~ a precedent, ~ (good) relations with / a (good business) relationship with, ~ a system for, ~ a timetable for
Estimate: ~ the cost of, ~ the time it will take to
Evaluate: ~ the success of
Examine: ~ a case, ~ a problem, ~ a situation
Exceed: ~ a budget, ~ your authority to
Exchange: ~ ideas about
Execute: ~ a policy, ~ a plan, ~ a strategy
Exercise: ~ authority over, ~ control over, ~ discipline, ~ influence over, ~ leadership
Exhibit: ~ at a conference, ~ at a trade fair
Expand: ~ operations

Experience: ~ a delay, ~ difficulties in, ~ a setback
Explain: ~ the situation to
Express: ~ a desire to, ~ an interest in, ~ an opinion about, ~ a wish to
Extend: ~ a deadline, ~ a (warm) welcome to
Extract: ~ information from

Face: ~ a challenge, ~ competition from, ~ a delay, ~ a difficult situation, ~ difficulties
Fail: ~ to meet a deadline, ~ to reach a target, ~ a test / an examination
Favour: ~ one alternative, ~ a course of action
Feel: ~ a (strong sense of) commitment to, ~ concern for
Fill in: ~ a form
Finalise: ~ the details of
Finance: ~ a project
Find: ~ an answer to a problem, ~ a job, ~ a solution to a problem, ~ a way to
Fix: ~ a deadline, ~ a meeting, ~ a price, ~ a target
Focus on: ~ the details, ~ the essentials, ~ the main issue(s), ~ the main problem
Follow: ~ a course, ~ instructions, ~ a programme, ~ orders
Force: ~ a decision
Forecast: ~ a result, ~ sales
Form: ~ a (good business) relationship with, ~ an opinion
Formulate: ~ a(n action) plan
Forward: ~ a message / an email to
Freeze: ~ spending on
Fulfil: ~ a commitment to, ~ an obligation to, ~ expectations
Function: ~ effectively
Fund: ~ research into, ~ a project

Gain: ~ experience of, ~ a good reputation, ~ recognition, ~ an advantage
Gather: ~ data, ~ information about
Generate: ~ sales, ~ growth
Get: ~ approval for, ~ compensation for / to, ~ a job, ~ permission for / to, ~ results
Give: ~ an assurance that / to, ~ details of, ~ feedback, ~ permission to
Go into: ~ production
Go over: ~ budget
Grant: ~ permission to
Greet: ~ a visitor
Guarantee: ~ a level of service, ~ quality, ~ satisfaction, ~ success

Handle: ~ a problem, ~ a sensitive issue, ~ a (difficult) situation, ~ a complaint
Have: ~ a meeting
Hold: ~ an interview, ~ a meeting, ~ the line, ~ talks with

Identify: ~ a problem
Implement: ~ a decision, ~ a directive, ~ a plan, ~ a policy, ~ a programme, ~ a project, ~ a strategy, ~ a resolution
Impose: ~ a solution, ~ restrictions on
Impress: ~ an audience, ~ a client
Improve: ~ communication(s), ~ an image, ~ performance, ~ productivity, ~ quality, ~ service

Increase: ~ efficiency, ~ market share, ~ output, ~ pressure on, ~ prices, ~ productivity, ~ sales, ~ (client) satisfaction
Incur: ~ a penalty
Influence: ~ a decision
Inherit: ~ a problem
Integrate: ~ a new colleague
Interpret: ~ the figures, ~ the findings
Introduce: ~ changes
Invent: ~ a reason
Invest in: ~ new equipment, ~ training
Investigate: ~ a problem, ~ a failure
Involve: ~ (more) people in
Issue: ~ a statement

Join: ~ a company, ~ a department
Judge: ~ a situation
Justify: ~ one's actions, ~ a decision

Keep: ~ a record of
Keep up: ~ the good work
Keep up with: ~ developments
Kick off: ~ a meeting, ~ a project

Lack: ~ the resources to, ~ experience
Launch: ~ a campaign, ~ a new initiative, ~ a product
Lead: ~ a discussion, ~ a project, ~ a team
Leave: ~ a message for
Lend: ~ support to
Liaise with: ~ a colleague, ~ an opposite number
Lift: ~ morale
Limit: ~ the damage
Look forward to: ~ hearing from you
Lose: ~ direction, ~ control
Lower: ~ expectations

Maintain: ~ a balance, ~ communication with, ~ a connection with, ~ contact with, ~ discipline, ~ an image, ~ good relations with, ~ one's position, ~ pressure on, ~ quality
Make: ~ an appointment, ~ arrangements for, ~ changes, ~ a claim, ~ a complaint, ~ a concession, ~ a decision, ~ a forecast, ~ an inspection, ~ a loss, ~ a mistake, ~ money, ~ an offer, ~ a payment, ~ a point, ~ a product, ~ progress, ~ a profit, ~ a proposal, ~ a suggestion
Manage: ~ people, ~ results, ~ time, ~ yourself
Maximise: ~ effectiveness
Measure: ~ results, ~ the impact of, ~ progress
Meet: ~ a challenge, ~ a commitment, ~ a deadline, ~ (customers') expectations, ~ (customers') needs, ~ a target
Minimise: ~ a loss
Mismanage: ~ a situation, ~ a project
Miss: ~ a deadline, ~ a target

Monitor: ~ an activity, ~ performance, ~ progress, ~ a situation, ~ a scheme, ~ a system
Move: ~ an appointment

Object to: ~ proposals to
Obtain: ~ an apology
Observe: ~ a rule
Obtain: ~ approval for, ~ a benefit, ~ permission for / to, ~ support
Occupy: ~ the position of, ~ the post of
Offer: ~ assistance / help in / to, ~ compensation for / to, ~ a discount
Open: ~ a meeting
Oppose: ~ a plan, ~ a proposal
Organise: ~ a conference, ~ an exhibition, ~ a meeting, ~ a seminar, ~ a trade fair
Outdo: ~ the competition
Overestimate: ~ the costs

Pay: ~ a debt, ~ an invoice, ~ a visit to
Penetrate: ~ a new market
Perform: ~ a task
Pick: ~ the best person for the job, ~ a winner
Play: ~ a role
Postpone: ~ a meeting
Predict: ~ failure, ~ success
Prepare: ~ for a meeting
Present: ~ a proposal, ~ figures
Process: ~ data, ~ information, ~ input
Promote: ~ an idea, ~ a product
Provide: ~ an estimate, ~ feedback on, ~ a guarantee, ~ help with, ~ support
Publicise: ~ an event
Publish: ~ details of
Put: ~ pressure on
Put forward: ~ a plan, ~ a proposal, ~ a project, ~ a resolution, ~ a solution
Put together: ~ a team

Query: ~ an invoice
Question: ~ a decision

Raise: ~ (the level of) awareness of, ~ an issue, ~ a point (in a meeting), ~ a question, ~ the energy
    level of, ~ expectations, ~ the level of motivation of, ~ prices
Rate: ~ a course, ~ a performance
Reach: ~ an agreement, ~ a compromise, ~ a decision, ~ a deal, ~ a goal, ~ a target
React to: ~ a demand for, ~ a request for, ~ the news that
Recall: ~ faulty goods
Receive: ~ a payment, ~ recognition for
Recommend: ~ a course of action
Recover: ~ a debt
Redraft: ~ a proposal, ~ a contract, ~ a letter
Reduce: ~ costs, ~ overheads, ~ the rate of absenteeism, ~ the size of the workforce
Refer to: ~ the minutes of the last meeting

Refund: ~ the price of
Reject: ~ a proposal, ~ a project
Remove: ~ a barrier / an obstacle (to progress)
Reorganise: ~ a company, ~ department
Report on: ~ progress
Request: ~ information about, ~ a meeting with
Rescue: ~ a project
Reserve: ~ the right to
Resist: ~ pressure from
Resolve: ~ conflict, ~ a dispute, ~ a problem
Respect: ~ someone's opinion, ~ someone's point of view, ~ a deadline
Restrict: ~ access to
Restructure: ~ a department, ~ an organisation
Retain: ~ control over
Review: ~ a situation
Revise: ~ a forecast, ~ estimates
Run: ~ a company, ~ a business, ~ a course, ~ an operation, ~ an organisation, ~ a risk, ~ a scheme
Run into: ~ difficulties, ~ problems
Run up: ~ debts, ~ a loss

Satisfy: ~ a need
Schedule: ~ a meeting
Secure: ~ a loan
Select: ~ criteria
Sell off: ~ (part of) a company
Send: ~ a (clear) signal to
Set: ~ a deadline, ~ standards, ~ a target
Set up: ~ an agency, ~ a committee, ~ a company, ~ a department, ~ an organisation, ~ a
   programme
Shelve: ~ a project
Shut down: ~ an operation
Sign: ~ an agreement, ~ a cheque, ~ a contract, ~ a deal, ~ a form
Simplify: ~ a task
Solve: ~ a problem
Sort out: ~ a problem
Stand up for: ~ yourself, ~ what you believe in
Start up: ~ a business
State: ~ the case for
Stick to: ~ your (original) position
Streamline: ~ an operation, ~ a procedure
Submit: ~ an estimate, ~ a proposal
Suffer: ~ a setback, ~ inconvenience
Suggest: ~ a solution
Supply: ~ details of, ~ an estimate
Support: ~ a policy, ~ a proposal, ~ a recommendation

Tackle: ~ a problem
Take: ~ action against, ~ appropriate measures to, ~ a break, ~ a decision, ~ an initiative, ~ a long

Appendices

time to, ~ the minutes of a meeting,~ steps to

Take part in: ~ consultations with, ~ a discussion, ~ a meeting, ~ a role play, ~ a simulation, ~ a seminar, ~ talks with, ~ a workshop

Take up: ~ a challenge

Target: ~ a prospective client, ~ a new market

Terminate: ~ an agreement

Track: ~ perfomance

Transfer: ~ expertise

Turn down: ~ an offer

Undertake: ~ an assignment, ~ research into, ~ a survey, ~ a task

Unleash: ~ potential

Update: ~ an image

Waste: ~ time, ~ money

Weigh up: ~ the advantages and disadvantages, ~ the alternatives / the options

Welcome: ~ a guest speaker, ~ a visitor

Wind up: ~ an operation

Withdraw from: ~ a market

Work on: ~ a project

Work out: ~ a figure for

Work to: ~ a deadline

Write up: ~ the minutes of a meeting

Answer key

Answer key

1 The individual at work

1

1	C	2	B, D	3	C	4	B
5	D	6	C	7	B	8	C

2

1	white collar	2	direct report	3	expatriate	4	shifts
5	retire	6	predecessor	7	counterpart	8	leave
9	unemployed	10	shop floor				

3

1	c	2	a	3	g	4	h
5	e	6	d	7	f	8	b

4

1	f	2	d	3	j	4	a
5	g	6	b	7	h	8	i
9	e	10	c				

5

People:	co-worker, opposite number, line manager
Contracts:	part-time, full-time, half-time
Types of work:	shift, seasonal, casual
Departures:	resign, retire, quit

2 Human resources policy and planning

1

1	human resources	2	empowerment	3	equal opportunities	4	promotion
5	diversity	6	disabilities	7	family-friendly	8	attendance
9	absence	10	benchmark				

2

1	e	2	i	3	h	4	j
5	b	6	a	7	c	8	g
9	d	10	f				

3

1	D	2	B	3	D	4	C
5	A	6	C	7	C	8	C
9	A	10	B				

4

1	termination	2	overstaffing	3	business process re-engineering
4	business partnering	5	alignment	6	outsourcing
7	sexual orientation	8	retention	9	human capital
10	ageism					

5

The lists are not definitive.

1 Move someone within the organisation: re-entry, resettle, promote, redeploy, ...

2 Change the structure of the organisation: delayer, demanning, downsize, offshore, outsource, social dumping, ...

3 Improve equality in the workplace: affirmative action, equal opportunities, equality management, discriminate (don't!), glass ceiling (remove!), positive action, quota strategy, ...

4 Develop HR and business and strategy: alignment, balanced scorecard, benchmark, business partnering, business process re-engineering, downsizing, human capital measurement, time and motion study, ...

3 Resourcing

1

1 panel	2 requirements	3 take on	4 reject
5 vacancy	6 appoint	7 pre-select	8 headhunt
9 intake	10 candidate		

2

1 apply, word of mouth	2 degrees, diplomas	3 vet
4 profile, executive search, agency	5 trial period	6 advertised
7 graduates	8 track record	

3

1 C	2 A	3 C	4 B
5 C	6 C	7 B	8 A
9 D	10 D		

4

1 g	2 f	3 b	4 h
5 c	6 e	7 a	8 i
9 d	10 j		

5

1 d	2 a	3 h	4 b
5 f	6 i	7 e	8 g
9 j	10 c		

4 Reward

1

1 C	2 B	3 B	4 D
5 A	6 C	7 D	8 D

2

1 b	2 j	3 g	4 a
5 f	6 e	7 h	8 c
9 d	10 i		

3

1 subsidised	2 childcare facilities	3 crèche	4 cover
5 index	6 eldercare	7 insurance	8 vouchers

4

1 a	2 h	3 c	4 d
5 f	6 g	7 j	8 b
9 e	10 i		

5

Blue-collar workers	White-collar employees	Senior management
Wage	Salary	Salary
Paid overtime	Perks	Stock option plan
Piecework	Profit-sharing scheme	Perks
Profit-sharing scheme		Profit-sharing scheme
		Golden handshake

6

1 Golden hello
2 Golden parachute
3 Golden offering
4 Golden handcuffs
5 Golden handshake

5 Developing people

1

1 C	2 D	3 B	4 C
5 B	6 C	7 A	8 A
9 C	10 D		

2

1 b	2 h	3 d	4 e
5 f	6 a	7 c	8 g

3

1 trainer	2 apprentice	3 mentee	4 coach
5 false beginner	6 tutor	7 facilitator	8 mentor

4

1 tailored (d)	2 in-company (c)	3 in-house (b)
4 off-the-peg (e)	5 vocational (a)	

5

Course	Learning	Skills	Training
course participant	learning curve	skills gap	continuing training
crash course	learning curve	core skills	adventure training
intensive course	learning organisation	hard skills	survival training
extensive course	learning style	interpersonal skills	training levy
sandwich course	blended learning	soft skills	assertiveness
	distance learning		training

6 Health, safety, welfare and environment

1

1 inspect	2 rehabilitate	3 convalesce	4 bully
5 harass	6 protect	7 injure	8 evacuate
9 contaminate	10 prohibit	11 ventilate	12 intimidate
13 pollute	14 counsel	15 abuse	16 discharge

2

1 abuse	2 harass	3 inspect	4 rehabilitate
5 injure	6 evacuate	7 protect	8 counsel
9 bully	10 discharge		

3

Potential danger in the workplace

Accident / solvent / hazard / asbestos / smoking / fire / slips, trips and falls / carcinogen / agent

Safety measures

Assembly point / goggles / breathing apparatus / check-up / machine guard / ergonomics / security / screen / first aid / muster station / warning

4

1 h	2 c	3 f	4 b
5 g	6 e	7 a	8 d

5

1 fatality	2 neglect	3 sick	4 rest breaks
5 stress	6 burn out	7 risk assessment	8 employee assistance programme

6

1 b	2 c	3 a	4 d

7 Employee relations and representation

1

1 B	2 C	3 A	4 B
5 D	6 A	7 C	8 B

2

1 f	2 c	3 e	4 h
5 d	6 g	7 b	8 a

3

1 e	2 b	3 f	4 d
5 a	6 g	7 c	8 h

4

1 industrial action	2 withdrawal of labour	3 down tools	4 walk out
5 unofficial action	6 stoppage	7 work-to-rule	8 strike
9 picket			

5

Disciplinary action
suspend / misconduct / misdemeanour / warn / discipline
Union roles
shop steward / convenor / general secretary / worker director / lay member / activist / militant
Union administration and management
ballot / affiliate / closed shop / branch / check off / disaffiliate / show of hands / subscription / motion / national executive / merge

6

1 blackleg	2 sweetheart deal	3 'them and us' mentality
4 poach	5 beauty contest	6 black

8 Employment law

1

1 d	2 b	3 e	4 a
5 c			

2

1 adjudication	2 allegation	3 compensate	4 legislation
5 comply	6 disclose	7 fine	8 rule
9 settlement	10 witness		

3

1 directive	2 panel	3 opt-out	4 amendment
5 rights	6 Data	7 statutory	8 submission

4

1 clause	2 restrictive covenant	3 breach	
4 opt-out	5 disclaimer	6 comply with	

5

1 g	2 i	3 f	4 b
5 j	6 e	7 h	8 a
9 c	10 d		

9 Communication and culture

1

1 house magazine	2 body language	3 change	4 stereotypes
5 eye contact	6 dress down Fridays	7 native speakers	8 mission statement

2

1	c	2	e	3	a	4	b
5	d	6	i	7	h	8	j
9	f	10	g				

3

1 power distance
2 uncertainty avoidance
3 transformational / transactional leadership
4 individualism / collectivism
5 monochronic / polychronic

4

1	b	2	a	3	b	4	a

5

1 functional silo (c)   2 open-door policy (a)
3 fog index (b)   4 active listening (d)

Index

Notes

1 Main entries in the book are in bold, followed by the page number.
For example: **absent** 33
2 Collocations with definitions are in non-bold, with the headword appearing first, and followed by the page number.
For example: absence, investigate 33
3 Terms given within the definitions of headwords are in bold with the cross-reference to the main term.
For example: **able-bodied**. See **disability**
4 Where the cross-referenced headword appears more than once, the relevant page number is given in brackets.
For example: comp and ben. See **compensation** (77)
5 Terms given within the definitions of defined collocations are in non-bold, with the headword appearing first, and followed by the cross-reference with the headword appearing first.
For example: application, speculative. See application, unsolicited.

Index

Index

Index

Index

Index